THE BUSINESS OF PUBLIC RELATIONS

THE BUSINESS OF PUBLIC RELATIONS

E. W. Brody

PRAEGER

New York
Westport, Connecticut
London

Library of Congress Cataloging-in-Publication Data

Brody, E. W.
    The business of public relations.

    Bibliography: p.
    Includes index.
    1. Public relations. I. Title.
HD59.B757 1987   659.2   86-30552
ISBN 0-275-92333-9 (alk. paper)
ISBN 0-275-92649-4 (pbk. : alk. paper)

Library of Congress Catalog Card Number:
ISBN: 0-275-92333-9
ISBN 0-275-92649-4 pbk.

First published in 1987

Praeger Publishers, 521 Fifth Avenue, New York, NY 10175
A division of Greenwood Press, Inc.

Printed in the United States of America

The paper used in this book complies with the Permanent
Paper Standard issued by the National Information Standards
Organization (Z39.48–1984).

10 9 8 7 6 5 4 3 2 1

For Sandy

Contents

Preface

Academicians have argued for years whether public relations meets the classic definition of a profession. The argument is now being overtaken by events; public relations has achieved maturity, and more. It is a field increasingly populated by professionals; by individuals who adhere to stringent ethical standards; who hold the public good above private gain. Contemporary efforts toward licensure and certification should enable them to purge public relations of less ethical practitioners.

Public relations since the 1960s has been growing at an unprecedented rate. At minimum, it is a business; more appropriately, it might be termed an industry. This trend appears likely to continue.

Larger counseling firms number their employees in the thousands and their revenues in the tens of millions, in one case more than $100 million. Practitioners number in the tens of thousands; some suggest more than 100,000. The combined memberships of the Public Relations Society of America and the International Association of Business Communicators soon will exceed 25,000. Their combined practice budgets almost certainly exceed $1 billion.

Not unlike many professions that have achieved similar size, however, public relations lacks a strong management cadre. Most who lead the nation's largest public relations organizations are practitioners by education, training, and experience. Their successes have been a product of good advice, good fortune, and a great deal of hard work. In many cases their experiences were more painful than need have been the case.

Knowledge of management in public relations practice is limited; most is anecdotal in nature. The Counselor Academy of the Public Relations Society of America (PRSA) has made some progress in this area through a series of monographs and other publications. Unfortunately, the Academy considers this material proprietary and it is available only to members. Requests for permission to reprint portions of its content have been declined.

Individual members of the Academy and others fortunately have been more forthcoming in PRSA seminars and in professional publications. Their descriptions of successful management techniques and this author's experiences during some 20 years of organizational and counselor practice are incorporated into this volume. Traditional and contemporary management techniques in finance, human resources, and other areas were added to complete the work.

This book is an effort to ease the paths of a new generation of public relations managers. Their performance will be a vital component in the success of tomorrow's public relations practices, counselor and organizational.

The title was chosen in an effort to differentiate between management of the public relations practice as opposed to the process. Process management has been dealt with at length and most capably in recent years by Professors James E. Grunig and Todd Hunt, Professors Norman R. Nager and T. Harrell Allen, and others. A few aspects of practice management have been addressed in more broadly written texts. Gerald J. Voros and Paul H. Alvarez discussed some aspects of financial management in *What Happens in Public Relations*. Other management concerns were addressed in Bill Cantor's *Inside Public Relations: Experts in Action*.

This text covers those subjects and others as components of a strategic management approach to public relations. It takes a systems perspective and emphasizes practice and human resources development as well as financial management. In the latter area, components range from the founding to the sale of a practice.

The seeds of the book were sown several years ago in a proposal to the Counselor Academy, which contemplated a monograph dealing with management of smaller practices. The result was overly long to serve as a monograph and lacked detail necessary for a text. With encouragement from colleagues in the academic and practitioner communities, that document became this book.

No work of this sort is accomplished in a vacuum. Any attempt to acknowledge all of the assistance necessary to complete a first book would be more than futile. There are a number of individuals, however, to whom I am especially indebted.

My many colleagues in the Department of Journalism and the College of Communication and Fine Arts at Memphis State University have been especially helpful. Dean Richard R. Ranta and Professors Gerald C. Stone and John DeMott created an atmosphere without which this book would have been impossible.

Equally supportive and encouraging have been many in other colleges and universities and in the practitioner community. They include Professor Dean A. Kruckeberg of the University of Northern Iowa, Professor Albert Walker of Northern Illinois University, Professor Frank Walsh of the University of Texas at Austin, Professor Adrian Headley of Arkansas State University and—most especially—Professor Norman R. Nager of California State University at Fullerton.

Practitioners who directly or indirectly contributed to this work included Harold Burson and Michael Morris of Burson-Marsteller, Paul S. Forbes of Paul S. Forbes & Associates, William C. Adams of Phillips Petroleum Company, David Ferguson of Hill & Knowlton, Andrew Edson of Padilla &

Speer, Inc., Brandon Davis of Federal Express Corporation, David G. "Jerry" Daly of Holiday Corporation, and Richard K. Long of Dow Chemical U.S.A.

The members and guests of the Public Relations and Marketing Special Interest Group (PRSIG) and PRLink (the computer utility of the PRSA) also made substantial although indirect contributions. Edward Bernays, Patrick Jackson, and others who have helped make these information utilities successful have made a major contribution to the professionalism of public relations.

I am especially indebted to Professors Dennis L. Wilcox of San Jose State University and Michael B. Hesse of the University of Alabama. Their comments and suggestions in reviewing the manuscript were invaluable. So, too, was the guidance provided by Alison Podel and her colleagues at Praeger.

E. W. Brody

REFERENCES

Cantor, Bill. *Inside Public Relations: Experts in Action.* Edited by Chester Burger. New York: Longman, 1984.

Grunig, James E., and Todd Hunt. *Managing Public Relations.* New York: Holt, Rinehart and Winston, 1984.

Nager, Norman R., and T. Harrell Allen. *Public Relations Management by Objectives.* New York: Longman, 1984.

Voros, Gerald J., and Paul H. Alvarez, eds. *What Happens in Public Relations.* New York: AMACOM, 1981.

1
Public Relations: A New Perspective

The nature and scope of public relations practice are constantly changing. The profession's pioneers were message or publicity oriented; their successors were concerned with the process: research, planning communication, and evaluation; and the focus later changed to organizational relations. Public relations practice today is viewed in an environmental context. Practitioners are concerned with organizations and the social fabric of which they are a part.

These were changes in emphasis in the public relations process; they were accompanied by less noticeable changes in public relations practice. Practitioners slowly have moved upward in organizational hierarchies; their operations and responsibilities have broadened; they have become involved in budgeting and employment procedures; in purchasing and legal matters. Management, in other words, has been growing in importance in public relations.

These developments have occurred because public relations has become less an art or science and more a business. More precisely, management of the *practice* has become as important as management of the *process*. As the twenty-first century dawns, it will become even more important.

Clients and employers in earlier and less turbulent times were tolerant of the weaknesses of public relations. Cost overruns were accepted as the price of creativity, results that defied measurement were satisfactory, a "good image" constituted adequate return on investment. These conditions no longer are acceptable. Practitioners are expected to produce measurable results in keeping with predetermined goals. Clients and senior managers demand reasonable returns on public relations investments.

These demands will compound in the months and years ahead. Practitioners are assuming a mediating role in society. Programs they fashion increasingly are designed to achieve accommodation between organizations and constituent groups over major social issues. Public relations is becoming one of senior management's dominant concerns.

This trend will continue as issues increase in number and complexity. Public relations practices will grow. Personnel will increase in number. Budgets will mushroom. Management as well as public relations skills will be required of practitioners. Organizational public relations managers will be expected to function as peers in the executive suite. Counselors will find their own organizations as demanding as those of their clients.

REQUIREMENTS OF MANAGERS

Change in society and in the role of public relations will require practitioners to acquire new knowledge and enhanced skills. They will be called upon to better organize and apply the resources at their disposal. They will be required to better design and execute strategic business plans. Greater management skills will be necessary in finance, human resources, and practice development. Enhanced marketing and sales abilities will be needed. New technologies will be challenging. Process control will require greater precision. Practice legalities will be more demanding. So will relationships between practitioners and their clients.

Perhaps most important will be growth and development in practices and practitioners—both must mature and prosper. These and other areas of managerial concern are discussed in subsequent chapters. Their content will be readily assimilated by those first equipped with several basic concepts, which include the laws of man and nature, relationships between organizations and their environments, strategic management, and a unified public relations practice model.

LAWS OF MAN AND NATURE

Public relations historically has been more concerned with the laws of man than nature. Some basic precepts of psychology, sociology, and economics occasionally have intruded. The primary focus, however, has been micro- rather than macrocosmic. Organizations have been viewed in terms of "publics" or "constituencies." Individuals have been seen as members of these groups. The message that "there is no general public" has been extended beyond its original intent. It has produced a tendency to view organizational relationships as informal networks or narrow streets.

No perspective could be less appropriate. Practitioners and managers today adopt simplistic practice models at their peril. Organizations—their own and others—are parts of a complex fabric subject to natural as well as human law. They are system components and must be viewed as such.

Systems Theory

Understanding natural and man-made systems and processes requires sensitivity to organizational dynamics. Natural systems are parts of the environment in which man-made systems function. Man's knowledge of natural systems is limited; nevertheless, it can enhance his insight into systems he creates and those with which he deals.

Knowledge of organizational-environmental linkages also is helpful. This especially is true where external environments are viewed as a set of suprasystems and internal environments are seen as a group of subsystems. The inadequacy of traditional management methods in coping with change becomes obvious when organizations are viewed in this context. So does the desirability of strategic management.

Organizations in Nature

Management is an organizationally oriented discipline, dealing primarily with man-made organizations. They exist and function around and within other human and natural structures. Some can be manipulated; others are resistant. Knowledge of both is necessary to success.

The components of man's natural environment are ordered and organized for consistency and cohesion in a way that defies duplication. This may account for man's inability to fashion perfect organizations. Man-made systems are more likely to fail, however, out of relative resistance to change.

Natural organizations are readily seen in plant and animal worlds, where multiple subsystems function as cohesive entities and as parts of greater ecosystems. They are not rigid systems. They are dynamic rather than static, reacting to natural or human intervention.

Organizations as Living Systems

The extent to which natural systems parallel those of human origin is open to argument. Organizations nevertheless increasingly are viewed as organic structures; as living systems. As such, they are bound up with nature's suprasystems and subsystems. Their functions as social or sociotechnical systems parallel natural or biological systems.

This especially is so with respect to linkages with internal and external environments, but other similarities also exist. Organizations are complex systems designed for specific environments. They adapt to environmental change. They may be stable or unstable. They consist of subsystems dealing in the processing, coordination, and control of information. Some suspect elemental dynamic processes govern the behavior of systems—social as well as physical and biological.

Contemporary organizations are near-infinitely complex. They are involved with two sets of environments—external and internal. The external include natural, human, political, socioeconomic, market, and technological. The internal include psychological, social, political, and technological. The former might be termed suprasystems of which organizations are part. The latter then can be viewed as subsystems. Neither can be held superior or subordinate as problem generators. Each component of each set is a possible source of multiple pressures.

Subsystems

Psychological. Of the four internal environments or subsystems of the organization, the psychological is the most complex. It includes the individual motivations, needs, values, attitudes, perceptions, beliefs, emotions, and personality structures. Those of every individual, from chief executives to most menially positioned employees, are involved. This level of complexity is noteworthy for two reasons: It raises questions as to the ability of organizations to function consistently on rational bases; and psychological subsystems create environments from which social subsystems emerge.

Social. The social subsystem is perhaps the most dynamic. It involves the collective aspects of human behavior in groups of all sizes. It also is more than the aggregate of individual bahaviors. "Organizational cultures" originate in this subsystem. They appear to be products of what has been described as a collective consciousness or intelligence. The roots of the informal power structures or political subsystems also are found here.

Political. Political subsystems generate the power and influence wielded by natural rather than formal leaderships. Individuals who constitute this leadership and the roles they occupy are created here. Formal leadership structures may or may not be based in the political subsystem.

Technological. The technological subsystem is no more independent than any other. It consists of the collective attributes of machines and the individuals and systems supporting them. Here are found the roots of mechanization, computerization, automation, and robotization. Most important in viewing organizational subsystems is their dynamic interaction—none of them function independently. Change in one impacts others. Each also interacts with the external or suprasystems in which organizations function. Relationships between organizations and their environments are conceptually illustrated in Figure 1.1.

Suprasystems

Natural. The natural environment consists of resources that man until recently took for granted. Included are raw materials, humans who work in the organization, the air they breathe, and the water they drink. World

FIGURE 1.1
Relationships between Organizations and Environments.

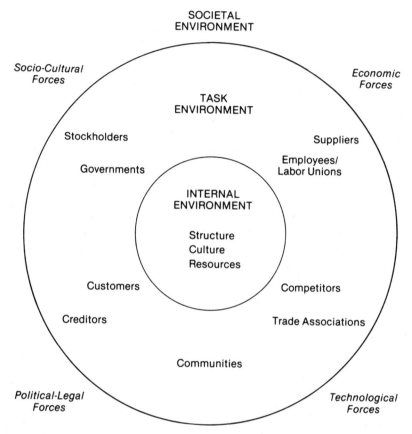

Source: From Thomas L. Wheelen and J. David Hunger, *Strategic Management and Business Policy*, © 1983, Addison-Wesley, Reading, Massachusetts. Reprinted with permission.

population and pollution problems and impending natural resource shortages originate in the natural environment.

Human. The human environment also is mixed. It contains elements most expect to find in this category and others many would be unlikely to mention. The former include all humans, employee and nonemployee, within and beyond organizational operational areas. The latter include their abilities and skills, educational levels, attitudes, and opinions. Changing human values and attitudes originate here. So do problems arising out of human obsolescence in the age of robotics.

Political. The political environment similarly extends beyond elected or appointed officialdom. It includes labor unions and other special interest groups. They exert indirect pressure on organizations through the political system. This environment, like others, includes contingent as well as existing groups. They include formal or informal groupings that form around emerging issues.

Social. The socioeconomic or social environment is dynamic as well. It spawns evolving concepts such as corporate responsibility—as it now exists and may exist in the future. The obligations and responsibilities of individuals and organizations to society and each other are established here.

Market. The volatile market environment includes competition, consumer behavior, changing consumer values, and other elements. These define the marketability of products or services. The market environment, like others, is vulnerable to external factors, as in the auto industry during the oil crises of the early 1980s.

Technological. The technological environment includes the collective aspects of machines as well as ancillary and support systems. Mechanization and automation in industry is one of this environment's more important dimensions. Discoveries, inventions, and innovations developed here directly or indirectly impact every other area. Moreover, seemingly small changes, such as development of the microprocessor, quickly can produce major impacts.

ORGANIZATIONS AND ENVIRONMENTS

A Complex World

External and internal environments—suprasystems and subsystems—together create the complex worlds in which organizations function. They interact dynamically within and across group boundaries. Understanding their interactions is vital in managing organizations. Existing and prospective interaction can be better understood by examining changes now beginning to be felt in the United States.

Changes promising to be most traumatic are associated with transition from the industrial to the postindustrial era. Evidence of the transition began to appear during the mid–1980s. Most visible were multiple plant closings and resultant unemployment. Although superficially akin to changes associated with economic cycles, they signaled permanent systemic change.

The origins of these changes were complex. They were in part technological; in part socioeconomic. Heavy industry had become less competitive, partly through technological change. Steel and auto producers with vintage production facilities were pitted against modern overseas plants. Some argued that the competition was between overseas labor forces committed to quality and domestic workers grown lethargic and apathetic over decades of technological superiority. Others pointed to product quality differences as a causal factor. Still others blamed environmental protection laws, which added to costs.

Systemic Change

Most now concede that the changes are structural rather than cyclical, permanent rather than transient. They continue to produce a "ripple effect," which remains to be measured in suprasystems and organizational subsystems. Hundreds of thousands of new jobs were created while steel and auto employment declined. They required less-skilled workers, however, and offered lower wages. They also were dispersed across the United States while steel and auto unemployment impacted selected areas. The result was what some called "rust bowls" comparable to the "dust bowls" of the Depression era. Unemployment extended across the industrial spectrum. Hundreds of thousands of white-collar as well as blue-collar workers lost jobs; and no reversal of the trend appeared to be in sight.

Organizational Reactions

These conditions produced predictable change in organizational subsystems or internal environments. Workers became more compliant and less militant on seeing that employment with huge corporations no longer offered lifetime security. Change was occurring, in other words, in the psychological subsystem. Concurrently, while the Democratic Party long had been considered the home of the working man, Republicans claimed the White House. Political systems were changing in the United States and in organizations. Workers were coming to understand that their economic welfare was inextricably linked to that of their employers. Unions and political positions they advocated suffered as a result.

Less measurable changes in organizations' social and psychological systems also were occurring. Changing external environments prompted change in organizational subsystems. Such changes will continue as a result of other external factors, some more predictable than others. The population of the United States is aging—the bulk of the electorate will be near or beyond retirement age by the year 2000. Through the political system, this change wil impact national social programs. Among them will be the nation's health care delivery system, growing ever more expensive with advances in medicine and technology. Change in this and other areas will produce organizational responses. The complexity of the systems involved makes them difficult to predict accurately.

Analytical Problems

Linkages among organizations, suprasystems, and subsystems defy simplistic analysis. They are clear enough, however, to permit on-going analysis and assessment of prospective impacts and alternative responses.

Where will problems arise? Few venture specifics but some trends are evident. Domestic society appears moving from concern over quantity to concern over quality. Rather than abundance, sufficiency appears to satisfy more individuals. A shift from uniformity to diversity is appearing in personal values and in recreational and purchasing patterns.

Traditional hierarchies in organizations are being replaced by problem-solving units and networking mechanisms. Numbers of management levels are declining and new corporate cultures are developing.

Education and training are assuming larger roles. Conventional behavior is yielding to experimental. The United States appears to be changing from a power and money society to a knowledge and wisdom society; from centralization to decentralization.

Control Problems

Conventional management systems are becoming less appropriate in the face of change. Continuing attempts toward total control have failed. They appear to generate barriers in organizations and between organizations and stakeholder groups. These conditions have produced a new approach to management—a process called strategic management.

STRATEGIC MANAGEMENT

A Dynamic Process

Management strategies have been defined as directional action decisions required to achieve organizational purposes; they are developed in keeping with problems or opportunitites; they are generated by suprasystems within limitations imposed by subsystems; they are the means by which organizations initiate actions to achieve their purposes; they must be based on and consistent with these purposes; they also must be subordinate to purposes and organizational environments. Strategic decision making thus becomes a continuing, dynamic process.

Directional action decisions include all those taken in establishing objectives, plans, and policies and in their implementation. They may be planned or spontaneous. They may involve new directions or reaffirm earlier-taken decisions.

Organizational purposes are the reasons why organizations exist and function. They must be consistent with demands and opportunities created by suprasystems and subsystems that constitute organizational environments. Writing in *The Practice of Management*, Peter Drucker provided a new insight into objectives when he declared the only objective of a business is to create a new customer. He linked organizations implicitly with their environments, external and internal.

Success or Failure

Organizational success or failure is governed by the ability to adapt; to maintain appropriate congruence or fit. This is difficult to achieve without anticipating change. Contemporary organizatons' ability to do so is questionable. Adaptability is not a major attribute of traditional twentieth-century organizations. Most were patterned after models created by Henri Fayol, Frederick W. Taylor, Max Weber and—more recently—Alfred P. Sloan, Jr. They have three primary components: (1) specialization of function, (2) individual accountability established by written rule and procedure, and (3) rigid control through hierarchical structure.

Such structures may be appropriate in stratified societies with low educational levels, limited human and natural resources, and slow rates of social and technological change. Few suggest these conditions exist today. Their disappearance requires strategic rather than traditional management techniques.

Strategic Management

Strategic management involves taking decisions and actions that determine long-term organizational performance. The process includes strategy formulation, implementation, evaluation, and control. It emphasizes monitoring and evaluating environmentally generated opportunities and constraints in light of organizational strengths and weaknesses.

Strategic planning is used at three organizational levels: corporate, business, and functional. At the corporate level, the process involves constantly reexamining organizational activities. It deals with the nature of businesses in which organizations engage and the flow of resources to and from them. At the business level, the process deals with divisions or other organizational subunits. It involves profit or operating margins and development and delivery of products and services. At the functional level, the emphasis shifts to developing strategies to improve performance.

Public relations units historically have been positioned at the functional level in organizations. More of them are now moving to the business level and management responsibilities are changing as a result.

Integration Necessary

The three levels require integration but use a uniform model involving external and internal environments. Both influence formulation, implementation, evaluation, and control of organizational strategies. Formulation involves defining organizational missions, objectives, strategies, and policies. Implementation requires developing programs, budgets, and procedures. Performance is monitored through on-going evaluation and control procedures. Feedback mechanisms are provided to complete the cycle.

The process applies to organizations and operational components. In public relations it is equally applicable in corporate and consultant practices.

Parallel Models

Strategic planning parallels contemporary public relations process models; the process is virtually identical in counseling organizations. Differences arise in organizational units only in that suprasystem goals and strategies already have been set. Public relations unit planning begins from these premises rather than an external perspective.

Other than in environmental orientation, strategic planning also parallels management by objectives as applied to public relations by Norman R. Nager and T. Harrell Allen.

The process proceeds from environmental assessment—internal and external—to developing goals and strategies. They are based on analyses of stakeholder groups. They require action and communication but external constraints exist. These include demographic, social, and technological trends originating in the several environments. The demographic will be most uniformly felt. Change concurrently can be expected from what consultant Paul E. Shay calls "the five driving technologies" of the twenty-first century:

1. Computers.
2. Factory and office automation with attendant pressures for new management methods.
3. New materials, especially composites such as those being introduced in the automotive industry; fiber optics, new plastics, ceramics in engines, and so on.
4. Biotechnology, especially in the synthesis of new substances, perhaps eventually in whole plant systems.
5. Health and medical technologies such as nuclear magnetic resonance and self-diagnostic equipment.

Coping with change will be no easy task, especially where practitioners attempt to apply traditional practice models and management techniques. Neither is well-suited to emerging environments.

Accelerating environmental change will hasten the changing role of public relations practice. The contemporary emphasis on communication will shift to mediation. Practitioners will serve as facilitators, assisting clients and employers in achieving accommodation with constituent groups. Strategic planning will become their primary tool. Communication will be more demanding as a result of media fragmentation. It nevertheless will assume a secondary practice role. Communication will be to strategic planning tomorrow what brochure development is to communication today.

These changes will dominate public relations practice in organizational and counselor settings. They will create new demands on both the practice and the process of public relations. The former will require more intensive application of sophisticated management techniques than to date has been the case. The latter will foster a new practice model applicable in organizational and counselor settings.

A UNIFIED PRACTICE MODEL

The process and practice of public relations involve different concepts. The process deals with solving public relations problems. Professional practice requires dealing with business management as well. Recent developments in process application have created greater practice diversity. The trend is most readily seen in proliferating special interest groups within the PRSA. In contrast, public relations organizations have been moving toward a unified practice model.

The Consultant Model

The consultant model of public relations management, as it will be called here, originated in counselor rather than organizational practices. Movement of organizational practices from functional to business levels makes it applicable to them as well. The model requires that all practitioners assume a consultant approach to their practices.

The relative uniformity of the model also requires terms be precisely and consistently used and understood. In this context, *consultant* is used in a generic sense. The public relations consultant may be an employee or manager within any organization engaged in any commercial, industrial, or institutional pursuit. The department or other organizational component in which he or she is employed is called an *organizational unit*. The term *counselor* refers to an employee or manager of a *counseling organization* or agency; a firm providing public relations services to multiple clients. The terms *practitioner* and *public relations professional* here include all engaged in professional practice in organizational and counselor settings.

Installing the consultant model requires functional rather than structural change in most organizational practices. Three primary areas are involved. First, public relations units become consultant groups in organizations, assuming proactive roles. Second, units are recast as profit centers rather than components of "overhead." Third, the function is positioned as a free-standing entity or organizatonal component reporting to the chief executive. The ideal vehicle is a multidisciplinary communication division.

Challenge and Opportunity

Such reorganization creates challenges and opportunities. Challenges arise since services no longer are provided "cost-free" to other operational components. Practitioners instead would sell services to personnel, marketing, financial services, management, and other components. Each is free to accept or reject proposed services and pays for them through interdepartmental voucher or otherwise.

Opportunities arise since well-managed public relations units generate profits in several forms. Managers are called on to deal with other departments on cost versus benefit bases. Professional services can be sold to cost-conscious managers on no other basis. They must be educated to the value of public relations services in achieving organizational objectives. Second, public relations managers become more cost conscious. Their operating expenses must be kept at the lowest possible levels consistent with quality to enhance profits.

Changing Perceptions

These conditions require change in traditional organizational models. More importantly, they change management perceptions of the public relations function. Change results in part from the value-for-value-received orientation of the consultant model. Of greater potential impact, however, is the public relations unit's "bottom line." No more convincing measure of performance exists.

The proactive consultant model requires one behavioral change of managers: client relationships must be established. This involves little more than a modified service orientation. Rather than waiting for work to come to them, managers would serve their interests and those of "clients" by identifying needs and proposing responses.

Effectiveness and Efficiency

The consultant model also tends to generate effectiveness and efficiency in public relations units. Where future "client" assignments are influenced by the extent to which current objectives are achieved, practitioners become intent on producing desired outcomes rather than merely "getting out the work." Fiscal accountability also encourages effort toward efficiency.

Recasting public relations units as profit centers rather than components of "overhead" is complex but productive. Complexity arises out of change in internal accounting procedures and reluctance on the part of practitioners and prospective "clients." Benefit potential encourages professionals to overcome these difficulties.

Executive Perspectives

Managers and financial officers are more comfortable with methods to traditional cost monitoring practices. They are applied in the consultant model. "Client" support is produced by applying resources to enhance operating performance.

A similar rationale facilitates related organizational changes. The objective of the process is productivity. Professional managers are comfortable in its application. They welcome changes in forms that enhance function. Changes are especially welcome where new structures permit better measuring results with traditional yardsticks: profits or, in the case of institutions, net operating revenues.

Profit Centers

The consultant model establishes public relations units as profit centers rather than components of organizational overhead. Services are designed to meet other organizational needs and sold at prices producing adequate returns for both parties. The unit becomes a business within an organization, responsible for applying resources to produce returns.

This approach first tends to produce dismay among corporate and institutional practitioners. Accountability remains foreign to many organizational units. The consultant model appears to create risk, which is counterbalanced by opportunities, which arise out of ability to demonstrate productivity in economic terms understood by management.

Criticism Avoided

Where public relations units contribute to organizational success, potential criticism over lack of measurable results is eliminated. The model creates certifiable data attesting to productivity. They justify expenditures and support requests for further resources in ensuing years.

The data are generated by applying accepted business practices in professional settings. Applications vary little from corporate and institutional situations to consulting practices. The same types of resources are applied to produce similar results. Results are measurable where quantifiable standards of performance are agreed upon.

Expansion Encouraged

The consultant model also creates benefits rather than difficulties for practitioners by encouraging organizational expansion. Rapid counselor firm growth in the mid–1980s was attributed to corporate/institutional decisions to minimize internal capabilities. Where economic as well as creative outcomes can be demonstrated, this trend might be reversed.

Other than as described above, the consultant model applies uniformly to corporate/institutional and consultant practices.

IN SUMMARY

Public relations is assuming a more dominant position in organizations and society. Organizational and counselor practices are growing in number, size, and complexity. Practice rather than process management as a result is assuming new importance.

Success in practice management requires that practitioners acquire new knowledge and skills concerning organizations, their constituencies, and the environments in which they function.

Areas in which greater proficiency is needed include strategic planning, business analysis, technology, organizational planning, finance, marketing, practice development, sales, interorganizational relationships, process and human resources management, public relations law, and career and organizational development.

Nature suggests and many concede that contemporary organizations logically and rationally must be considered living systems. This perspective is especially enlightening where organizations are viewed as components of broader fabrics; as functional parts of multiple environments or supra-systems. The organization concurrently can be viewed internally as composed of additional environments or subsystems.

Conditions in society support these theoretical constructs. Multiple social, moral, and ethical issues remain to be resolved in the United States. Resolution of one in many cases leads to several others of equal or greater magnitude. They compound organizational difficulties and make strategic planning and environmental assessment essential to success.

A unified practice model based on counselor practice and called the consultant model enables practitioners to best deal with their changing environments. The model casts practitioners in consultant roles regardless of practice settings. It provides a mechanism through which organizational practices can demonstrate their value and realize their potential.

ADDITIONAL READING

Didsbury, Howard F., Jr., ed. *Communications and the Future: Prospects, Promises and Problems*. Bethesda, Md.: World Future Society, 1982.

Dizard, Wilson P., Jr. *The Coming Information Age: An Overview of Technology, Economics and Politics*. New York: Longman, 1982.

Drucker, Peter. *The Changing World of the Executive*. New York: Time Books, 1982.

Drucker, Peter. *Innovation and Entrepreneurship: Practice and Principles*. New York: Harper & Row, 1985.

Drucker, Peter F. *Managing in Turbulent Times*. New York: Harper & Row, 1980.

Drucker, Peter F. *The Practice of Management*. New York: Harper & Row, 1954.

Grunig, James E., and Todd Hunt. *Managing Public Relations*. New York: Holt, Rinehart and Winston, 1984.

Haigh, Robert, et al. *Communication in the Twenty-First Century*. New York: John Wiley, 1981.

Louv, Richard. *America II*. Los Angeles: Jeremy P. Tarcher, 1983.

Mitchell, Arnold, *The Nine American Lifestyles: Who We Are & Where We Are Going*. New York: Macmillan, 1983.

Nager, Norman R., and T. Harrell Allen. *Public Relations Management By Objectives*. New York: Longman, 1984.

Naisbitt, John. *Megatrends: Ten New Directions Transforming Our Lives*. New York: Warner, 1982.
Paluszek, John. *Business and Society: 1976–2000*. New York: AMACOM, 1976.
Toffler, Alvin. *The Adaptive Corporation*. New York: McGraw-Hill, 1985.

2

The Consultant Model Applied

Models are tools. They usually are simplistic devices created to engender insights into more complex concepts. Ideally, they enhance understanding of reality. They equip users to better grasp and apply basic concepts in a complex world.

The consultant model of public relations practice is no different. It is intended to induce understanding of public relations' role in complex commercial, industrial, and institutional environments.

Models' utilitarian value depend on user understanding of business and management. Concepts involved must be understood in theoretical and applied contexts. So must contemporary social dynamics and their impacts on organizations. They together enable public relations managers to develop and apply strategic management principles to enhance their practices.

AN ENVIRONMENTAL APPROACH

Environments

Public relations practice is complex for manager and practitioner. Managers' tasks are especially difficult because they must deal with two sets of environments:

1. Organizational environments, consisting of suprasystems in which public relations units function and subsystems of which they are a part.
2. Environments in which elements function. This is the case whether the public relations unit is an organizational component or a counseling firm. In the former case, "clients" are other organizational components.

This book is concerned with management of public relations practices rather than public relations processes. It focuses on public relations units' suprasystems and subsystems. For organizational units, suprasystems consist of organizations of which units are a part. Their subsystems are departmental components. Counselor firms' subsystems also are departments. Their suprasystems—other than where they are subsidiaries of larger organizations—are identical to those of other free-standing enterprises. Despite organizational differences, they offer identical services to clients and employers.

Organizational Purposes

Public relations organizations exist to produce accommodation between clients and constituent groups. Public relations planning begins with results desired. Every action is designed to produce a predetermined reaction. Public relations strategies are integrated sets of plans and programs that marshal and deploy organizational resources. They are designed to achieve goals and objectives. They function within environments and in relation to competitors. They maximize strengths and minimize weaknesses. Their success requires understanding environments in order that users may capitalize on organizational strengths.

Practice Models

Public relations practices—organizational and counseling—differ only in positioning. Counseling firms are free-standing business units; some are subsidiaries of larger organizations. They deal with internal and external environments as described earlier. Organizational unit positions vary since their external environments consist of the infrastructures of their organizations. Although differing in size and scope of operation, their primary internal environments are virtually identical to those of counseling firms.

Viewed as organizational models, then, public relations organizations' basic forms are almost identical. Managers' concerns are similar as well, varying only in that organizational managers must be more closely attuned to environments of other departments. All are prospective clients. Managers' external concerns thus are somewhat more complex than in free-standing counseling firms.

Significant numbers of larger counseling firms are subsidiaries of other organizations—most often advertising agencies. The counseling firm's position then is not unlike the organizational public relations unit's. The suprasystem is the parent firm rather than the organizational community.

A Systems View

Public relations units should be viewed as systems. Their suprasystems are the organizations of which they are components or, for free-standing counseling firms, the business community. Their subsystems are internal operational groups. The model applies to large units and small; to corporate public relations organizations with divisional subsidiaries and to small freestanding counseling firms. In the latter case, subsystems can be defined as professional and support groups. Where the "firm" consists of a single counselor, subsystems can be viewed as including vendors to which counselors turn for design, typography, printing, and other services.

Public relations units' internal and external environments generally are consistent despite variation in structures. External environments include natural, technological, political, human, socioeconomic, and market structures. Internal environments include social, psychological, political, and technological structures.

While varying situationally in importance, all are elements with which managers must deal effectively if the organization is to succeed. Success can be defined in many ways; most often in public relations it is measured in terms of growth and stability. Growth usually is calculated in human and monetary terms—in numbers of personnel and profit dollars. Stability refers to turnover in personnel and/or clientele.

The New Model

Definitions of success should apply uniformly to both organizational and counselor units. They traditionally have been applied primarily to counselor organizations, while organizational units have been objects of benign neglect.

With increasing economic pressures in the early 1980s, these circumstances began to change. A uniform public relations practice model emerged. It casts organizational public relations units in a pattern identical to the counselor firm's. Prospective clienteles, consisting of other organizational components, are more limited than the counselor firm's. Otherwise, units are functionally and environmentally identical.

In the "consultant model," organizational public relations units become "profit centers." They develop and market services to other organizational components, such as sales, marketing, and personnel departments. Their revenues originate in intraorganizational transactions. Their success then can be measured by the same criteria applied to counselor organizations.

Applying the Model

Applying the consultant model renders organizational public relations units operationally identical to counselor organizations. Managers' primary concerns become identical as well, as do management's objectives. Organiza-tional units, like counseling firms, are managed as businesses: organizations created by individuals to provide goods and services to others.

The consultant model recognizes increasing consistency in public re-lations practice across counselor and organizational units. Where variations arise, as in the case of existing and prospective clienteles, they are identified as such. Otherwise, readers may assume the text refers to counselor firms and organizational units.

CLASSIC COMPONENTS OF BUSINESS

The primary components of business are land, labor, and capital. Land refers to natural resources as well as real estate. Labor consists of the people who produce the products or services. Capital includes money and the machin-ery, equipment, tools, and other devices that help people perform better.

These components are interdependent; each relies on the others. All are influenced by technology, the application of knowledge to production. Some consider technology a "new" component of production.

Natural resources can be extracted only with trained labor and so-phisticated equipment. Labor can be optimally productive only with ample natural resources and appropriate tools. Equipment can be produced only with labor and natural resources.

Whether viewed as a fourth component of production or an associated factor, technology influences all other components. It increases work force efficiency, it enhances ability to extract natural resources, and it adds to the productivity of machinery.

Managers' Roles

Management's classic role in organizations involves four functions: planning, organizing, directing, and controlling. For organizational subunits, a fifth function is added: reporting. Successful public relations practice in coun-seling and organizational settings requires optimal performance in all these areas.

Planning

Simplistically, planning is a two-step process. It involves setting objectives and deciding how to attain them. The detailed process is only slightly more complex. It requires that organizations establish multiple major objectives, which typically deal with products and/or services, profit levels, and growth—all are pertinent to public relations regardless of type of practice unit. Profit in organizational public relations may be merely the difference between internal charges and operating costs. It nevertheless is a significant indicator of unit performance and a major determinant in subsequent allocation of resources.

Setting Objectives

Planning involves major objectives and one or more sets of subobjectives. In small organizations, the latter may serve only as mileposts on the road to major objectives. In larger units, they may be assigned to lower management levels as specific goals.

Determining how to achieve objectives is more complex. The process involves defining alternative courses of action and determining which will be most productive at the lowest cost. This is accomplished by examining cost-benefit ratios.

Cost versus Benefit

Cost-benefit ratios are determined by analyzing action plans and their underlying assumptions. In developing new services, for example, any of several might be selected. Probabilities for successful introduction are calculated based on assumed economic conditions, competitive factors, and so on. Probabilities, most often expressed in percentages, are applied to investments required. Anticipated return on investment (probability × dollar amount) governs in selecting services to be developed.

Organizing

Organizing is a process by which plans are implemented. It involves dividing work into small units for assignment to individuals or groups of employees. The process is a series of steps that vary with unit size, organizational structure, and task complexity.

Organizing begins when plans have been completed and resources allocated. It involves analyzing plans and delegating authority and responsibility to get jobs done. The process is essential regardless of unit size.

Unit Sizes

Most units, organizational or counselor, are established with a single professional employee. Planning, organizing, and subsequent management tasks are undertaken by the professional. He or she subsequently may handle production, distribution, and other functions.

The process nevertheless should be followed precisely in the interest of long-term organizational development. In one-person units, professionals often spend more time as technicians than managers. If they aspire to management, technician tasks ultimately must be assigned to others. Conscious, consistent process application clarifies and separates roles and paves the way for rational organizational development.

In larger organizations, where roles have been separated and appropriate structure exists, further responsibilities accrue to managers. Organizations depend on teamwork. Cooperation and understanding between and within operational units is vital. Creating and maintaining a psychological climate conducive to success then becomes a primary managerial responsibility.

Organizational Culture

This psychological climate has been called a corporate or organizational culture—a set of values and performance standards to which employees willingly subscribe. It is neither developed nor maintained without effort.

Organizational cultures are created by leaders with visions of the future. They must have the ability to convey their visions to others with such conviction that they will accept them as their own. While no small task, this is essential to long-term success. Where individual counselors elect to remain "solo practitioners," for example, they must obtain similar commitments from vendors on whom consultancies depend.

A sense of long-term organizational development thus must be established early in the life of the unit. Conscious effort to develop policy and procedure through strategic management principles is essential in establishing conceptual matrixes to facilitate rational development and organizational growth.

Directing

Directing is the management function dealing with guiding and supervising subordinates. It traditionally has been accomplished on face-to-face bases with employees as they perform their tasks. This has been less and less the case in recent years, especially in public relations.

Basic changes in organizational structure started developing in the United States in the 1980s under competitive pressures, primarily from abroad. The near-death of Chrysler Corporation and similar events in other industries forced managers to reexamine traditional models, which then included multiple layers of middle managers in oversight roles.

Alternative Model

The primary alternative was a model successfully applied by the Japanese, where a strong organizational culture is the primary governor of individual behavior. The model became especially attractive as computers assumed the information transfer role of middle managers. Their capabilities in data storage and analysis rendered obsolete management echelons previously needed to gather and transmit information.

These conditions encouraged the relatively "flat" organizational charts sought after in commerce and industry today. They also tended to deemphasize management skills indigenous to directing: communication, motivators, and leadership. Of the three, communication is most important.

Communication

Communication is critical in directing employees, especially in flat organizational structures. Minimal managerial/supervisory oversight is implicit in these designs. They assume employees are knowledgeable, skilled, and motivated, although this often is not the case.

Humans must know what is expected of them to function productively in organizations. Qualitative and quantitative standards must be established and understood. Opportunity must be created for ample two-way communication.

Without adequate communication, managers' efforts to motivate are predestined to failure. With communication, the reverse is not necessarily true. Another ingredient is necessary: managerial understanding of reward systems and motivation.

Motivators

Money, fringe benefits, working conditions, meaningful work, and a feeling of accomplishment traditionally have been management's primary motivators, but they are no longer adequate. A new generation of workers is coming into the labor force, a generation that demands what Naisbitt and Aburdene call a "nourishing environment for personal growth."

Members of this generation believe work should be fun, challenging, and stimulating. The best of them seek psychic and literal ownership. Managers ignore these factors at their peril.

Leadership

Change in motivational roles is reflected in the third component of successful directing: leadership. Leaders no longer can succeed as figureheads, dealing largely with policy matters and staying remote from daily concerns. They must develop and convey motivating views of the future to establish strong corporate cultures. They must adapt management styles to employee preferences. Flexibility now is essential and will be even more important through the remainder of the century.

Controlling

For all the reasons organizing and directing are increasing in importance, controlling is declining in significance. Controlling traditionally involves monitoring performance and correcting deviation. Typical tools include budgetary and quality control systems as well as personal evaluation.

Monitoring

Monitoring is almost automatic for most functions in most organizations. Computers provide instant analyses of financial performance data. They monitor production rates, inventory levels, and similar factors. Only in public relations and other creative fields does monitoring retain some importance. The reason is simple: Creative and similar qualitative elements are not amenable to quantitative measurement. Indirect indicators of performance exist, however, and increasingly are coming into use.

Sensitivity

Monitoring will continue to be important in public relations practice, but with an unusual twist. Change in the work force and in workers' intangible values require greater sensitivity in rendering management judgments. Successful managers must learn to criticize constructively with gentility and discretion. They must create nurturing environments or find themselves at the mercy of artistic "prima donnas" in competitive personnel markets.

Reporting

Reporting is a highly developed skill among public relations counselors, but this is not often the case among organizational practitioners. These circumstances have been changing under economic pressures, however, and soon will be as common in the latter group as the former.

Given strong strategic planning, reporting is the simplest of management tasks. Strategic plans deal with finite objectives. They prescribe temporal frameworks in which they are to be achieved and appropriate reporting points "en route."

Guidelines

The primary reporting guideline is simple and functional: "no unpleasant surprises." Clients—counselor and organizational—must be informed of the progress of work undertaken in their behalf. "Informed" is subject to interpretation. Where performance matches plan, little reporting is needed. Digression demands prompt reports.

This principle is readily seen in agreements between counselor organizations and vendors such as printers and photographers. Expressed informally, they prescribe: "We expect our work to be delivered on dates specified. If you encounter circumstances that cause delay, we expect to be notified immediately. Our clients are more receptive to notification that work will be delayed than to apologies after delivery dates."

Successful reporting processes anticipate problems and report and deal with them promptly. Nothing less is acceptable in any organization.

Skills

All managerial functions are within the capability of those equipped with essential skills. They have been categorized as technical, conceptual, and human. They most often have been listed in that order. In the new work environment, priorities will be reversed. Public relations continues to be a "people business." It also remains a creative business, but with greater challenges than in the past. Maintaining adequately educated, trained, and motivated personnel complements may be first among them but newcomers will intrude.

CONTEMPORARY MANAGERIAL ROLES

Classic management components are helpful models for public relations practitioners. Functional views of contemporary managerial roles prove more enlightening. They apply to all organizations and fall into six categories: (1) organizing resources for optimum productivity, (2) producing services and products, (3) managing human resources, (4) marketing services and products, (5) financing operations, and (6) controlling operations. Today, a seventh category must be added: environmental assessment. A decade ago, management functions safely could be viewed strictly from organizational perspectives. Managers could concentrate on meeting internal needs. There existed little risk of unpleasant surprises from external sources. These conditions have changed radically. Managers now must be concerned with organizational environments. Social and political trends demand organizations be viewed as components of community, nation, and world rather than self-contained entities.

Within seven categories, then, fall every management component applicable to public relations practice. Few differences exist between corporate/institutional departments and consulting firms. They arise primarily where new organizations are contemplated. Public relations counselors then must deal with organizational questions inapplicable to corporate or institutioinal practice. Uniformity otherwise prevails.

Organizing for Productivity

Organizing in public relations practice varies little from other enterprises. It is designed to bring resources together to achieve objectives. Management decisions are required as to scope of organizational activities, their grouping into logical frameworks, and their assignment to people. Essentials of the process are delineating objectives, coordinating, and delegating authority. Little variation exists across organizations in basic categories: corporate/institutional and counseling practice.

Organization in counseling primarily is a product of size. Several legal structures are available, and each implies organizational variation but differences are more perceived than real. Organization is more critical in corporate/institutional practice, especially as to functional positioning in the organization. The consultant model requires staff rather than line positioning. Public relations ideally is among if not preeminent in a unit dedicated to communications disciplines. Managers should report to principal operating officers.

Producing Goods and Services

Public relations services and products—corporate or institutional as well as counseling—essentially are similar. The basics of production—inputs, transformation or throughputs, and outputs—are identical. Variation arises as a function of unit size and organizatioinal communications need. Production planning generically deals with the location, capacity, and layout of facilities involved. The process in public relations involves evaluating internal versus external resources and the relative merits of in-house production versus subcontracting.

The latter decisions are governed by anticipated volume and the nature of internal resources. Practitioners in corporate or institutional practice often find significant economies by better-using or establishing internal resources. The same principle applies in counseling but on more limited bases. Counselors achieve best results by concentrating efforts in primary operational areas. Internally generated demand for specific products or services seldom justifies additional free-standing profit centers.

Managing Human Resources

Human resources management techniques are uniform across organizations. Motivation and leadership are the key elements involved. Others include personnel practices, employee training and development, wage and salary administration, and benefits programming. Managerial latitude in these areas varies more with organizational size than type. Less significant but noteworthy are contingent organizational needs in management-labor relations.

Attention also is necessary to variation in personnel categories. Many feel their creative colleagues require extra delicacy in "care and feeding." Others consider variation in employee relationships a greater source of difficulty.

The Marketing Function

Whether labeled "business development," "marketing," or "sales," acquiring additional business always is a counselor concern. Under the consultant concept, it equally concerns corporate/institutional practitioners. Their circumstances differ in few respects. Organizational consultants' prospects and geographic scope are circumscribed by the organization they serve. Counselors' prospects are near-limitless, bounded only by ethical parameters and self-imposed geographic or practice limitations. Organizational opportunities are few, however, only in relative terms. Practitioners find growth potential in personnel and labor relations, dealer/distributor relations, supplier relations, and so on.

This approach involves marketing in the traditional sense of that word. Marketers identify customer/constituent/client needs, develop products or services to meet those needs, and deliver them on mutually advantageous economic bases. Public relations practice differs traditionally only in that need for public relations services seldom is expressed. Practitioners find it necessary to identify problems and induce use of services in their solution.

Financing Operations

Financing in traditional public relations practice differs from counseling firm to corporate/institutional department. Similarities outnumber differences under the consultant model. Most significant among the latter is need for "start-up" capital. Entrepreneurial practitioners must find or provide necessary capital. Parent organizations meet this need for corporate or institutional practitioners. Subsequent concerns follow similar paths with few exceptions. The consultant model requires a return on investment in both situations.

In close-held rather than publicly owned counseling firms, the term "profit" becomes ambiguous. Profits as defined by the Internal Revenue Service are minimized. Net income to principals is the primary goal. "The bottom line," in contrast, measures success in publicly held firms and in corporate or institutional departments. Counselor practices also differ since they ultimately are disposed of while corporate/institutional units presumably function in perpetuity.

Controlling Operations

Every organization and subunit ultimately must evaluate performance and draw up future plans based on the evaluation. The procedure is a control process. It involves two components: decision making and control. Both apply to all public relations operations.

Decision making includes analysis, defining alternatives, selecting courses of action, and implementing decisions. Certainty, risk, and both objective and subjective probabilities must be considered. Control requires developing standards, measuring results, and taking corrective action. Both processes require information. Much of it is generated as accounting and data. The balance is created through production reporting.

Environmental Assessment

Much has been written about managing public policy, public affairs, and public issues. The underlying concept is neither new nor revolutionary. Strategic management long has been a component of business practice; so has environmental assessment. Strategic management differs from public affairs or public issues management in one respect: It encompasses all trends or issues. Public issues management focuses on those amenable to government intervention.

Environmental assessment in strategic management is concerned with external and internal organizational environments. The former include impacts of changing social, moral, and ethical standards on workers as well as legislatively or administratively mandated change in wage rates, fringe benefits, and such. Successful managers thus deal with organizational suprasystems as well as subsystems. Through them they deal with change in contemporary society.

SOCIETAL CHANGE

Public relations managers share the problems of those directing other enterprises. They also must deal with emerging difficulties unique to public relations practice. Three promise to be especially troublesome: (1) increasing public skepticism of media content; (2) continuing decline in the efficacy of mass media as channels of communication; and (3) growing numbers of social problems that defy solutions.

Decline in public confidence in the media apparently is an ironic outcome of the Watergate affair, which brought the downfall of President Richard Nixon. Watergate and related events produced general deterioration in confidence in institutions and corporations. By the 1980s the media were afflicted as well.

Media Problems

Independent studies by organizations of print and broadcast journalists showed public confidence in their content at less than 45 percent. Audiences concurrently were deteriorating.

The decline apparently was being produced by a combination of factors, foremost being media proliferation. Television networks were under siege by cable systems. The Federal Communications Commission was preparing to license low-power television broadcasters as well. Among print media, daily newspaper circulation was being eroded by business newspapers, city and state magazines, and increasing market penetration by nationally circulated dailies such as the *Wall Street Journal*, the New York *Times*, and *USA Today*.

Magazines apparently were contributing to declines among newspapers and broadcast audiences. Specialized publications were proliferating in such diverse subject areas as computers and health. Reincarnated versions of *Life* and the *Saturday Evening Post* were seeking to reinvigorate the mass magazine concept.

Finally, new information sources were proliferating. Computer owners were spending more time with information utilities. They ranged from CompuServe Information Service and The Source to specialized data bases such as Dialog and Mead Data Central's Nexis.

No end is in sight. In France, virtually every home has a videotext unit. In the United States, relatively inexpensive videotelephones are coming into more common use in business. Even the political establishment has joined the information age, vaulting the Potomac via satellite to maintain closer contacts with constituencics.

A Matter of Logic

While quantitative data were lacking, logic and anecdotal information tended to confirm the extent of the problem. Logically, individuals' available time for acquisition of mediated iniformation is relatively inflexible. Where new media prosper by attracting audiences and advertising support, they must be assumed to have been gained at the expense of others. More convincing are comments such as those of a former Proctor and Gamble executive in *Business Week*: "the mass audience delivered to the mass merchandiser by the mass media simply no longer exists."

The problem doubtless has been compounded by another technological development that created considerable media impact: the videocassette recorder or VCR. The VCR destroyed broadcaster control over what viewers see and when they see it. Without reliable data, it nevertheless is logical to assume that many use VCRs to watch entertainment programming during periods in which networks are broadcasting news.

Emerging Issues

These trends reduced public relations practitioners' ability to convey messages to mass audiences through mass media. They also developed at a time in which more issues preoccupying the nation defy solution.

A few examples illustrate the latter point. Public outcries against nuclear energy and environmental pollution have increased. Other than polluting fuels, however, there is no practical alternative to nuclear power. Public complaints also have focused concurrently on use of chemicals to increase food supplies and higher grocery prices. Concurrent resolution again appears impossible.

Finally, there are issues raised by definitions of the term "social responsibility." The Reagan administration's retreat from social welfare programs with admonitions to private enterprise to assume responsibility created pressure on the business community. How should business respond? How shall priorities be set? How much is enough? These and other questions demanded responses none seemed prepared to deliver.

Against this backdrop, public relations managers must deal with all the problems and opportunities that arise in any business. Liability insurance costs have been increasing. Availability of capital, constricted in the early 1980s, eased in mid-decade but could again become a problem. These and other factors must be considered by managers in developing strategic plans for their practices.

DEVELOPING PRACTICE STRATEGIES

Strategic planning is essential to successful public relations practice. This is so regardless of the size of the consultant or corporate organization. The process may be relatively informal. In smaller organizations it may involve outside counsel. It must be comprehensive in nature, however, and the process is as important as the product.

Beginning the Process

Successful strategic planning begins with agreement on a planning outline. Simplicity is preferable but the process must address every functional area. In consultant organizations, these include financial, human resources, staff development, client services, fees, new business development, and organizational structure. To the extent they are controllable at the department level, these factors should be examined in the course of corporate and institutional strategic planning as well. Corporate and institutional plans vary, however, as to new business development. Here the outer boundaries of the organization serve as geographic limits. External environmental assessments in keeping with departmental strategic plans deal with organizational environments or suprasystems within which departments function.

Mission Statements

Most strategic planning processes include reviewing mission statements, analyzing external and internal environments, and developing objectives and strategies for each functional area. Strategies include target and periodic review dates.

Mission statements define the purposes for which organizations exist and functions they perform. They should specify what organizations want to be. The kinds of clients they want to serve, expressions of service philosophy, and general statements describing the manner in which success will be achieved and measured also are necessary. Finally, mission statements are designed for permanency. They become fixed beacons for managers' continuing guidance.

Environmental Assessment

Results of internal and external environmental assessments, including statements of relative strength and weakness, are the informational foundations of strategic plans. External environments consist of conditions in which organizations function. In public relations practice, changes always are pertinent. Impacts vary with the nature of the organization. Corporate units are concerned with their positions in context with other communication disciplines. Counseling firms are concerned with relative position among consultancies. Strategic planners in both cases seek opportunities for productive growth. Needed services not currently provided constitute opportunities for public relations departments. Specialized services not available in a community or region create similar opportunities for counselors.

Internal assessments vary little from counseling to corporate organizations. They deal with strengths and weaknesses; with growth rates and staff capabilities; with training and development programs, client mixes, and the like. The emphasis again is on detecting opportunities for growth or improvement.

Objectives and Strategies

Opportunities identified in internal and external assessments lead to development of objectives and strategies. They specify goals planners want to achieve and steps to achieve them. Objectives must be expressed in realistic terms. They should be achieveable within specified temporal frameworks. Moreover, they must be flexible.

Strategic plans "cast in concrete" become more troublesome than productive if goals and strategies must be accomplished at any cost. Planners should control plans rather than the reverse. Time factors especially require flexibility. Progress can be erratic. Proportionate progress cannot and should not be expected on quarterly or even annual bases. Plans should be road maps to assist organizations in moving from where they are to where they want to be rather than objectives in themselves.

Action Plans

Action plans must be developed from strategic plans. The latter speak in general terms; the former specify steps to implement strategies. They identify individuals responsible for each step and establish review points necessary during implementation processes. Action plans and detailed strategies should be drawn for each functional area.

The process facilitates periodic review and update procedures. Responsibilities are clearly defined together with pertinent review points. Strategies, while subject to revision in keeping with subsequent environmental assessments, are in place. Finally, where plans are communicated to all members of organizations and their roles are defined, a clear sense of direction is established.

IN SUMMARY

The consultant model of public relations practice casts organizational practitioners and counselors in near-identical roles. Both seek productive solutions to clients' public relations problems in circumstances that reward success.

The model requires adherence to new and traditional management techniques. Planning, organizing, directing, controlling, and reporting fall in the traditional category. They are supplemented in contemporary practice by techniques drawn from strategic management. Environmental assessment is most important among them.

The strategic management process bases all subsequent activities on constant monitoring of organizational environments, internal and external. It requires practitioner sensitivity and responsiveness to change. The requirement applies to practices and client organizations.

The process is especially appropriate in contemporary public relations practice. It focuses practitioner attention on contemporary trends and requires appropriate response. Trends of most concern in public relations include media audience fragmentation and multiplying social problems.

Strategic planning begins with development of a mission statement. Environmental assessment leads to creation of appropriate goals and practice strategies. Action plans designed to induce measurable behavioral change among constituent groups then are prepared and implemented.

ADDITIONAL READING

Albert, Kenneth J., ed. *The Strategic Management Handbook*. New York: McGraw-Hill, 1983.

Drucker, Peter. *Management: Tasks, Responsibilities, Practices*. New York: Harper & Row, 1974.

Gannon, Martin J. *Management: An Organizational Perspective*. Boston: Little, Brown, 1977.

Haner, F. T., and James C. Ford. *Contemporary Management*. Columbus, Ohio: Merrill, 1973.

Hickman, Craig R., and Michael A. Silva. *Creating Excellence: Managing Corporate*

Culture, Strategy and Change in the New Age. New York: New American Library, 1984.

Marsteller, William A. *Creative Management*. Chicago: Crain, 1981.

Naisbitt, John, and Patricia Aburdene. *Re-Inventing the Corporation*. New York: Warner, 1985.

O'Toole, James. *Vanguard Management: Redesigning the Corporate Future*. Garden City, N.Y.: Doubleday, 1985.

Wheelen, Thomas L., and J. David Hunger. *Strategic Management and Business Policy*. Reading, Mass: Addison-Wesley, 1983.

3

Preparing for Tomorrow: Strategic Organization

Public relations practice is changing. Few are so venturesome as to predict the shape of tomorrow's public relations organizations. They inevitably will be far different than today's.

A PROFESSION IN TRANSITION

Although enshrouded by confusing terminology, the nature of the profession is in transition. Practitioner roles are shifting from technician to expert prescriber; computers and associated technology are becoming common in day-to-day practice; and public relations is becoming a management function in fact as well as theory.

Environmental Pressures

Accelerating change in public relations practice originates in multiple environments. Some exert pressure on public relations organizations. Others produce new and expanded client demands.

The latter trends are most pervasive. They originate in the political environment, where the federal government has sought to shift responsibility to the states. They arise in the technological environment, where new industries are being spawned by biotechnology and robotics as well as computers. In the market environment, product life cycles are growing shorter and marketers are frustrated by weakness in communicatons channels. The social environment is generating problems as organizations seek to define social responsibility. In the human environment a shortage of workers soon will develop as the baby boom era nears retirement.

These pressures are compounded in public relations. Organizations demand more of public relations departments and counselor firms. Measurable results are required. New movements toward licensure and certification also are afoot.

These trends demand change in management philosophy within the profession. Managers until recently were able to concentrate on solving client problems. Now they must act to insure that their own organizations remain viable as well.

Organizational Models

Organizations providing public relations services traditionally have been cast in one of two models. One is the counseling firm, which consists of one or more professionals and a variety of support personnel providing services to general or specialized clienteles.

The second is the public relations department, which is an organizational component. Like the counselor firm, it consists of one or more professionals and various support personnel. Unlike the counselor organization, it provides services only to the parent organization.

Increasing numbers of organizations maintain internal and external public relations resources. The latter usually handle special tasks or support organizational staffs in emergencies.

Reductions in numbers and/or sizes of organizational public relations units has been accomplished through consolidation, in conjunction with mergers and acquisitions. More multidivisional companies handle public relations through single corporate staffs. Such arrangements usually are accompanied by increased use of counselor organizations.

Specialized Tasks

Special counsel may be needed in any of several situations. Perhaps most common are governmental relations problems. Pressing needs often arise in governmental relations where organizational headquarters are distant from seats of government. Other specialized assistance may be required in dealing with overseas problems, with the financial community, or with ethnic groups.

Emergency Situations

When the word "emergency" is mentioned in public relations practice, many think immediately of Tylenol, Love Canal, Three Mile Island, and Bhopal. These are but a few of the types of crises with which public relations deals.

Unfriendly takeover attempts, product liability problems, and battles to fend off unionizing efforts also are included. The latter may appear routine to the average individual; to organizational executives, they are crises.

Contemporary thought suggests these problems will occur with increasing frequency. Writing in the 1985 edition of *Public Affairs Review*, Ian I. Mitroff and Ralph H. Kilmann identified "five generic types of corporate tragedies or disasters that have been happening on a scale wide enough to preclude denial of the phenomenon":

1. Product or service tampering, as in the case of Tylenol.
2. Inability to predict or control environmental circumstances, as with Proctor & Gamble's Rely Tampon.
3. Major catastrophes such as Union Carbide's in Bhopal.
4. Guilt by unwarranted association, as in Atari's problem with an X-rated cartridge produced by another party but compatible with Atari video equipment.
5. Logotype problems such as the recurrent rumors that Proctor & Gamble's man-in-the-moon logo was somehow satanic.

The problems, these authors suggest, will continue. They also contribute to a growing need for public relations services. There is no assurance, however, that traditionally organized counselors or organizational units are prepared to provide them.

The Nature of Public Relations

Among basic problems with which public relations organizations must contend is a matter of definition. Too few have ever addressed a question of vital importance: "What business are we in?"

Definition Problem

They are in the public relations business, of course. Most have grown and prospered, however, as generalists rather than specialists. They have undertaken virtually any and every assignment that comes to hand.

Some have specialized but they are relatively few. Many apparently specialized organizations are less than they appear. Some are specialized divisions of general practices. Others are more specialized in name than in practice.

Labeling Problem

Compounding difficulties in defining the nature of the business is a labeling problem. In recent years, public relations has borne many labels: "public affairs" has been prominent in government; "external affairs" and "public issues" have been used in some companies; Of late the term "issues management" has become popular. Definitions of these terms differ little from that of public relations. Considerable confusion nevertheless has arisen.

Promiscuous use of the term "marketing" has compounded the problem. Strictly interpreted, marketing involves two basic steps. The first is research to determine consumer needs and desires. The second is developing products or services to meet those needs and desires. Communication techniques—especially advertising and public relations—then are used to convey information about products or services to prospective consumers.

The foregoing should not be taken as denigrating any discipline. It reflects semantic problems practitioners encounter in dealing with clients— existing and prospective. They can be overcome by approaching organizational development, marketing, and sales processes in terms of client needs. Counselors occasionally avoid all mention of public relations in less sophisticated markets. They instead focus on solutions to problems with which clients are concerned, leaving others to define terms.

Developing the Strategic Plan

Organizing public relations practices under any name follows a consistent pattern. It serves counselor and organizational practitioner alike in proposed and existing practices. The pattern is based on a business plan capitalizing on organizational strength and competitor weaknesses. The developmental process involved is called strategic planning.

Strategic planning involves a series of steps to produce optimum results with available resources. They include:

1. Environmental assessment
   a. External
   b. Internal
2. Identifying prospect industries
3. Identifying specific prospects
4. Analyzing competitors' strengths and weaknesses
5. Cataloging organizational resources
   a. Creative
   b. Physical
   c. Financial
6. Establishing goals
7. Determining strategies
8. Allocating resources
9. Implementing the plan
10. Monitoring results and making adjustment

There is no magic in the number of steps listed. Others might expand the list or outline the process in fewer steps. The process rather than any list of components should be practitioners' primary concern. As in practice development, it applies strategic methods to insure logical and rational planning. One approach to the strategic planning process is diagrammed in Figure 3.1.

FIGURE 3.1. Strategic Management Model.

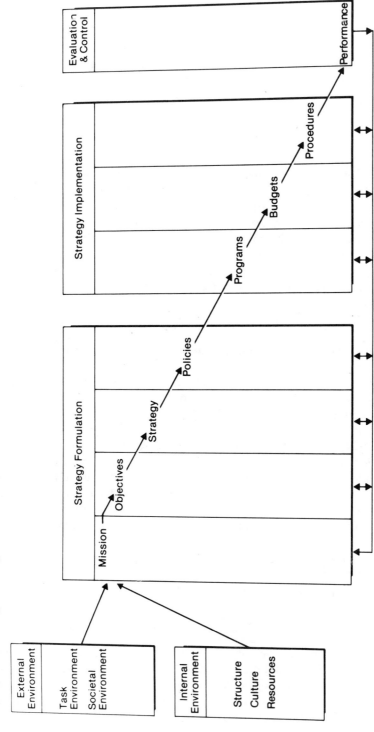

Source: From Thomas L. Wheelen and J. David Hunger, *Strategic Management and Business Policy,* © 1983, Addison-Wesley, Reading, Massachusetts. Reprinted with permission.

37

Environmental Assessment

Multiple environments must be examined in applying strategic planning techniques to public relations. Internal and external environments are included. External assessment is more complex in public relations than in other organizations.

Counselor Practice

Multiple external environments require attention. They include those of the business community and the practice. Competitor organizations must be listed with the nature of their practices. Special attention must be paid to the nature of their clienteles and services they render.

Counselors' internal assessment processes also require precise focus. Primary attention must be given to organizational capabilities, technological as well as human. Assessment outcomes must specify organizational productivity levels in relation to potential. Two questions are paramount. Are resources optimally productive? Can they be redeployed to enhance productivity?

Organizational Practice

Environmental assessment in organizational practice is similarly complex. External assessment again involves multiple environments: the practice environment, consisting of the organizational suprasystem; the set of suprasystems within which other organizational components function; and the environment of the organization as a whole.

Public relations' "competitors" in organizational practice are other communication subunits of the organization. They include advertising, sales, promotion, and marketing. The extent to which law, accounting, and other organizational subunits may be impinging on the traditional public relations practice area also should be examined. Accountants have been seeking to develop social index or statistics that might be made part of "social accounting systems." Proliferation of lawyers has encouraged some to expand counseling services beyond legalities.

Internal assessment in organizational practice parallels the counselor pattern. The primary questions again involve existing and potential productivity levels. Responses must identify specific areas of potential improvement.

Research

The environmental assessment process should be a starting point for ongoing research. Precise methodologies will vary with circumstances. Focus group interviews often are a logical first step. They enable practitioners to ascertain the extent to which key constituencies are concerned over emerging issues identified through assessment.

Thereafter, formal survey research may be appropriate. This especially is true where diverse populations are involved and issues are evolving rapidly. Repetitive surveys at frequent intervals then may be desirable.

Identifying Prospects

The prospect identification process is identical for counselor and organizational practitioner other than in one respect—prospects in the latter case are confined to the organization. The identification process consists of two parts in both practice formats. The first involves functional areas. Organizational practitioners examine other organizational components while counselors focus on industry groups. The second phase requires specifying individual prospects. Prospects' existing and potential needs are paramount in each situation.

Counselor Practice

Counselor prospect identification steps require responses to a series of questions:

1. What commercial/industrial/institutional groups are using public relations services within the geographic area the counselor serves or will serve?
2. In what sectors can environmental factors be expected to create demand for services?
3. What organizations in the several groups are without professional counsel?
4. Which will most need counsel

Organizational Practice

With one exception, organizational practitioners' prospect identification process parallels that of counselors. Which organizational components are using public relations services? Which are apt to need them in the near term? In the long term?

The exception deals with existing and/or proposed counselor relationships. It requires several further questions. To what extent can services currently provided by counselors be handled internally? To what extent *should* they be handled internally?

Internal versus External

Internal versus external development of public relations services is a matter that has troubled many managers. The question essentially is economic. Assuming service quality is equal, can organizational public relations needs be better met through an internal department? Through a counselor organization? Through a combination of the two?

Each approach has advantages and disadvantages. Most involve relative quality and cost. Considered in the abstract, the differences are almost meaningless. They can be analyzed only in light of organizational need.

Cost

Given equal practitioner knowledge and skill levels, services delivered by internal units tend to be less costly. Most counselor organizations base charges on multiples of personnel wage rates. Multipliers usually are no lower than three. Cost must be viewed, however, in context with volume and consistency of need. Where relatively little specialized service is required, employing full-time personnel is impractical. This also is true where a great deal of service is required in a short time, as in the case of a crisis or transient legislative or regulatory problem.

Geography

Another element bearing on the internal versus external service question is geography. Travel and accommodation costs must be added to wage rates of those handling assignments in distant locations. These may be acceptable where assignments are infrequent. As frequency—and cost—increase, what once was economically handled internally may better be assigned to external counsel.

Managerial Philosophy

Management philosophy also requires evaluation in determining the extent to which organizations should use internal or external resources. Senior managements during the 1970s tended to prefer internal staffing. Public relations managers were cast more in facilitator than consultant roles.

The pattern changed with the recession of the early 1980s. Economic conditions induced reexamination of internal organizations. Many were reduced in size. Remaining practitioners were more often in consultant than facilitator and technician roles. The latter functions more frequently were assigned to external counsel.

Neither approach can be labeled "right" or "wrong." Preferences of organizational and public relations managers govern. "Outsourcing," as it is known in the auto industry, frees managers to fulfill the consultant roles to which they aspire. They can be expected to encourage the practice, but not without price.

Increased use of external counsel demands greater care in their selection. Comparative evaluation of counseling organizations is not the easiest of tasks. Each has strengths and weaknesses. Their resources vary. So do the skills and bodies of knowledge they command.

The "path of least resistance" tends to lead organizational and public relations managers to concentrate external assignments with one or a relatively few counselor firms. Those seeking optimum results exercise caution.

Over time, counselors increasingly may find themselves working "side by side" with colleagues in the same manner as advertising agencies assigned different products by the same manufacturer.

Competitive Factors

Strategic planning creates an organizational design calculated to achieve managers' objectives. A review of practice opportunities is the first step. To establish action priorities, constraints also must be assessed. They include internally and externally created limitations.

Limitations

Constraints on practice potential are created in part by competitors. In counselor practice, they may have preempted industries or predominant organizations in those industries. Their relative strength may be so great as to reduce initially perceived potential. Similar conditions apply in organizational practice. An advertising or marketing department may be handling product publicity. Financial services may have a prior claim on shareholder relations. Such conditions pose a series of research questions for public relations managers.

1. To what extent are perceived needs being met in specific industries or practice areas?
2. Are prospects in those sectors already equipped to meet those needs.
3. Are all services necessary to need satisfaction available in the marketplace?

Screening Prospects

These questions can be viewed as screens through which prospect lists must be passed. Each eliminates some prospects. Where perceived needs largely are being met, little potential exists for new services. Where primary prospects are well-equipped but others are not, further investigation may be appropriate. Where all needed services are not available, they must be offered productively.

By pursuing the questions to logical conclusions, managers develop two types of prospect lists. For counselors, the first includes organizations in industries where significant levels of need exist. The second lists specific prospect firms. In organizational settings, the first list consists of other organizational subunits. The second itemizes services not available from organizational sources.

SERVICES AND RESOURCES

At this point in the analytical process, managers should be able to respond tentatively to the question posed earlier: "What business are we in?" The public relations business, of course, but greater definition is needed. Will the organization specialize in financial public relations, in employee communication, or in one or more other practice areas.

Decisions should be made on the basis of market conditions. Which services are in greatest demand? To what extent is demand satisfied? What does the environmental assessment process suggest as to emerging demand? Short term? Long term?

Finally, how can assets be deployed to produce services selected at maximum profit? Whether "revenue over expense" on an organizational unit's year-end statement or "cash in the bank" for a counselor firm, the bottom line is critical. It is tangible evidence of success in terms senior managers understand.

Resource Analysis

Resource analysis is a two-part process through which managers prepare to make decisions vital to the long-term health of the practice. The first part is an analysis of organizational resources. The second is an analysis of external resources.

Internal analysis deals with two of the primary components of business: labor and capital. External analysis examines vendor organizations' capabilities.

Human Resources

Successful human resources analysis requires precise responses to questions about skills and bodies of knowledge:

1. Which are available in the organization?
2. Which are consistently required and amenable to short-term acquisition through
   a. Employee training/education?
   b. Expanding the personnel complement?
3. Which are intermittently required and might better be obtained through external sources?

Knowledge and Skill

Summaries of personnel attributes should be readily available. Where data do not exist, they should be developed through knowledge/skills inventories.

Few employees exercise all their skills or apply all their knowledge in any position. All must be known to managers if human resources are to be applied productively. Where knowledge or skills must be strengthened to produce new services, three alternatives exist: employees can be educated or trained, new employees can be hired, or counselors can be called upon to provide the services.

Education/Training

Several techniques can be used to produce short-term improvement in employee skill and knowledge levels. Self-study using library resources is a viable option where knowledge rather than skill is required. Most libraries have required texts or can obtain them through loan services.

More formal techniques are appropriate where extensive knowledge is necessary and time factors are not critical. Most professional organizatons offer seminars and short courses for members and others. Technical schools, community colleges, and four-year colleges and universities also offer continuing education programs. Managers should investigate availability of appropriate programs at nearby institutions.

Adding Personnel

Early expansion of organizational personnel to provide new services involves risk. Offering a service without the capability to provide it is equally risky. Failure to offer services where demand exists is an unacceptable alternative, however, and managers must proceed in the face of some risk.

Risk can be minimized in at least two ways. One exists where staffs are to be expanded or vacancies exist. Position descriptions can be redrawn and work reallocated to accommodate individuals with required skills or knowledge. In the alternative, the work can be subcontracted, which also entails risk. The nature of the new service becomes known to outsiders; subcontractors may prove unreliable or inept. This approach nevertheless may be appropriate in the absence of adequate capital.

Where personnel are added, screening profiles should be developed specifying knowledge/skill levels necessary in developing new services. Formal human resources planning processes are used in larger organizations.

Capital Resources

In business, capital is more than money. The word is defined to include machinery, equipment, and tools that humans use in producing products or services. Managers' decisions determine the form in which assets are held. They can be maintained as money in the bank, as humans on the payroll, or as equipment for employee use.

Money

Cash in the bank, or uncommitted in the budget, tends to comfort managers. it makes little or no contribution toward achieving organizational objectives. Money market interest rates are inadequate to compensate investors for business risks.

This does not mean managers should "bet the store" on risky ventures. Cash reserves are essential. Borrowing is expensive when interest rates are low. When they move rapidly upward, the business may be at risk.

Money must be invested to produce a return. It can be invested in human or capital resources. The decision making involved must be based on two factors. The first is return on investment. If the manager invests in personnel, what return can be expected? The second is risk. If the new service is not accepted in the marketplace, what might be lost?

Equipment

The same questions apply to equipment. They must be asked—and answered—as to each opportunity identified through the assessment process. Only then can informed decisions be made.

Analyses of equipment needs parallel those used in the personnel area. What return can be expected? The question should be applied to the service for which equipment would be purchased and to other applicatons. How much will it be used? What will be the cost per hour of use? How will these costs relate to additional revenues? To savings in labor?

Complete analyses of alternative resource applications enable managers to reach logical conclusions. This especially is so where external resources are concurrently examined.

External Resources

Managers can defer acquiring resources by contracting with outside vendors for products or services. Many vendor services long have been used in public relations practice, others are relatively new in the marketplace—all can be acquired externally. They include copywriting, graphic design and illustration, photography, typography/composition, printing, audio-visual production, and meeting/convention services.

To a greater or lesser extent, public relations organizations buy all of these services. Rankings vary from one practice to another. Multiple variables govern the extent to which a practice uses external services. They include availability, specialization, and technological factors.

Availability. Most listed services are available in most communities. Availability—and quality—tend to vary with community size. Highly specialized services such as computer-generated graphics tend to be least available.

Specialization. Specialized services are not confined to "high tech" areas. Architectural photography is not readily available in many communities; nor are specialized writing skills such as technical writing and speech writing.

Technology. Technology used in public relations is not necessarily "high" technology. High-speed automated reproduction of products ranging from black-and-white photo prints to audio and video tapes is concentrated in a few high population areas.

Managers need total production systems. They can and should combine internal and external resources to meet client needs. Needs must be met on timely bases within established quality standards and budgetary limits.

GOALS AND STRATEGIES

Goals and strategies to achieve objectives are organizational road maps. Goals are destinations to which managers seek to take organizations. Strategies are directions to be followed in reaching those goals.

The organization without goals and strategies essentially is uncontrolled. It lacks direction. Its decisions are made on ad hoc bases. What it achieves will have been accomplished more by coincidence than design.

Setting Goals

Organizational goal-setting is a relatively simple process. It conventionally begins with a look backward. Where the organization has been and the extent of the progress it has been making contribute to realistic goal setting.

Goals traditionally are set in terms of sales or profits. They can be established more specifically in public relations. Numbers and types of accounts to be gained during the ensuing period often are projected as goals.

Realism Essential

The nature of goals is less important than the level of realism management employs in setting them. Goals must be attainable. They must be realistic. Organizational subunits and individuals charged with achieving goals tend to ignore any that appear beyond attainment.

Goals often are established in percentages based on prior years' performance. The goal for the new year equals the prior year's performance plus a growth percentage. Specific goals then are fixed in terms of types of clients and/or services. These are based on factors previously discussed: results of the environmental assessment process, identification of prospects, competitive strengths and weaknesses, and availability of resources.

Ranking Alternatives

These elements are viewed collectively rather than individually. Potential expansion in an area where competition is relatively strong might be assigned to relatively low priority. So might new services requiring a high percentage of uncommitted resources.

Management decisions must be based on value judgments derived from information gathered earlier. With goals established, strategies then are selected.

Selecting Strategies

Strategies applicable to developing public relations practices are diverse. They vary with the nature of practices.

Organizational Strategies

In organizations, strategies are limited by organizational boundaries. Traditionally, they also are limited by organizational goals. Practice expansion often involves little more than providing additional services requested by senior management.

Under the consultant model, fewer constraints apply. Public relations managers are free to solicit additional "business" from both existing and prospective clients. Prospective clients are other organizational units perceived as needing professional services. The unit's obligation to senior management is to provide services throughout the organization as needed and within limits imposed by resulting revenues.

Practice expansion opportunities exist in almost every organization. Managers need only identify them. Goals established for other organizational units yield clues to practice opportunities. Almost any change in organizational course or structure creates public relations needs. These opportunities must be exploited if public relations units are to achieve objectives. They usually are expressed in terms of growth and enhanced measurable outcomes.

Counselor Strategies

Near limitless numbers of strategic paths are open to counselors. They vary with the nature of the practice (general versus specialized), the geographic scope of the practice, and other factors.

General practice managers may elect to open units specializing in one or more emerging industries. Those operating in confined geographic areas may expand service areas, perhaps by opening new offices.

Others may pursue opportunities created by environmental change. Increased use of public relations techniques among professionals in recent years created such an opportunity. It permitted expansion of many practices and encouraged founding of new counselor firms specializing in service to professionals.

Implementing the Plan

The final steps in strategic planning are inextricable from the goal-setting and strategy selection processes. They proceed in light of available resources. As strategic decisions are made, resources are allocated as well.

"Checkpoints" or review dates should be built into plans as they evolve. These may be fixed dates or relate to completion of various phases of the plan. They are necessary for two reasons: plans do not always proceed as envisioned, and external events can intervene, requiring strategy adjustments.

Except in unusual circumstances, executing strategic plans begins on predetermined dates. They usually are the first day of a calendar or fiscal year. Between final approval and starting dates, managers must allocate responsibility for execution.

ALLOCATING RESPONSIBILITIES

Working with employees and vendors requires public relations managers to function in different worlds. Employee-employer and customer-vendor relationships differ. The primary point of difference is dependency. Employees' economic welfare is bound up in their jobs. Failure to comply with conditions of employment places a job at risk. This level of dependency rarely exists in customer-vendor relationships. Managers lack ability to compel performance.

Internal Responsibilities

Transferring responsibility within organizations is known as delegation. Successful delegation requires transferring responsibility and authority in equal parts. Recipients must, of course, be capable of handling the tasks at hand.

Managers' ability to delegate is limited by several factors. Organizational size and personnel quality are primary among them. Basic decisions as to systems to be used also are made during early planning.

Organizational Alternatives

Two alternatives usually are available to managers: One is a team approach to client needs; the other is an individual approach. Most public relations organizations use a combination of the two.

Under the team approach, professionals from several organizational subdivisions work together to meet client needs. Decision making is collegial in nature. The system tends to suffer for two reasons. First, responsibility is divided. Second, creative concepts tend to be compromised.

In the individual approach, single professionals handle client contact and decision making. They draw on other organizational resources as necessary. The system eliminates compromises inherent in the team approach. At the same time, however, potential for error compounds.

In larger organizations, a compromise often is used. A junior manager— in counselor organizations, an account supervisor—coordinates multiple individually assigned projects.

Impending Change

Managers now have some latitude in determining which approach to use. This latitude is apt to be restricted, however, as impending human resources shortages develop. Creative individuals are more demanding of organizations than most. These pressures can be expected to compound.

Managers' tasks will be further complicated by pressure to create nurturing environments. They require challenging work yielding greater employee satisfaction. These may prove difficult to establish.

Attitudinal Problems

Contemporary practitioners and managers might best be characterized as entrepreneurial communicators. Many are products of journalism. Individual enterprise and self-sufficiency are valued in both professions. Individual competition, which breeds a tendency toward secrecy, is endemic. Shared professional values are well-developed and mutually accepted. These cultural elements are among primary behavioral governors.

Journalistic culture was transplanted into public relations, for better or worse, by those who made the professional transition. Values involved served practitioners well while they were practicing individually in organizations or counseling roles. Self-reliance, follow-through, and related attributes helped them accomplish professional objectives. As organizations grew, these characteristics tended to become counterproductive.

The self-sufficiency and individual enterprise instilled in journalism induced similar expectations of others in public relations. Few managers have been secretive by design, or have they often created the openness and sharing of ideas and concepts necessary in public relations practice. Instinctive competitiveness apparently tends to produce "sink or swim" conditions for novices. They are expected to absorb cultural and performance standards by osmosis in the journalistic tradition.

These conditions may contribute to turnover among newcomers and to management problems for senior practitioners. The latter tend to arise as they seek to expand individual practices.

External Responsibilities

Where carefully developed, vendor relationships are more easily managed despite lower dependency levels. Successful and durable relationships exist where vendors are selected on the basis of capability and competitiveness, organizational expectations are clearly defined, and relationships are mutually beneficial.

Managers can obtain levels of vendor service difficult to generate internally where these conditions are fulfilled. All prerequisites must be met, however, if this is to be the case.

Dependency is critical in dealings with vendors. It is not normally part of such relationships but can be induced and becomes compelling. The "frog and puddle" analogy is applicable. Public relations organizations are better served as large frogs in small puddles than where the reverse is true.

The principle applies especially to counselor organizations, which cannot bill clients for vendor excuses. The frog and puddle analogy suggests several managerial steps.

Limited numbers. First, vendors should be limited in number. Sufficient work then can be placed with each to enhance the size of the frog. The process also reduces numbers of people with whom practitioners must work.

Careful selection. Second, vendors should be selected for types of work in which they specialize. Specialists usually excel in their specialties. Other work tends to be of marginal quality. In photography, for example, good portraiture and good architectural photos seldom originate from a single source. In printing, those specializing in four-color process work rarely perform well where work is less demanding. Quality may be high but prices tend to be excessive. Several vendors may be used where specialized work is concerned but numbers should be kept to a minimum.

Mutual advantage. Third, mutually advantageous arrangements should be actively developed. There is no reason, for example, why routine printing work should be handled on a rush basis. Managers should see that printers have more than ample time to complete routine work. This practice creates a basis for working agreements that might be expressed as follows: "Whenever and wherever we can, we're going to give you more than enough time to do our work without pressure. In response, when we find ourselves pressed, we expect you to reciprocate." Another important point can be made in like manner. "When we have agreed on a delivery date, we expect it to be kept. If you encounter a problem that will create a delay, we expect to be called *at least* 24 hours in advance of that delivery date. It's relatively easy to call a client a day ahead of time and tell him a job will be late. When he calls the day after the deadline and says it hasn't arrived, we have a major problem."

Quality levels. Fourth, quality levels must be accurately specified. While difficult, this objective can be accomplished. Definitions of "high quality" vary. Samples can be used if necessary. Only with clear definitions can managers establish criteria by which outcomes can be judged and standards enforced.

Prompt payment. Finally, there is the matter of money. Vendors appreciate prompt payment. Public relations organizations should be sufficiently funded and organized to permit mailing checks within 48 hours of receipt of invoices. Typical vendor relationships become close working relationships where this practice is followed.

Conflicts of Interest

Conflicts of interest can involve organizations and vendors as well as employees. This especially is true for creative personnel. They frequently are asked to "do a little job on the side" to supplement their incomes.

Employees

Efforts to control employees' activities off the job can create legal risk. Employees can be barred from performing services for competitors, but beyond this limitation, control efforts become perilous.

Courts in recent years have granted employees ownership rights in their jobs. In addition, noncompete agreements may be less binding than employers suppose. Consultation with attorneys is advisable before action is taken.

Vendors

The volume of federal and state statutes and regulations bearing on public relations practice continues to grow. Confidentiality of information imparted to vendors thus is increasingly important. Concepts created by consultants for employers or clients can become worthless or counterproductive if they come into competitors' hands. Vendors should be cautioned on these points and held accountable for lapses.

IN SUMMARY

Public relations practice, like society, is in the process of change. More specialization is developing. Corporate disasters are becoming more numerous. The practice is being redefined and broadened, and it is moving higher among organizational and executive priorities.

Successful practice management requires more sophistication than once was the case. It demands the same environmental assessment procedures employed in behalf of clients and employers. Succeeding steps must be followed as well.

Practice opportunities require careful analysis. They are emerging in counselor and organizational practice. Many organizations are assigning more public relations work to outside counsel, the logic and rationality of which are open to question. Cost and geographic factors are paramount in making judgments. Comparative evaluation is necessary for those who elect to use counseling organizations.

Strategic planning in these circumstances involves a series of steps. Competitive factors must be analyzed. The assessment process then must be directed inward to evaluate the public relations unit. Resources and services must be cataloged for examination in parallel with practice opportunities.

Only then can goals be established and strategies determined. Managers must determine how resources are to be allocated. Decisions must be made as to whether organizational needs are to be satisfied internally or externally.

Finally, responsibilities must be assigned internally and externally before strategic plans are implemented. Strong relationships with reliable vendors are a major practice asset.

ADDITIONAL READING

Aldrich, Howard E. *Organizations & Environments*. Englewood Cliffs, N. J.: Prentice-Hall, 1979.

Glueck, William F. *Organization Planning and Development*. New York: American Management Association, 1971.

Hall, Richard H. *Organizations: Structure and Process*. Englewood Cliffs, N.J.: Prentice-Hall, 1977.

Hickman, Craig R., and Michael A. Silva. *Creating Excellence: Managing Corporate Culture, Strategy and Change in the New Age*. New York: New American Library, 1984.

Mitroff, Ian I., and R. H. Kilman. "Why Corporate Disasters are on the Increase and How Companies Can Cope With Them," *Public Affairs Review*, 1985.

Nager, Norman R., and T. Harrell Allen. *Public Relations Management by Objectives*. New York: Longman, 1984.

Toffler, Alvin. *The Adaptive Corporation*. New York: McGraw-Hill, 1985.

Wheelen, Thomas L., and J. David Hunger. *Strategic Management and Business Policy*. Reading, Mass: Addison-Wesley, 1983.

4
Making the Critical Decisions

Successful public relations units develop through careful planning. This is the case whether an organizational department or a counseling firm is contemplated. The planning process requires that several variables be closely examined. There must be sufficient need for public relations services. A detailed business plan is necessary. The size and scope of the practice must be determined, as must the organizational structure and necessary facilities.

ESTABLISHING NEED

Sufficient need and demand for services must exist to justify projected investment. The two are not identical. "Demand" implies needs recognized by prospective users of services. "Need" suggests some may not be aware public relations services can be used in resolving existing or prospective problems. Need analyses begin with environmental assessment. What follows is a series of steps similar to those specified by Control Data Corporation's Quentin J. Heitaps, in Bill Cantor's *Inside Public Relations: Experts in Action.*

Environments

Careful scrutiny of pertinent environments is vital to successful decision making. Internal and external environments are involved. Prospective organizational units should be designed to deal with existing needs and those the environments may generate. Would-be counselors must have resources to meet environmentally generated needs of current and future clients.

The issue in both cases is a matter of return on investment. Will anticipated return be sufficient to justify the risk? Can the same resources create equal return at less risk elsewhere?

Critical Questions

The decision to proceed thus should be based on answers to a series of questions:

1. What environmental trends are impacting or threatening to impact the organization or client organizations.
2. What are their needs?
3. What services will be necessary to satisfy those needs?
4. With what bodies of knowledge and skill can the public relations unit initially be equipped?
5. To what extent will the organizational unit be able to meet
   a. Existing need?
   b. Prospective need?
6. For what services will the unit be forced to turn to external vendors?
7. What prospective clients require services the counselor will be able to provide?
8. What environmental trends suggest additional services may be required in near or long terms?
9. Which of the additional services will the counselor be able to provide without investing in further resources?
10. What capital investment will be required?
11. What operating expenses will be incurred on monthly or annual bases?
12. When will the new organization become profitable?

A preliminary needs assessment is essential. It must generate data adequate to permit accurate economic projections. They are necessary to determine if the unit will be economically viable in a reasonable time. Variables involved include volume of work available, value of the work, and investment needed to produce services involved. Few organizations suddenly encounter sufficient need to justify developing a public relations department; nor does sufficient unsatisfied demand for services exist in most communities to assure entrepreneurial success.

Surveys Appropriate

A mail survey of prospective clients in geographic areas that counselors propose to serve can be invaluable. Survey instrument design is important; it should deal with specific services rather than public relations in general. Too few prospective clients are aware of the scope of professional practice.

Those unfamiliar with research designs will find it helpful to consult an expert or an appropriate text. Surveys should address need factors carefully to obtain accurate data. Respondents often will provide names and addresses if copies of results are offered. Many may do so despite their identifying themselves as prospective clients.

Designs should permit including a cover letter and all questions on one 11 × 17-inch sheet folded to four 81/2 × 11-inch pages. A return envelope with postage prepaid should be included.

Telephone surveys can be used but tend to be difficult for two reasons: Decision makers are hard to reach through this medium, and interviews are time-consuming. They may be considered an imposition by individuals whom counselors should not offend.

Surveys also are appropriate in organizational practice but informal in-person interviews are preferable. Numbers of prospects are few and practitioners seek as much information as possible. Interviews also serve as sales devices, helping to acquaint prospects with available services.

Developing a Plan

Survey data enable researchers to estimate practice development potential. They provide quantitative indicators of potential among types of organizations surveyed. The information facilitates design of development plans based on practitioner knowledge and skill.

Plans should specify organizational groups of greatest potential and services to be offered. Economic estimates then should be conservatively prepared. Numbers of clients to be signed over 12 to 24 months of operation and resulting revenues should be estimated. They enable practitioners to project dates on which break-even points will be reached. One question then remains: Are resources available to absorb losses that accrue until break-even points are reached?

Similar approaches can be used by senior managers weighing the merits of creating internal public relations units. Volume of need projected over 12 to 24 months can be calculated. So can the cost of acquiring services externally. These should be weighed against projected expenses involved in operating the internal unit for a like period.

Alternatives

Several options are open to entrepreneurs establishing new enterprises. Use of counselors is an obvious alternative for organizations. "Moonlighting" can serve as a market test for entrepreneurs. Economic risks are sufficient in either case to justify caution.

Part-time, free-lance, or moonlighting opportunities exist in most markets. Many young organizations without resources to employ or retain professionals will engage part-time help. As they mature, they tend to employ professionals and later may retain counsel as well.

The Decision

When need has been established, a question remains: Can need satisfaction produce adequate revenue to support the practice?

ECONOMIC DECISION MAKING

The decision to establish a public relations practice is more readily made in organizational than counselor settings. Senior organizational managers can readily estimate need and cost. They presumably have adequate resources to sustain a practice until it is profitable. Prospective counselors often are handicapped by lack of resources and uncertainty over break-even points.

Risk attendant to launching counseling organizations can be minimized in several ways: A detailed set of financial projections should be prepared, alternatives in acquiring facilities and equipment should be examined, and sources of additional funds should be considered.

Financial Projections

Financial projections for proposed counseling practices most readily are calculated in budget form on monthly bases. The budget might be outlined as follows:

Expense

Item	*Monthly Cost*
Salaries	$
Withholding/FICA	
Office rent	
Telephone	
Utilities	
Accounting & legal	
Automotive expense	
Dues/subscriptions	
Travel/accommodations	
Depreciation	
Miscellaneous	
Contingency	

Unless one or more clients already have been signed, there will be no revenues. Even where a clientele exists, revenue flows will not begin for 30 to 60 days unless retainer fees are billed in advance. Listed expenses thus accrue without revenue for most of the first several months of practice. Losses decline as revenues increase until the break-even point is reached.

Revenues

In calculating revenues, prospective counselors must be guided by best estimates of receipts (rather than potential) for the first year, and numbers of dollars available to sustain the practice for that period or longer.

Expenses listed above anticipate start-up capital. This is evidenced in the word "depreciation." Depreciation consists of losses sustained as the value of furnishings and equipment declines. Presence of the word implies an investment in this area. Where start-up funds are limited, early investment needs can be minimized by financing or leasing. Interest costs tend to make these devices less attractive than they appear.

A more comprehensive approach is illustrated in Figure 4.1. The example applies to a retail rather than a service business. With appropriate modifications, it can be used to project public relations practice needs as well.

Financial Alternatives

Where staffed and equipped offices are essential and resources are limited, several alternatives exist. Furnishings and equipment can be rented or leased. Advantageous lease-purchase agreements are offered by many vendors. Title to items involved is transferred at the end of the lease period, and little or no initial investment is required. Lease payments often can be written off as operating expense.

Rentals create less economic advantage since lessees gain no equity in furnishings or equipment. They merely permit conservation of financial resources during the early life of the business. An accountant should be consulted as to the tax implications of leasing and renting before commitments are made.

Operating and furnishings/equipment funds also can be borrowed, but this approach seldom is productive. Most lenders require monthly payments that drain limited capital. Borrowing from relatives or friends on long-term bases may relieve early financial pressures; presumably, however these funds will have to be repaid.

Alternative funding sources available in manufacturing, distribution, and retailing usually are not accessible to counselors. Such loans are secured by equipment, materials, and inventories. These do not exist in public relations practice.

Prospective counselors also may elect to accept a partner or partners, active or silent. They will be forced in most cases to yield control of the business in the process. This risk may be unacceptable unless those involved are well known to one another.

When economic questions have been resolved, yet another challenge awaits: development of a business plan.

FIGURE 4.1.
The Optimum Start-Up Plan.

Estimated monthly expenses

	Your estimate of monthly expenses based on sales of $_____	Your estimate of how much cash you need to start your business (see column 3)	What to put in column 2. (These figures are typical for one kind of business. You will have to decide how many months to allow for in your business.)
	Column 1	Column 2	Column 3
Salary of owner-manager	$	$	2 × column 1
All other salaries and wages			3 × column 1
Rent			3 × column 1
Advertising			3 × column 1
Delivery expense			3 × column 1
Supplies			3 × column 1
Telephone and telegraph			3 × column 1
Other utilities			3 × column 1
Insurance			Payment required by insurance company
Taxes, including social security			4 × column 1
Interest			3 × column 1
Maintenance			3 × column 1
Legal and other professional fees			3 × column 1
Miscellaneous			3 × column 1

Source: From Herbert S. Meyers, *Minding Your Own Business: A Contemporary Guide to Small Business Success*. Homewood, Ill.: Dow Jones-Irwin, 1984. Reprinted with permission.

THE BUSINESS PLAN

Every organization needs a business plan, and public relations organizations are no different. The planning orientation of the public relations process seemingly would encourage business planning as well; nevertheless, plans appear no more plentiful here than elsewhere. Their absence in organizational practices often is rationalized, because the practice is viewed as part of a larger organization. Planning presumably can be left to senior managers.

Business plans are more common among counselor organizations, appearing more frequently among larger firms although arguably are more needed in smaller organizations. Their absence often is blamed on lack of time. More often than not, lower priorities are assigned to planning than to other functions. Billings for the current month or year are perceived as more important.

Elements of the Business Plan

Business plans consist of six components: (1) a definition of the business and its objectives, (2) a description of the management structure, (3) a definition of services to be provided, (4) marketing plans, (5) departmental plans, and (6) financial plans. These components and the knowledge to amalgamate them into a cohesive whole produce the business plan. It is not easily constructed; weeks or months may be required but the investment is worthwhile regardless of time required. It repays developers many times over the life of the enterprise.

Defining the Business

Components of the business definition should be familiar, since they are based on the five Ws of journalism: who, what, when, where, and why.

"Who" requires a response to the question, "What business are we in?" If the term "public relations" is part of the organizational title, the unit's name will suffice. Beyond this point, more effort is required.

"What" refers to the nature of the business. What are its purposes? What services will it provide? What markets will it serve, and what percentage of market will it capture? What profit margins are anticipated and when will they be achieved?

"When" refers to timing in several contexts. It includes organizational timeline projections such as starting dates and calendar-oriented factors such as demand for services.

"Where" refers to geographic scope—local, regional, national, or international.

"Why" refers to motivational factors. In public relations under the consultant model, this question can be answered in a single word: profit.

Management Structure

Organizations require structure—a truism that may escape the notice of practitioners in organizational and counselor settings. Need compounds as organizations grow and ultimately demands attention. Growth problems tend to decline to the extent organizational structure has been developed.

Appropriateness of structure is a function of the nature of the practice. Public relations unit structure in organizations must be integrated with the parent firm. In counselor firms, more latitude exists. The unit may be a subsidiary of another organization. Only occasionally will it be a component of another communication firm. In either case, managers usually have more design latitude than in larger organizations.

Organizational Components

The components of an organization are its operational units. Each may consist of one or more individuals. Each is assigned specific functional duties and responsibilities. Organizational planning thus begins with a listing of existing and planned functions.

To facilitate planning, public relations managers usually find it appropriate first to list all functions with which their organizations are involved. Services and products acquired from internal or external sources should be included. A typical list might include the following:

1. Administration
2. Finance
3. Development/marketing/sales
4. Client services
5. Production
   a. Copywriting
   b. Photography
   c. Graphic design
   d. Typography/composition
   e. Printing
   f. Audio/video
   g. Special events

Organizational Charts

In counselor organizations, these components might be established in an organizational chart. Charts are vital planning tools. While the firm's founder(s) may handle all designated functions at the outset, additional personnel ultimately will be employed. Organizational charts, supplemented by time estimates for listed functions, assist managers in two ways: They help in establishing hiring priorities, and they assist in developing primary and secondary skill/knowledge criteria for individuals to be hired.

As a practical matter, charts can be rendered to reflect organizational development plans. Existing operational units then are placed in boxes with solid lines. Functions delegated to vendors are indicated with broken lines. Proposed functions are shown and numbered in order of anticipated development.

In organizational practice, charts differ in only two respects: First, the linkage of the department with the organization must be established; second, where resources from other departments are to be used, these relationships should be shown. Vendor relationships also may be shown for long-range planning purposes.

Scope of Services

The nature of services the organization will provide and the constituencies it will serve must be specified. Change in organizations, their public relations units and counselor firms assure that the practices ultimately will extend beyond assumed boundaries. They nevertheless must be specified to guide developmental processes.

Specificity Essential

Will the organization provide employee relations, customer relations, governmental relations, or shareholder relations programs? Will it handle employee publications, the ombudsman function, lobbying, and preparation of the annual report? Will it serve the health-care industry, the construction industry, and the transportation industry?

Organizations inevitably depart from specific definitions of services. Practitioners respond when senior managers or client firms' executive officers ask that speeches be written. When opportunities occur beyond initially defined practice boundaries, counselor organizations respond as well.

Flexibility Necessary

Organizational and counselor units over time may modify originally defined parameters. Such changes should be made by design rather than by chance. Opportunities can be identified through environmental assessment.

Recent change in the health-care sector, for example, created opportunities for practitioners in organizational and counselor roles. Organizational practitioners broadened the scope of their practices in response. A number of counselors focused major developmental efforts in this sector.

Results generally have been salutary. Developmental efforts were optimally productive, however, only where previously existing plans were modified. Revised plans then reflected expanded objectives or substitution of an emerging market for a previously targeted sector.

The Marketing Plan

Neither the scope nor nature of services to be offered by public relations organizations can be accurately defined without market analysis and planning. The process equips managers with data necessary to attack specific market segments. It requires identifying current and prospective customers and competitors. Market potential then can be estimated. Targets can be selected, sales estimated, and strategy defined.

Market Analysis

Analysis addresses a series of market questions: Is there a need for proposed services? Who are the prospective users? Do they recognize their needs? Do they understand the role of public relations?

Can prospective users be listed by name and location? By anticipated rate of usage? By ability and willingness to pay?

Can you identify competitors and specify rates they are charging? Can you itemize their strengths and weaknesses; their successes and failures? Can you define the market in numbers of prospective clients and dollar potential?

Strategy Development

With all necessary information in hand, practitioners are ready to develop organizational goals and strategies. Strategies are governed by circumstances—the nature of services to be offered, of groups to be served, and of competition all must be considered.

Ries and Trout suggested three principles in offensive marketing warfare: be mindful of the leader's strength, find a weakness and attack at that point, and launch the attack on as narrow a front as possible.

Consider, for example, the new counseling firm committed to employee communication services and facing competition from well-established counselors who dominate among larger prospective clients. A strategic opportunity was created for such a newcomer with development of "desktop publishing." The new technology uses computer-driven laser printers in economically creating employee newsletters for small organizations. The implied strategy: attack the lower end of the market (smaller firms with which competitors are not concerned). Establish a base for expansion.

Observers of the marketing wars should recognize the strategy. It was employed by the Japanese to enter the "economy" end of the U.S. auto market. After capturing much of this segment, they expanded upward in auto size and pricing.

Multiple strategies may be contained in the marketing plan. Each must be based on market conditions, general economic climate, competitive factors, and receptivity to proposed services. Analyses of these factors permit accurate estimates as to pricing and sales/marketing tactics.

Departmental and Financial Plans

Departmental plans begin with chief executives' assignment of responsibilities under marketing plans. They include lists of specific tasks, resources required for each, and time estimates. They may require capital and operating investments.

Operating investments consist of human and material resources implied or implicit in tasks assigned. Capital investments include any depreciable assets necessary to task completion. Capital investment often can be minimized or eliminated through subcontracting. Leasing rather than purchasing also can conserve working capital.

The departmental plan and resultant budget are extensions of the marketing plan. They also constitute the organization's financial plan. Department budgets are not always generated in this way. Senior management may allocate funds through a "top down" as opposed to a "bottom up" approach.

Business plan development equips practitioners to make subsequent decisions. The first among them deals with the ultimate size of the practice.

SIZE AND SCOPE

Maturation of public relations practices does not necessarily imply growth in personnel or facilities. Mature practices should be more profitable than fledgling organizations. Profit need not be a function of size. Many practitioners, according to counselor Rendall P. Ayers, prefer to maintain smaller organizations. There also appear to be developing, as New York *Times* columnist Philip H. Dougherty has written, a new stratum of regional firms.

The organizational size question should be addressed early. The options involved are extensive and can best be illustrated in terms of extremes: large and small.

Organizational Size

Small organizations often consist of individual practitioners with minimal support personnel. A well-organized secretarial service in some instances can provide all essential support. The function readily can be handled in organizational settings by a practitioner-manager and a secretary. Both cases imply extensive use of external resources.

Commitment to organizational growth, in contrast, implies developing internal resources. The organization ultimately may include graphic design, photography, typography, printing, and other ancillary units.

There is no magic in either approach. Neither necessarily will be more or less productive or profitable than the other. Managers are best advised to follow the beat of their own drummers after considering relative advantages and disadvantages.

Pluses and Minuses

Problems and pitfalls arise in public relations organizations large and small. Their significance is a function of managerial perspective.

Impact of Size

Managers in smaller organizations can continue as practitioners; they need not become administrators. All professional duties not assigned to vendors then are performed by the practitioner.

This approach is a mixed blessing in counselor situations. Solo practitioners or proprietors of small organizations lack job security as well as support personnel. Also absent are peers with whom ideas and problems can be discussed. On the other hand, considerable sense of accomplishment and extrinsic reward attaches to such situations. Most practitioner time is devoted to public relations practice rather than managing others.

Economic Factors

Small counselor organizations find profitability more easily achieved. Efficiency tends to decline with size. When individuals fill multiple roles, overhead factors are reduced but practice development is more difficult. Larger organizations are more visible; they have greater depth of experience and more contacts. Smaller firms can offset these factors with more aggressive sales efforts oriented toward assignments matching practitioner expertise.

Alternative Approaches

Practitioner objectives determine strategy in counselor and organizational practice. Rapid growth requires aggressive strategies. Those who prefer smaller organizations can be more conservative, but this orientation need not reduce ultimate rewards. Profit in small practices tends to be greater as a percentage of revenues than in larger organizations.

Conservative practitioners spend the bulk of their time servicing clients. They seek to defer growth and enhance profits. Growth creates temporary reductions in profit and efficiency. Individual practitioners can realize annualized billings in six figures and take home the bulk of those revenues.

The aggressive organization is growth oriented from its inception. Staff, space, and equipment are required immediately. Managers spend the bulk of their time selling rather than servicing clients. In the economic area, substantial early capital investment and overhead may reduce profit for years.

GETTING ORGANIZED

Decisions on practice size are primary determinants of organizational structure. In counselor organizations, a legal form must be selected. Organizational units must be positioned within existing structures. Working relationships must be established. Space and equipment must be acquired.

Organizational Structures

The first question requiring attention involves the structure of the enterprise. While perspectives differ, it applies to organizational and counselor units.

Internal Units

Unit placement in organizations should be a primary concern. Should public relations be a free-standing department or an operational unit? To which senior manager should the director report? Given senior management commitment to public relations programming, placement may be relatively unimportant. The primary requirement is more a matter of ability to provide a full range of professional services than of position on an organizational chart. Where senior management is not conversant with public relations capabilities, the unit may come to be viewed only as a source of technical support. Conceivably, it may be subordinated to another communication discipline.

Since senior managements can change—for better or worse—public relations units should be free-standing rather than subordinate to advertising, marketing, or other departments. Public relations by nature is a staff rather than a line function. Unit managers—regardless of title—should report directly to chief executive officers.

Counselors

Counselors' comparable decisions deal with legal rather than structural issues. Counseling firms can be sole proprietorships, partnerships, corporations, or a combination of these. Sole proprietors and partners can, and should, incorporate. Corporate structures create two advantages. They economically insulate individual(s) involved. Only capital invested in the corporation is at risk. Personal assets seldom can be seized to satisfy corporate indebtedness. Incorporation also protects the corporate name.

Corporations require names. When a secretary of state has recorded a name, it will not be granted to another corporation, nor will out-of-state corporations be permitted to operate in issuing states under the same name.

Corporate income taxes need not be a problem to the fledgling business. Federal tax laws permit corporations to elect "Subchapter S" status. Corporate tax returns still must be filed, but profits or losses "flow through" to the owner(s). They are added to or subtracted from other personal income. Taxes are paid on individuals' net income.

Other Preliminaries

Prospective counseling firm proprietors require assistance in law, accounting, insurance, and banking. The professionals involved should be carefully selected. They vary as to specialty. Firms vary in size and their members vary in compensation.

Guidance in selecting legal, accounting, and other professional counsel is available from several sources. Colleagues may be best among them. Their experience can be invaluable. Assistance also may be obtained from pertinent professional organizations.

Law

Counselors require legal advice on several points early in their practices. Primary among them are pitfalls that exist in any business. Attorneys can provide guidance as to how these can be avoided or limited. Early assistance also is advisable in drafting counselor-client agreements. Little further legal help will be needed until personnel are hired. A noncompete agreement then may be necessary.

Accounting

Accounting assistance is a continuing need. Certified public accountants' services are preferable because they tend to be more credible with the Internal Revenue Service. Their practices usually are relatively complex, and the resultant knowledge levels benefit all clients. Certified public accountants quickly can set up counselors' books; thereafter, they can expeditiously maintain those books and prepare tax returns. Counselors inexperienced in accounting find these processes unduly time-consuming.

Bookkeeping and accounting needs are reduced where computers are used. Others find it convenient to deliver copies of checks, deposit slips, and client statements to accountants. Bookkeeping and tax returns can be completed from these documents at minimal cost until growth requires an office manager.

Insurance

Insurance advice also is needed. Equipment and furnishings should be covered. Business interruption insurance (fire can destroy records of little tangible value) also may be worthwhile. Errors and omissions insurance (the public relations equivalent of malpractice insurance) is available but expensive. Most counselors attempt to limit their risks through "hold harmless" clauses in client agreements. Legal decisions suggest they provide less protection than is perceived to be the case.

Risk reduction is the rule, especially in casualty and health areas. Automotive, fire, and health insurance coverages usually are necessary. They are less expensive where substantial "deductibles" are used. The principle involved is called "self-insurance." Insureds accept a portion of the risk in return for reduced premiums.

Banking

Strong working relationships with commercial banks also are important. Like most organizations, banks tend to specialize. Public relations practitioners are best served by those emphasizing service to business. Accountants and insurance specialists often can identify such institutions and make appropriate introductions.

Counselors thereafter should develop strong personal relationships against the day when assistance is needed. Bankers can be helpful in many ways other than lending. They can obtain information concerning prospective clients and their financial capabilities. They can provide advice concerning practitioners' financial and business development plans. They also can be sources of new business leads.

With cultivation, the counselor's banker, attorney, accountant, and insurance agent can constitute an informal board of directors. Each has a stake in the practice. Counselors can be sources of referrals for these professionals.

Organizational Relationships

Organizational practitioners face different requirements. Functional internal relationships to facilitate departmental success are their first concern. Among departments with which rapport is essential are management, marketing, advertising, personnel, development/planning, sales/sales promotion, legal, and accounting.

Early calls on department managers fulfill two objectives: Working relationships must be established, and these individuals are prospective clients. Also worthy of early exploration are internal resources that may be of value to the department. These include copywriting, photography, graphic design/illustration, typography/composition, printing, and audio-visual production. Many such services exist in organizations, and each can be of benefit to the public relations unit. Duplication is expensive.

When the internal assessment is complete and foundations for functional linkages established, practitioners can proceed to examine space and equipment needs.

PHYSICAL FACILITIES

Both organizational and counselor units require offices and furnishings. Several variables deserve practitioner attention. Among them are location, utilitarian versus esthetic factors, and—for counselors—contractual concerns.

Location and Utility

Office locations are important to counselors and organizational practitioners. In many cases, their first concern should be utilitarian rather than esthetic.

Convenience

Counselors must balance convenience against "the right" location. They have only time to sell. Time spent in traffic jams is not saleable. Except in larger cities, most narrow their choices to sites convenient to major highways. Any attempt to be "close to the clients" is doomed to failure. Their office locations change over time; and account turnover also tends to render such decisions obsolete.

On the other hand, a "good" address and the appearance of strength and stability it may convey can be important. The relative value of address, convenience, and similar factors can be accurately assessed only in specific situations.

In organizational settings, the same principles hold true. The public relations department should be situated close to the organization's executive offices. Practitioners find they spend considerable time with senior executives.

Utility

Because clients and prospective clients seldom visit public relations offices, they tend to be functional rather than elaborately decorated. Moreover, office appearance is not a valid indicator of professional skill. Practitioners spend much of their time in clients' offices. Some have operated successfully without offices of their own. As in the case of address versus convenience, however, esthetic decisions can be taken only in light of specific circumstances.

Counselor Alternatives

Multiple office alternatives are available to fledgling counselors.. They range from the "dining room table" to counselor-owned buildings. Facilities tend to evolve as practices develop. They can be outgrown through practice growth, especially during early years. Unless committed to maintaining a "solo" practice, counselors are best served by maintaining flexibility. Their alternatives include no offices, shared offices, rented or leased offices, and counselor-owned offices.

No Offices

The "no office" option can be handled in one of several ways. Least expensive and least desirable is a business telephone installed at home and equipped with an answering machine. Personal telephones answered informally by family members are unbusinesslike. Electronic answering equipment is little better—it frustrates callers and many will hang up.

Variations on the "no office" option include answering services, but they are also less than satisfactory. Their personnel often are ill-trained and disinterested, and these attributes are apparent to callers and reflect upon practitioners. Secretarial firms offering telephone answering services are a potential alternative. Since satisfactory call handling encourages greater use of other services, telephones are better-handled.

Access to occasional typing, word processing, duplicating, and related services also is helpful, but hourly costs are relatively high. Quality levels tend to vary with cost, however, and skilled personnel require little time to complete most tasks. Usage may be expensive but often is less than costs involved in equipment leasing or ownership. Larger cities offer "office suites." These are multiple single offices—furnished or unfurnished—with support services available. They differ from secretarial services in that support facilities and services usually are available only to tenants.

"Co-op" Arrangements

Cooperative office arrangements also are worthy of consideration. These "space-sharing" situations may include use of telephones, office equipment, and so on. Counselors over the years have associated with design studios, printing organizations, and advertising agencies. Associations with colleagues are most advantageous, but involvement with advertising agencies has produced varying results. Several such "marriages" have ended in divorce. Advertising agency affiliations may provide work for counseling firms; they also may discourage assignments from organizations that have strong ties to competing advertising agencies.

"Associations" is used here as the term is applied by attorneys. They often share offices, secretaries, and equipment while maintaining independent practices. The principal benefit arises out of attendant "mutual support" agreements. They may provide for assistance during periods of overload, illness, or vacation. Taken to this point, the professional provides resources and support otherwise available only in larger organizations.

Rentals and Leases

Rental and leased offices usually are less expensive than "office suites." Almost without exception, they are unfurnished. Space cost declines while capital investment tends to increase. Furnishings can be rented but costs are relatively high.

Rental offices involve no long-term commitment since they often are rented on month-to-month bases. Leases seldom are written for terms of less than 12 months. Rates vary with location, building amenities, and market conditions. Renewal options should be included to protect rates over extended periods.

Drawbacks and advantages exist in rental and lease arrangements. Rental rates can be raised or arrangements can be canceled at any time. On the other hand, counselors are free to vacate, usually on 30 days' notice.

Under leases, they usually are "locked in" for the duration. This can be a problem where practices experience unforeseen growth.

Purchased Space

Offices also can be acquired by purchasing buildings or parts of buildings. The latter involve condominium or cooperative arrangements. Advantages and disadvantages again arise. Substantial tax benefits are possible, especially where counselors own buildings individually and lease them to their firms. When space is outgrown and relocation is necessary, market conditions can produce losses if property must be sold.

Early purchase arrangements are inadvisable unless practice development plans call for small organizations. The only exception to this rule occurs where counselors are well-financed and can afford to retain facilities as investments.

Start-Up Cost

All of the foregoing factors must be considered in establishing a budget; in determing "how much it costs" to go into public relations practice. Organizational practices often require little other than the salaries of those involved where space and minimum equipment are available. Counselor practices may require tens to hundreds of thousands of dollars. Six-figure budgets are not unusual where several practitioners join to launch a new firm at "the right address" with well-furnished offices, several support personnel, and no clients.

MONITORING PROGRESS

Most who establish or become managers of public relations organizations spend considerable time developing plans. Some go so far as to create comprehensive business plans. Few reap the benefit of these efforts.

As day-to-day business pressures develop, plans tend to be set aside "for the moment." Accountants' financial statements first wait days, then weeks, and finally months to be reviewed. Business development projects are treated in similar fashion. Control deteriorates and the organization begins to drift.

A very different approach is required. It requires that practitioners apply in their businesses the same monitoring techniques they use for clients. Periodic review dates—preferably monthly—must be set and observed. Progress toward goals and strategies must be consistently measured. Where timetables are not being met, adjustments must be made.

Outcomes must be consistently compared with plans. Where objectives are not achieved, time must be taken to analyze "the reasons why." Where they are accomplished, factors that contributed to success must be identified. As these processes are consistently applied, successes multiply while failures are avoided. In their absence, practices succeed only by chance. Failure becomes as likely an outcome as success.

IN SUMMARY

Public relations organizations should be founded on the basis of need established through research. Research designs should encompass environmental assessment in several dimensions. Trends suggesting developing needs must be examined. So must perceptions of prospective constituents or clients. Need assessment results then can be applied in developing economic projections. These must show acceptable break-even points within existing economic limitations. Research also provides data for use in practice development programs.

When the decision to proceed has been made, several steps are necessary to assure optimum success potential. A business plan must be developed. Structures must be established to support an organization of predetermined size and scope.

Counselors also must establish legal, accounting, insurance, and banking relationships. Organizational practitioners must develop intraorganizational relationships. Both contribute to practice success.

Space and equipment needs then must be addressed. Prescribed budgets may limit organizational practices but needs essentially are comparable to those of counselors. Counselors' prospective physical environments range from a room at home to a fully-staffed office. Here and in equipment selection, economic resources will govern.

When the organization is launched, practitioners must establish and observe monitoring procedures. They require periodic reassessment of progress. It must be measured against previously established goals and strategies. Causes of success and failure must be identified so that the former may be repeated and the latter avoided. Potential for success otherwise is substantially reduced.

ADDITIONAL READING

Albert, Kenneth J., ed. *The Strategic Management Handbook*. New York: McGraw-Hill, 1983.

Cantor, Bill. *Inside Public Relations: Experts in Action*, edited by Chester Burger. New York: Longman, 1984.

Gallesich, June. *The Profession and Practice of Consultation*. San Francisco: Jossey-Bass, 1982.

Greiner, Larry E., and Robert O. Metzger. *Consulting to Management: Insights to Building and Managing a Successful Practice*. Englewood Cliffs, N.J.: Prentice-Hall, 1983.

Heitpas, Quentin J. "Planning," in Cantor, Bill, *Inside Public Relations, Experts in Action*, edited by Chester Burger, New York: Longman, 1984.

Holtz, Herman. *How to Succeed as an Independent Consultant*. New York: John Wiley, 1983.

Meyers, Herbert S. *Minding Your Own Business: A Contemporary Guide to Small Business Success*. Homewood, Ill.: Dow Jones-Irwin, 1984.

Ries, Al, and Jack Trout. *Marketing Warfare*. New York: McGraw-Hill, 1986.

5
Technology:
A Competitive Edge

Fledgling public relations organizations once experienced difficulty in competing with entrenched colleagues. Success remains difficult to achieve, but the competitive gap has been narrowed by technology. The microcomputer is responsible—it radically expands individual productivity; it serves as secretary, researcher, bookkeeper, design assistant, and planner.

Computers and other electronic equipment have become essential to the practitioner. Their labor-saving potential is beyond the grasp of those who have not explored the new technology. Surprisingly, other than in a few large corporations such as 3M Company, few have thoroughly exploited the new technology.

As McKinsey & Company's Richard N. Foster points out, such circumstances create opportunity. Management must be exceptionally skilled, he says, to defend, attack, or counterattack on the basis of technological strength.

COMPUTERS

Computers are machines. Their operating instructions are contained in programs or software. Thousands of programs are available to prospective users. Computer performance is controlled by two factors: the extent to which needs are specified before purchases are made, and the care taken in software selection.

Prospective users should begin with detailed needs analyses. Needs should be arranged in priority order and expressed in quantitative and qualitative detail. Software or programs should be selected before hardware is purchased, because software requires specific hardware. The range of applications open to practitioners is broad and expanding rapidly. They include word processing, accounting, information management, telecommunications, research, graphics/printing, planning, and other uses.

Computers can enhance the productivity of public relations organizations in each area through time savings. They are produced in the accounting area by equipment that monitors expenses charged to clients.

Software Limitations

If there is a drawback in applying computer technology to public relations it is in the software area. Through the mid–1980s, no software program had been developed specifically for public relations applications. Further, according to consultant Howard Benner, none is apt to be developed. Public relations practitioners, Benner told a PRLink conference CompuServe on March 4, 1986, are too few to make software development economically viable.

This does not mean no software exists to meet practitioner needs. Programs abound for computer applications commonly undertaken in public relations. What does not exist is a single multipurpose program designed for the profession. Several have been custom designed for larger counseling firms; they are occasionally offered for sale to colleagues.

Word Processing

Word processing applications include preparing letters, proposals, reports, and other documents. Some programs enable users to generate individually typed form letters for solicitation and other purposes. Computers thus replace conventional typewriters and equipment once required for automated letter writing.

The System

Systems (hardware and software in combination) permit reuse of documents in whole or part without disturbing originals. "Boiler plate" sections of proposals, reports, and other documents can be readily reused. "Cut and paste" proposals prepared by typewriter require considerable time. They can be created and printed in letter-perfect form in minutes by computer. "New" and "old" versions can be retained in electronic form for subsequent use.

Eliminating Retyping

Most beneficially, documents created by computer need to be "keyed" only once. Drafts can be modified as necessary by electronically manipulating originals. "Spell check" programs are available and often are included in word processing software. Retyping is eliminated. A key stroke sends documents from computer to printer.

This process is valuable in developing complex documents requiring multiple revisions over extended time periods. Corporate annual reports are good examples. Between first draft and printing, they proceed through dozens of revisions. Each may require incorporating suggestions from multiple reviewers. Computer users can proceed from a half dozen sets of changes to a complete revision in hours. First, an electronic copy is made of the original. All changes then are incorporated into the copy. Where comments or suggestions are in conflict, alternatives can be inserted in parentheses. Finally, the new document is printed. Recommended changes in a 20-page document from a half dozen reviewers can be completed in hours.

Preparing multiple letters is no more complex. Most systems enable users to maintain mailing lists and generate letters through a single program. Users create letters, select appropriate lists, and press a few command keys. The computer generates individually typed letters and companion envelopes. Continuous-form stationery is available and relatively inexpensive in plain or preprinted forms.

Caution

Only one word of caution is necessary. Preliminary analysis of applications is essential in selecting software. Programs are relatively inexpensive and subsequent replacement is not a problem. Major costs nevertheless may arise in two areas: Files created by one program may not be compatible with another; and changes in software may require hardware changes.

Accounting

Savings potential through computer-based accounting systems is as great as in word processing. Prospective users again should plan to invest substantial time in examining available software. The process in accounting is complex. Users' needs and those of their accountants must be considered. For optimum economy, their systems must be compatible.

New Relationships

The computer is modifying functional relationships between public relations and accounting firms. Accountants once performed bookkeeping as well as accounting functions for practitioners. Bookkeeping can be less expensively handled internally where computers are used.

Accounting requirements in smaller practices may not justify investing in computers. Where acquired for other applications, they can create further time and cost savings in accounting.

Compatibility

Practitioners' first concern should be compatibility of proposed systems with those of their accounting firm. Operating efficiency requires that data be electronically transferable from one system to another. "Rekeying" should be avoided. This requires that practitioners' systems generate files compatible with accountants' computers. Data can be provided to accountants on floppy discs.

Telephone transmission is preferable but in most cases is not essential. Exceptions most often arise where public relations units are components or subsidiaries of larger organizations. Conformity to parent systems then may be a necessity. Systemic prerequisites may limit hardware choices. Software selection in word processing and other areas may be restricted as a result. These circumstances require analyzing system compatibility early in software selection processes. Those responsible for parent organizations' computers are practitioners' best source of information.

Multiple Applications

Multiple applications exist for computer systems in accounting and bookkeeping. They include time and expense records for client billing, payroll, payables, receivables, and other business applications.

In individual situations, rational—as opposed to technical—applicability is a function of existing and projected practice size. Where organizations deal with a few dozen clients, relatively simplistic accounting packages such as OneWrite may be adequate. When clients number in the hundreds, Lotus 1, 2, 3, would be a wiser choice.

Optimum economy is produced through multiple uses of data entered. Employee wage rates, for example, can be used in calculating pay checks, charges to clients, tax withholding forms, budgets, client statements, financial statements, and so on. The rate should have to be entered into as few files as possible. With appropriate software, it need be entered only once.

Most accounting data also are used in multiple applications. This has led professional organizations to handle more accounting work with their own computers. Data for audits, tax return preparation, and other functions handled by accountants are transferred to them at the close of operating periods.

Information Management

Data management probably will be last among computer applications adopted in public relations other than in larger organizations. Systems involved are relatively complex. Most public relations practices are relatively unsophisticated. Ultimately, however, data management is apt to become first on practitioner lists of most valued computer functions.

Range of Applications

Data management systems are applicable in multiple situations. They range from mailing list management to sophisticated trend analyses. With the advent of the issues management concept, trend data analysis became a critical practice component. Issues management involves on-going "environment assessment." The process requires monitoring trends that may impact the organization.

Monitoring is achieved through cyclical research. The process is used to assess changing attitudes and opinions among stakeholder groups concerning organizations and pertinent issues. Data management systems enable computer users to conduct sophisticated analyses of resultant data. With appropriate software, results can be presented in graphic as well as tabular form for management review.

Management Tools

Data management systems also can be applied to the public relations practice. They are especially helpful to public relations managers who lack adequate educational or experiential backgrounds in management. Most come from creative or sales backgrounds. They tend to neglect business monitoring practices necessary to successful management.

Some recognize these deficiencies and entrust economic monitoring to qualified accountants or managers. Others maintain perilous existences without benefit of adequate oversight. Carefully selected, contemporary computer software can reduce dependence on outsiders in the first instance and strengthen management in the second.

Telecommunications

"Telecommunications" functions contribute less individually to organizational efficiency than other computer-based activities. Collectively, they are of considerable value. They include electronic data transmission, research, telecomputer conferencing, and message receipt and delivery. Electronic data transmission potentially is the most productive of the several telecommunications applications. Like the others, it involves use of a telephone line linked to the computer by a modem (modulator/demodulator) to permit computer-to-computer data transfer.

Computers in Typesetting

The data often is the text of a communication tool such as a brochure transmitted to a client for review or a typographer for typesetting. Savings arise in both instances. Travel between counselor and client offices can be limited where text and messages can be exchanged by computer. Savings compound in dealing with typographers, many of whom can load electronic data directly into computers that control their typesetting equipment. Both "turnaround" time and cost are reduced. In addition, "what you send is what you get." Typographical errors indigenous to rekeying data largely are eliminated. In more sophisticated systems, complete pages of newsletters, leaflets, and similar items can be transmitted. Typographers' computers then handle typesetting and composition, eliminating another step in the production process.

Portable Computers

Computer-based telecommunication systems also enhance traveling practitioners' ability to serve clients. "Laptop" computers with built-in modems can communicate with office units from hotels or airports. Letters, memoranda, reports, and the like can be transmitted at any hour or stored for later transfer to other computers.

Research

Comparable advances in public relations research also have been achieved. Modem-equipped computers give practitioners direct and immediate access to thousands of data bases from their desks and motel rooms. Complete encyclopedias, texts of back issues of the *Wall Street Journal*, and the New York *Times*, and even the electronic files of the U.S. Department of Agriculture are accessible. Annual directories of "electronic data bases," as they're called, cover virtually any subject of professional interest. They enable practitioners to conduct research quickly for proposals, reports to clients, and similar documents.

PRSIG/PRLink

Research capabilities also are expanding exponentially with the growth of SIGs or special interest grouops. These are components of CompuServe Information Service (CIS), The Source, and other information utilities. CIS features include PRSIG (the Public Relations and Marketing Forum) and PRLink. The latter utility is sponsored by the Public Relations Society of America. Both provide extensive data files, on-line conference facilities, and electronic bulletin boards.

Electronic bulletin boards are a valuable information resource. They are maintained by hundreds of SIGs and cover a broad range of topics. Special interest groups in the computer area are maintained by users of most brands of computers and many software packages. Computer users tend to be highly responsive to requests for information on any topic. Even technical questions posted on bulletin boards are likely to draw a half-dozen answers in a matter of hours.

Avoiding "Telephone Tag"

Traveling practitioners are among the more prolific users of bulletin boards. They use these resources to avoid playing "telephone tag" with those who call their offices. Bulletin board messages can be labeled to make them accessible only to individual recipients. Users thus can deliver detailed messages and receive detailed responses without intermediaries.

Graphics and Printing

Ability to generate graphs and illustrations for reports and proposals has been a major computer attribute for some time. Technological advances in recent years compounded this advantage. Two are most significant. The first is software, that permits users to create newsletter, flyer, and brochure layouts on their screens. The second is the laser printer, which duplicates screen content on paper at near-printing quality.

Instant Newsletters

Used for years in newspaper publishing, the software became available for microcomputers in the mid–1980s. The first of the laser printers appeared at approximately the same time. They together permit fast, economical production of short-run newsletters and other material. Practitioners can handle copywriting, layout, typesetting, and printing "in house" in minutes. The only weakness in the "system"—doubtless only temporary—is inability to produce photographs. Users requiring photos still can use laser printers as typesetting devices to produce camera-ready line copy for lithographers.

Instant Slides

Other sophisticated software packages that also appeared in the 1980s permit users to create specialized lettering, drawings, and graphs in full color on computer screens. About the same time, there appeared an instant camera capable of producing 35 mm slides of the screen.

Practice managers can take advantage of these and other developments by familiarizing themselves with computer technology. Time must be invested, however, in selecting computer system components. Purchases cannot be handled in the manner most use in acquiring automobiles. One need not be technically knowledgeable to drive a car. Neither must one know what goes on "under the hood" to operate a computer. While automotive operating systems are near-identical, this is not the case with computers. Prospective buyers must acquire sufficient knowledge to select systems that best meet their needs.

Planning

Among the newest applications of computers are project planning and analysis. Perhaps a half dozen sophisticated programs have been written in this area; more undoubtedly will follow. Those available have demonstrated their applicability and value.

They permit rapid development and modification of work flow charts in any of several formats. Critical path method (CPM) and others are available. More important, data recorded entered for charts is readily "taken off" in other formats.

The programs will generate calendars based on the chart showing projected delivery dates. Users thus need not refer to relatively cumbersome charts to maintain oversight and control. When projected dates are not met, charts and calendars can be reproduced quickly in updated form. Users insert actual dates into electronic records and push "print" buttons.

These programs are overly sophisticated for simple tasks such as news release or script preparation. They can be helpful, however, where complex projects such as annual reports or trade show development are undertaken.

SELECTING THE COMPUTER

Computer systems involve two basic components: hardware and software. Physically imposing hardware appears most important, but the reverse is actually true. Software contains the instructions that make systems perform. Since all software is not compatible with all hardware, any system search begins with software. Prospective users first must decide what tasks they want performed. These should be listed in priority order and described in detail. Software then must be selected. Most software packages specify hardware requirements. Buyers need only select from among those brands that will run the software and meet the requirements.

Software Selection

Software selection begins with performance specifications. Prospective users must specify desired results with precision. In word processing, specifications might include or exclude features such as boldface type, underlining, indexing, and the like. In information management, numbers of variables that users will want to track are critical. In mailing list management, list size and numbers of variables to be used in sorting for different applications are important.

Software specification thus begins with results desired, or with end products. The accounting area permits a similar illustration. If employee tax withholding forms are to be generated at year's end from periodic time card entries that also will be used to generate client charge sheets, this should become a program specification.

Multiple less-sophisticated functions can be economically handled with integrated software packages such as Symphony or Jazz. Programmer compromises essential in designing such packages require they be less complex than single-purpose programs. Single-purpose programs may be preferable where considerable sophistication is necessary.

Beginning the Search

With software specifications in hand the practitioner's software search can begin. A library with back issues of computer magazines is a logical starting point. Publications such as *PC* and *PC World* periodically review software in major application categories. Reviews often include tabular comparisons of popular features. This information permits prospective buyers to "narrow the field" of packages available.

The search then should proceed to a software store, a retail outlet specializing in software rather than hardware. Most hardware outlets handle relatively little software; many lack adequate information about available software; some appear prejudiced toward packages they have available. Software outlets handle most popular items and have access to most available programs. Software sellers also are more knowledgeable; they can provide more help should users experience difficulty after the sale. Sales are final when buyers open sealed plastic envelopes containing floppy discs. Few software packages function perfectly, so subsequent problems are not unusual.

Individual users can provide helpful information concerning programs, but their experiences usually are limited. Rarely will individuals learn several programs in one application area.

Other Sources

Further information may be available from colleges or schools using multiple software packages. Faculty members at business colleges often have hands-on experience with many of them. Some public technical schools maintain computer laboratories open to the public. Prospective users can experiment with programs at nominal fees.

Leading computer magazines also are helpful. Announcements and descriptions of newly released software are published several months before packages are available. Articles typically are written as reviews that evaluate programs and documentation.

Documentation

Software consists of two components: floppy discs and instructions or "documentation." The latter term is appropriate since instructions usually are complex. Bulk, however, is not a valid indicator of quality. The best of programs is of doubtful merit when accompanied by documentation difficult to understand and apply.

Program documentation ranges from excellent to abysmal. Better-documented programs often include on-screen "tutorials." They lead users through step-by-step "dry runs." Their existence is not an indicator of documentation quality; nor is documentation necessarily uniform within "packages." Software producers add "extras" to single-purpose programs to enhance sales appeal. Additional functions may be better or worse documented than basic programs. Information on documentation provided in reviews tends to be sparse. Experienced users are better sources as to documentation quality.

Buying decisions ultimately should be made by those who will use the software. Weeks or months may elapse between the start of the search and the purchase. Longer periods of study may be self-defeating. A major university once pondered so long that most word processing programs being considered were superseded by new versions before a decision was reached.

Computer Specifications

Buyers should obtain program specifications before purchasing hardware. They should include the identities of major manufacturers whose equipment will run the program; the amount of memory recommended by the software producer; and any recommendations as to equipment configuration.

The latter point deals primarily with storage systems. Some programs are so voluminous they may be delivered on as many as six floppy discs. Manipulating this number of floppies is inconvenient. Users find hardware with hard discs preferable to two floppy drives.

Additional memory is more economically acquired at the outset than afterward. Users invariably "under buy." Programs tend to run lethargically where software requirements approach hardware capacity.

Memory capacity decisions should be taken before hardware shopping begins. Shoppers then can avoid having to visit dealers several times to "compare oranges to oranges." Hardware specifications govern prices, although substantial increases in memory cost relatively little.

Software safely can be purchased or ordered while hardware negotiations are in progress. Those reading computer magazines will notice mail-order prices considerably lower than retail. These prices can be used as bargaining points with software stores. In most cases, the mail-order process is safe and economical. Most "support" comes from software producers rather than retail outlets.

Hardware Selection

Hardware also is discounted by mail-order houses. Mail-order prices can be found in newspapers such as the New York *Times* as well as computer magazines. They can be used for comparative or bargaining purposes, but a preliminary tour of hardware stores should come first.

Several decisions narrowing the range of possible hardware selections can be made before the tour. Possibilities worthy of consideration, assuming software compatibility, are IBM, IBM compatibles, and Apple. More important than brands is availability of service or "support," as it's called. Prospective buyers should be wary of brands for which there are few dealers in the community or where dealers maintain no repair facilities. Some handle warranty work only on equipment they sell. Others may be on shaky economic ground. Buyers need honest, reliable, financially stable dealers with service facilities who handle brand(s) of equipment finally selected.

Equipment Brands

Qualified dealers can be found in most communities; brand selection is more difficult. IBM and Apple dominate the market. IBM clones collectively are a factor as well, but there are no Apple clones worthy of note. Practitioners will find it difficult to avoid selecting from one of these groups and may well find it hard to avoid IBM or a clone. Independent software developers (most software is produced by independents) focus their efforts on IBM and compatibles for higher sales potential. Some modify products to run on Apple and "off" brand hardware but they are relatively few.

When brand and dealer have been chosen, peripherals must be selected and a price negotiated. Prices should include installation. Some dealers also provide training, but usually it is unnecessary where software is well documented.

Peripherals

Technically, the computer is contained in the central processing unit (CPU). It consists of floppy disc and/or hard drives, which provide the memory. Programs and input data (words or numbers) are stored and manipulated by the CPU. Other components of the system are peripherals. They include printers, modems, and other ancillary items. Some place CRTs (cathode ray tubes or screens) and keyboards in this category. They need not be produced by computer manufacturers. Most—including IBM—do not produce a full line of peripherals.

Systems at minimum require a CRT and a printer—letter quality or dot matrix—in addition to the CPU. Most CPUs come with keyboards. CRT selection is a matter of preference. Characters on most CRT screens appear in green or amber. Clarity is more important than color.

Public relations practitioners usually select letter quality printers. They are slower, more expensive, and more costly to operate than dot matrix units. They require nonreusable and relatively expensive carbon ribbons. Dot matrix printers use more durable fabric ribbons. Many buy both types of printer and use dot matrix units for drafts.

A modem also may be part of the initial purchase. Modems are necessary to link computers to online data bases and information utilities for research purposes. Hayes is the acknowledged leader among modem manufacturers. Prices vary little among producers.

Finally, for those who elect CPUs with hard disc drives, a tape backup system is advisable. While hard drives are relatively problem-free, it is possible to "crash" the drive, destroying all recorded data. Reconstruction can be time-consuming and expensive.

Start Up

Learning to use computers need not be traumatic. Quality of program documentation and on-screen tutorials govern ease of learning. Systems should be "up and running" for word processing purposes in hours. Other applications take more time. In one case, caution is required. Where accounting systems are being converted from traditional to computer formats, the two should be operated in parallel for a time to insure satisfactory outcomes. Major problems can arise when a computer fails to produce client statements on time.

The organization's transition into the computer age will be time consuming. Transient problems are almost inevitable. The change nevertheless is essential if the organization is to succeed in the age of information. Productivity improves radically where computers are used. Professional time savings of as much as 30 percent are not unknown. Ratios of professional to secretarial personnel have shifted from 3:2 to as high as 10:3.

OTHER TECHNOLOGICAL DEVICES

While computers have become all but essential tools in public relations, other devices are equally worthy of consideration. Computers or microprocessors to some extent are involved in most of them. Of special interest are office copiers, electronic equipment control devices, cellular telephones, and facsimile systems.

Office Copiers

A high-quality office copier is essential. By "high quality" is meant equipment that will produce copies indistinguishable from originals. They are especially important where a computer is not available. High-quality copies can be distributed to clients instead of originals. Revisions can be made in originals when necessary, limiting retyping requirements.

Two optional mechanical features also should be considered: an automatic feeding system and a collator. They together permit multiple copies of multipage documents to be made stapler-ready with minimum manual assistance.

Controllers and Recorders

Electronic controller-recorders can be linked to a broad range of office equipment to monitor and/or record usage. They generate detailed data for billing purposes in electronic or printed form.

Controller-recorders can be attached to postage meters, copying machines, and telephones (to log long distance calls). They require that users insert code numbers to activate equipment. Telephone-type key pads or plastic cards with encoded magnetic strips are used as activating devices. Code numbers can be assigned to individual users or clients.

At the end of any period—usually a month—controllers print lists of user codes and recorded data. Data can show numbers of copies, amount of postage, or cost of long distance calls. These devices also can be configured to transmit data to computers used to generate client statements.

Users estimate costs billed to clients have as much as doubled when these devices are installed. Where 40 to 50 percent of costs were recovered prior to installation, at least 90 percent are recovered afterward. Copier, postage, and telephone costs can involve thousands of dollars each month.

Cellular Telephones

Counselors who cover large geographic areas by automobile find cellular telephones valuable. They permit constant contact with clients and others. They enable counselors to call ahead to confirm appointments and adjust appointment times where necessary. Perhaps most important, they permit productive use of driving time. Operating costs are relatively low and equipment can be purchased or leased.

Portable computers have proven similarly productive. Many now are equipped with built-in modems and can be used to transmit memoranda, correspondence, and other data from any remote site to office computers. Where professional personnel are traveling, such equipment quickly pays dividends in enhanced productivity and improved client service.

Early portable computers were operable for communications purposes only when linked to telephone lines. Some now include transceivers that make them usable in conjunction with cellular telephone systems.

Facsimile Systems

Information transmission by facsimile system also is increasing in popularity. Equipment is relatively inexpensive. Where vendors and clients are similarly equipped, it creates private systems identical to Federal Express Corporation's now defunct ZapMail.

IN SUMMARY

The microprocessor or chip at the heart of the computer and other devices is revolutionizing office practices. This especially is the case in public relations, where computers are amenable to multiple uses. Among them are word processing, accounting, information management, telecommunications, research, graphics and printing, and planning.

Those contemplating use of computers should begin by selecting software to meet specific needs. Hardware specifications provided with software then can be used in making hardware selections.

Other electronic devices worthy of early consideration by public relations firms include sophisticated copiers, equipment usage monitors, cellular telephones, and facsimile systems.

ADDITIONAL READING

Alperson, Butron L., et al. *The Fully Powered PC*. New York: PC World Books, 1985.

Alvarez, Bil. *Expanding Your IBM PC: A Guide for the Beginning*. Bowie, Md.: Brady Communications, 1984.

Bear, John. *Computer Wimp*. Berkeley, Calif.: Ten Speed Press, 1982.

Foster, Richard N. *Innovation: The Attackers' Advantage*. New York: Summit, 1986.

Sachs, Jonathan. *Your IBM PC Made Easy*. Berkeley, Calif.: Osborne/McGraw-Hill, 1984.

Willis, Jerry, and Merl Miller. *Computers for Everybody: 1984 Buyers Guide*. Beaverton, Ore.: Dilithium, 1984.

6

Managing Organizational Growth and Development

Public relations organizations seek continuing profitable growth. This is the case for counselor and organizational practitioner alike. Achievement requires practitioners concurrently to expand their practice, create practice balance, apply human resources on cost-efficient bases, apply financial resources productively, manage time efficiently, and demonstrate results. Managers must work toward these objectives simultaneously. Each is more complex than it appears.

PRACTICE COMPLEXITIES

Practice Expansion. Practice expansion requires sale and delivery of additional services to existing clienteles and/or expanding the client base. Practice development, marketing, and sales efforts each contribute to achieving these goals.

Practice Balance. Balancing the practice creates a stable foundation for growth. Organizational practitioners must look to unserved internal constituencies. Counselors must see their practices are sufficiently diverse to insulate against economic fluctuations and client attrition. Both must monitor indicators generated by environmental assessment as to emerging constituencies.

Human Resources. As practices expand, more and more hours are necessary to provide client services, but numbers of hours available are limited. Managers nevertheless must provide quality services on timely bases. Practice development must continue as well. Problems attendant to practice growth thus are similar to those that arise during organizational retrenchment. Managers are called upon to accomplish more and more with less and less.

Financial Resources. Expansion also creates economic stress. Financial resources are finite, and they must be conservatively applied, especially in growth situations. A manager's principal dilemma most often involves allocation. Should more resources be committed to staff expansion? How much additional operating capital will be required to handle additional business?

Staff expansion involves more than wage and fringe benefit dollars. Personnel require office space, equipment, supplies, and so forth. Even where they will generate sufficient billable hours to cover all of these costs, associated revenues will not commence for at least 30 to 60 days.

Managing Time. Time management arguably is the most neglected essential to public relations success. Neglect apparently arises out of managerial assumptions that employees will function efficiently. The assumption is tenuous at best. Sound time management can be induced, however, where managers install appropriate systems.

Demonstrating Results. Amidst multiple immediate demands pressing on managers, more mundane matters tend to be neglected, and often more important matters are among them. Demonstrating results to clients on continuing bases is a prerequisite to business retention. Failure to maintain on-going research and reporting systems can produce attrition among existing accounts while managers work to acquire new ones.

Balancing Demands. The greater the organization's success, the more pressing these problems become. This especially is so in the fledgling counselor organization. *Public Relations Journal* in 1986 reported that incoming Anthony M. Franco, president of Anthony M. Franco, Inc., of Detroit launched his firm with $4,000, half of which was borrowed. Others have started with sparser resources.

Potential for difficulty is equally prevalent in organizational practice for different reasons. Parent organizations' stability may protect public relations units from disaster. Whether they will provide all resources necessary to optimum growth is another matter. Managers are challenged to accomplish more with less, at least until proof of productivity is established and a new budget is prepared.

PRACTICE PRIORITIES

Management priorities in public relations vary from hour to hour and day to day. Unforeseen client problems assure this will be the case. In general terms, however, practice objectives remain unchanged. They include discharging responsibilities to existing clients, acquiring new clients, and applying human and economic resources productively.

None is as easily achieved as stated. Responsibilities to existing clients include on-going environmental assessment and counseling as well as timely delivery of services. Acquiring new clients in part is a function of service to existing clienteles. Reputations are created by quality of service and results. They must be supplemented by on-going practice development, marketing, and sales efforts.

Managers must apply human and economic resources to see that these objectives are met. Sales efforts must continue without impairing client service. The organization must move ahead according to plan.

Practice Beginnings

Public relations practice management is consistent across organizations. Organizational practitioners' needs and priorities differ little from those of counselors. Significant differences arise only early in the practice, when counselors are more concerned with economic matters and sales activities. Organizational practitioners are more free to concentrate on programs supportive of organizational objectives. Resources presumably will have been provided by their organization. Early priorities then might be categorized as follows:

A. Organizational practice
    1. Client service
    2. Staff development
    3. Practice development
B. Counselor practice
    1. Client service
    2. Practice development
    3. Practice management

Organizational Practice

Early staff development in organizational practice might better be termed resource assessment. It involves reviewing internal resources and identifying prospective external resources. Graphic design, photography, and printing services are early concerns.

Practice development needs create no immediate pressures; nevertheless, they should be part of practitioners' early tasks. Internal environmental assessment must begin immediately. Data produced identify prospective clients and their needs.

External environments also require early attention where the organization has not previously undertaken an environmental assessment effort.

Counselor Practice

Counselors' primary concerns are client service and practice development. Practice development arguably might be dominant. Managing economic and human resources is of near equal import.

Environmental assessment procedures presumably began before the firm was established. Where this was not the case, they must be installed immediately. Environments requiring attention include those of clients and the counselor firm.

Firm environments are most important where counselors are solo practitioners and must externally delegate considerable responsibility. Time limitations usually require delegating accounting responsibilities to accountants. Counselors also turn to vendors for many support services. They include graphic design, photography, printing, and others.

Most will have established vendor relationships and negotiated agreements before launching their practices. Where not been done beforehand, these relationships quickly become vital in maintaining practice productivity.

Developing Organizations

Counseling and organizational concerns become more uniform as practices develop. When early needs have been met in organizations, two other areas require greater attention: practice development and staff development.

Practice development involves marketing and sales efforts to expand the scope of departmental services. Existing and potential client needs presumably have been identified at this point through environmental assessment.

As practices develop, managers encounter staffing needs identical to those of counselors. Personnel must be recruited, trained, and assigned to handle specific tasks. The process must be managed within available resources.

Mature Organizations

Other than where counseling organizations expand geographically, public relations units inevitably achieve maturity. Organizational units at this point are providing complete services to all prospective clients. Counselor firms—other than in larger cities—are in similar circumstances. Their clients include every commercial/industrial/institutional group. Services have been expanded to the outer limits of public relations practice for all clients.

Managers' primary concerns then turn to improving practice results. Greater profits derived from stable clienteles become their primary objective. The same goal applies in organizational situations under the consultant model.

EXPANSION AND BALANCE

Expanding and balancing public relations practices must be handled concurrently, but these combined tasks are not easily accomplished. The path of least resistance is tempting; it may entail growth in narrow industrial groups. Concentrating on relatively few large accounts also can be attractive. Both involve risk.

Practice Expansion

Counselors and organizational practitioners use different approaches to practice expansion. Counselors are constrained only by limited resources. Organizational practitioners are circumscribed by organizations. Expansion procedures nevertheless are uniform in planning and application. The planning process involves three steps: (1) identifying prospective clients, (2) ranking them according to priorities, and (3) designing a system that allocates time and effort to marketing and sales in keeping with priorities.

Identifying Prospects

Prospects in organizational settings include all departments involved in communication: executives, human resources management, sales, marketing, and advertising. Others also may be involved. In publicly owned corporations, investor and stockholder relations responsibilities may be assigned to the financial sector. In decentralized organizations, functions may be delegated to divisional staffs.

Emerging Prospects

Every organizational component should be viewed as a prospective client. Their needs are readily identified through environmental assessment.

Many organizations launched organizational development programs during the mid–1980s. They were intended to create nurturing environments in anticipation of labor shortages. Responsibility in some cases was assigned to human resources departments; in others, new operational units were established. Considerable employee communication was involved in either case.

The same period spawned multiple problems in financial circles. They included organizational changes as a result of banking deregulation, public questioning of credit card interest rates, and questionable overseas loans. Takeover attempts, greenmail, and related problems compounded as well. Each generated public relations and/or communication needs.

Environmental assessment and prospect identification thus must be ongoing processes. Organizational problems ebb and flow; so do public relations needs.

Counselor Planning

The process is more complex for counselors. Organizational practitioners can focus environmental assessment processes on organizations. Counselors must monitor events and trends of concern to clients, prospective clients, and consultancies.

Automotive industry change, for example, added importers and their suppliers to counselor prospect lists. Domestic manufacturers' needs compounded. Market share loss created human resources and market problems. All were amenable in part to remediation through public relations programs.

Existing clients compound counselor planning tasks, because they tend to be overlooked as prospective sources of additional business. This should not be the case. Environmental trends impact existing and prospective clients alike. Failure to monitor prospective needs of existing clients opens their doors to competitors. Counselor Kent McKamy offered a preventive formula during an on-line PRLink computer conference on July 10, 1985:

- Be interested and curious; keep asking questions.
- Don't assume you know it all.
- Don't become a "carry-outer" of orders. Stimulate the relationship.
- Keep doing good work.

Practice Balance

Balanced public relations practices involve diverse clienteles. Diversity insulates practitioners from multiple client losses through economic or organizational change. Ample potential for balance exists in organizational and counselor practice.

Organizational Balance

The anticipated scope of young organizational practices tends to be overly narrow. Most are established in response to senior managers' perceived needs. Their perceptions may depart from reality as a result of two factors: First are pressures that prompted organizing the public relations unit—they are of primary and immediate concern; second is lack of managerial understanding of the scope of public relations practice.

Practitioners are morally and ethically responsible for correcting these misperceptions. Public relations departments can provide speech writing as well as media relations services, for example, to senior management. Human resources managers and others may have similar needs.

Total Needs

Public relations managers must address total organizational needs. Human resources, marketing, and other departments require special attention. They constitute opportunities in developing diverse and balanced practices.

Practitioners whose roles are limited to serving senior managers are vulnerable in two ways. First, conscientious departmental and unit managers ultimately will satisfy needs in one of two ways. They will develop communications capabilities within their departments or seek outside counsel. Second, senior management changes may introduce new philosophies less sympathetic to public relations.

Counselor Balance

The need for practice balance is no different among counselors. Where organizational practitioners may tend to concentrate on serving senior managers, counselors may be tempted to focus on a few business/industrial sectors. The temptation is natural. Counselors acquire working knowledge of industries they seve; they become known in those industries; and practice development is more easily accomplished there. A high price may be paid when industries involved go into recession.

Problem potential can be reduced by balancing practices. Counselors' environmental assessment efforts should produce indicators of new client potential. Such should have been the case with banking deregulation, with changes in the healthcare delivery system, and with auto industry problems.

Counselors need not neglect industries in which they are established and known. To avoid economic vulnerability, however, their development efforts must emphasize previously unserved constituencies.

Another Perspective

Balance also is needed in another context. Risk attaches to unusually large accounts, which are welcome in every practice but can lead to problems. First, although easily avoided, is a tendency to overconcentrate resources on large accounts. Where smaller clients' interests are sacrificed, they may drift away.

More important is potential loss of counselors' economic independence. Clients that dominate counselor practices in a sense come to own them. Client dismissal of counselors who permit this condition to develop can destroy practices. Perhaps worse, counselors may be tempted to compromise standards or ethics to guard against disaster.

The Big Account

Such conditions can be avoided only by maintaining practice balance. When the "big account" comes into the shop, diversification efforts should be redoubled. Smaller accounts must be sought more aggressively. Existing clients must be better-served to guard against perceptions of neglect.

These efforts often must be undertaken under trying circumstances. Big accounts tend to drain away uncommitted professional time. New personnel often must be hired and trained. Assimilating new accounts requires extra effort, and extraordinary effort may be necessary when they are exceptionally large. The counselor organization's long-term security demands concurrent efforts to balance the account mix.

Formulas Lacking

Attempts have been made to establish mathematical formulae defining the balanced practice. While no published data exist, many counselors attempt to insure that no single account generates more than 5 percent of total profits. Some are willing to accept larger percentages. Most probably would accept conditions in which the big account generated 5 to 10 percent of profits with one condition: Revenues from all accounts in the industry must be a small percentage of total revenues. Vulnerability to account turnover thus is a function of two factors: account size, and total volume of business originating in an industry.

APPLYING HUMAN RESOURCES

Managing human resources is a challenge in the best of circumstances. Organizational growth compounds the difficulty in one sense while creating opportunities in another. Problems arise because growth and diversification require new knowledge, skills, and talent. Opportunities are created since growing organizations better can meet the aspirations of their personnel.

Knowledge, Skill, and Talent

Practice development plans should permit practitioners to predict those bodies of knowledge, skill, and talent the organization will require. Forecasting tends to be difficult—no one can predict the manner in which practices will develop. Best estimates of organizational need may not be accepted by department and unit managers. Sensitivity to emerging trends among prospective clients varies.

Unforeseen intervening factors also can distort anticipated need patterns. Oil shortages triggered by the Organization of Petroleum Exporting Countries were exemplary of the latter element at work. Such problems should not be permitted to interfere with developing and implementing a human resources plan. It will not be perfect; it will require modification in response to environmental change; yet it is essential to successful management.

Plan Development

Human resources plans should be in place almost from the founding of the practice. They should be completed at the latest along with counselors' practice development plans and organizational practitioners' initial needs assessments. Human resources plans, in addition, should be based on human resources knowledge/skill/talent inventories, internal/external resources inventories, and internal/external human development resources.

Plans in final form evolve from responses to a series of questions. They must be posed and answered in context with the information specified above.

1. What will be the organization's short-term and long-term needs?
2. Which can be filled by existing personnel?
3. Which can be least expensively filled through external sources?

Operational Alternatives

Anticipated need factors influence selection of strategies to meet human resources needs. Education and training programs can generate required knowledge and skills where ample time exists. External sources may be used or new employees hired when needs are more immediate. Employer-funded continuing education programs are an investment in the future. They are especially important in the face of rapid societal change and should be provided in the long-term interests of the organization as well as its employees.

The most readily available alternative to meet education-training needs is a process called cross-training. It is most helpful where demand for existing services is growing. The process involves tutoring of one or more employees by another.

Cross-training should be an on-going procedure. It enhances the value of personnel, enriches jobs, and contributes to personal growth. Most important to management, it creates greater organizational flexibility by expanding employee capabilities.

Internal and external education-training programs also should be considered for this purpose. They are especially valuable when needs are not pressing and completion can justify improved compensation levels.

Anticipated work loads should be considered in examining two other options: employing additional personnel or use of vendors. Adding personnel is most easily justified where work volume is growing rapidly. Vendors are more economical where growth rates are slower or where skill/knowledge needs are highly specialized and little used.

Generalists can be more practically supplemented by specialists as organizations grow. In smaller organizations, specialization is a costly luxury. It limits internal capabilities and constrains individual growth and development.

Structural Development

Growth also implies increasing need for structure. Practitioners can successfully supervise all operations when organizations are small. Supervisory tasks become more burdensome as they grow and appropriate structure becomes essential.

Most management specialists suggest limiting "span of control." The term refers to numbers of employees reporting to one supervisor. Opinion varies but few suggest that a supervisor can successfully manage more than seven subordinates.

Beginning Points

Supervisory development arguably should begin with an organization's first employee. Delegation certainly should begin at that point. Individual employees should be encouraged to accept responsibility. Many prospective supervisors have been identified in this manner.

One successful consultant calls the process "constant testing." He describes his approach in this manner. "I assign the work and tell employees to let me know if they encounter difficulty. I also tell them if I don't hear from them I'll expect the work to be completed as assigned by a specific time and date. Occasionally, I have a problem, but I've found no better way to start the developmental process."

Organizations tend to stagnate in the absence of developmental programs. "That's why so many firms bog down in the $1 million (annual fee revenue) range," says the Chester Burger Company's Alfred Geduldig. Founders can't give up their quality control roles and "the boss is still reading copy at midnight," he told a Spring 1986 PRSA Counselor Academy meeting, in Phoenix.

Education and Training

Organizational practitioners may find help in human resources or training departments. Training programs may be available to meet departmental needs. Where they do not exist, public relations managers and others in the communication disciplines often can encourage development. Some employees provide formal educational benefit programs. Their use by promising employees should be encouraged.

Counselors experience more difficulty developing effective managerial structures. In small organizations, they tend to have little time to develop training or educational programs. Resources to fund programs also are limited. These circumstances often require hiring more experienced personnel as needs arise.

Conditions vary in medium to large counseling firms. The larger usually develop their own programs. Others depend on professional development seminars sponsored by the PRSA at national and local levels.

Uncomplicated management structures are preferable, according to industry consultant Dan Baer, but management talent must be developed or acquired for organizations to prosper.

Caution

Managers should be aware of varying definitions of "personal growth" and "opportunity" in developing organizational structures. Many individuals, and especially those in creative areas, have no interest in supervisory or managerial positions. They prefer to practice their professions. Provision must be made to meet their needs and desires lest they seek more satisfying circumstances.

APPLYING ECONOMIC RESOURCES

Use of dollars available to public relations practitioners is limited; each can be spent only once. How they best can be expended in practice development thus is a source of concern. Most available dollars ultimately are invested in human resources, which always is the case in the practices. Other needs intervene in early years, all concerned with productivity.

Essential Needs

Every organization requires certain essential components. In addition to personnel, they are space, furnishings, equipment, and supplies. Dollars are merely a medium of exchange that can be transformed into any of these forms.

Managers must cope with competing demands for resources with limited dollars. A single standard ultimately applies: productivity. Which investment will be most productive?

Organizational Variables

Many investment decisions are taken by senior managers for organizational practitioners. They have little influence over amounts of space allocated to them, especially at the outset. Their supplies usually are drawn from central departments against prescribed budgets. Their furnishings and equipment are provided, often in keeping with inflexible, organization-wide standards.

Over time, however, organizational managers can influence allocation of these resources. Knowledge of their relative productivity is necessary to direct that influence appropriately.

Relative Productivity

Relative productivity refers to differences in end-product quality or quantity achieved through alternative investments. A few examples drawn from counselor practice will be enlightening.

Most counselors are sensitive to graphics, especially as applied in stationery and business cards. "They make the first impression on many clients and prospective clients," says one of them. "It's not an area in which to cut corners."

As a result, blind embossing, steel die engraving, foil stamping, and other costly processes are comon. So are more expensive printing papers.

Since few clients visit counselors, however, offices tend to be more functional than decorative.

People versus Equipment

Personnel and equipment "trade-offs" are painfully deliberated. This especially is so in light of burgeoning computer technology. Decisions are more easily made where managers focus on end results rather than costs.

Computers enhance practice productivity. They reduce need for secretarial personnel and speed up processes and procedures. Time of acquisition thus should be the primary purchase variable.

If computers increase practitioner productivity by 30 percent—an oft-quoted figure—logic suggests they be acquired when organizations consist of two to three users. Benefits may not be immediately apparent to senior management in organizational settings. They often are unfamiliar with public relations practice and explanations may be required. Counselors should immediately recognize the benefits involved.

TIME MANAGEMENT

Time is the most perishable of commodities. The misspent dollar can be replaced; the lost hour never can be recovered. Management must insure every hour is invested productively. Only managers' time may be involved at the outset. Managers literally may be "one man bands," handling every task from environmental assessment to typing statements. Their tasks compound in number and complexity with organizational growth. Subordinates' time must be managed, directly or indirectly.

Relative Values

Men and minutes are created equal only in limited ways. Men vary anthropologically, intellectually, and physically. Minutes vary as to application potential. There are daytime minutes and nighttime minutes; weekday and weekend minutes; high-potential minutes and low-potential minutes. The latter variation is most significant in light of a concept taken from real estate.

This concept suggests that land should be dedicated to its "highest and best use." The term "highest" refers to a real estate scale on which prime commercial use is at the higher end of the scale and agricultural use at the lower. "Best" is another matter. It refers to economic productivity; to the revenues land will produce.

Scarcity and Utility

Variation in the value of time is created by scarcity and utility. Utility refers to the range of uses to which time can be put. Business telephone calls, for example, generally can be made between 8:00 a.m. and 5:00 p.m. on business days. They seldom can be completed between 5:00 p.m. and 8:00 p.m. and on nonbusiness days. From a commercial standpoint, then, utility of business hours is greater than that of nonbusiness hours.

Business hours also are fewer than nonbusiness hours, so scarcity makes them more valuable as well. Within the business day and business week, similar variations arise. Mondays and Fridays tend to be laden with distractions and are least amenable to use by consultants for sales calls. Early morning, lunch, and late afternoon hours are least desirable on other days of the business week. Prime selling hours thus might be defined as 9:30–11:30 a.m. and 2:00–4:00 p.m. Tuesday through Thursday.

Highest and Best

These 12 hours potentially arc most productive iin the practitioner's week. They can be used for sales or other purposes but those other purposes can be equally served in hours of lesser value.

Beyond the 12 prime or Category One hours—assuming a 40-hour work week—are 28 others. Many can be used for client contact; for meetings to obtain information, discuss work in progress, and such. These Category Two hours can be defined as including the first and last hours of Tuesdays, Wednesdays, and Thursdays. In some cases the last hours of Mondays, the first hours of Fridays, and a portion of the periods between 11:30 a.m. and 2:00 p.m. might be included. Some clients or prospective clients are amenable to business lunches. Perhaps another 10 to 12 hours are involved.

The remainder of the work week, consisting of Category Three hours, seldom can be used for sales or client contact activities. It can be dedicated, however, to maintaining contact with vendors, meeting with accountants and other consultants, returning telephone calls, and handling administrative duties that require the presence of employees.

Beyond the Call

Beyond the "normal" work week are Category Four hours, which nonmanagers are free to devote to families, hobbies, and other pursuits. Managers in relatively young organizations are not so fortunate. A perceptive individual once said workers are "paid for what they do between 8 and 5 and promoted for what they do between 5 and 8." In fledgling organizations, tasks not accomplished during the traditional work week must be completed during other hours.

Managing Time

Managers' most relentless enemy is waste, especially waste of time. Vulnerability is compounded by the nature of public relations practice. The "product" is not mass-produced. The "production line" includes multiple components—especially clients and vendors—beyond managers' control.

Postponed appointments, photo sessions delayed by weather, printers' equipment breakdowns, and many other factors produce delays.

Appointment scheduling problems and procrastination by prospective clients create difficulties in sales efforts. Almost any problem arising in a prospective client's day can induce cancellation of an appointment. Public relations managers and practitioners thus find it difficult to maintain schedules.

Flexible Scheduling

The potential for wasting time is considerable. In the absence of systematic control, time set aside for canceled appointments is more apt to be wasted than productively applied. Few manage to shift from planned to unplanned activity without losing time. This weakness can be overcome through flexible scheduling.

Flexible scheduling is a systematic approach to time management. Systems can be maintained in written or electronic (computer) form. They usually consist of one or two calendars. One must be portable; the second can remain in the user's office. The portable calendar may be a single sheet supplemented by a desk calendar or a portable calendar book (See Figure 6.1). Portable or desk computers can be substituted where users prefer.

Objectives

The nature of the tools is best left to individuals involved. Only one prerequisite exists: Users must have at hand a list of all tasks to be completed during current and ensuing weeks. They then are equipped to shift attention from one to another without pause. Where one task is delayed or postponed, another can be immediately substituted. Time that otherwise might have been lost is put to productive use.

The underlying principles are simple. The system assumes that best-laid plans will go astray. Where later-scheduled tasks are substituted for those delayed, time is well-used. The system is not designed to insure every planned task is completed in any day or week. It instead assists users in completing a day's tasks each day and a week's tasks each week. Little time is wasted and productivity is high where these objectives are achieved.

INSURING THE FUTURE

Ability to demonstrate results is essential to durable public relations organizations. Most practitioners accept this premise and related reporting responsibilities. Reports are readily prepared by skilled writers—a category to which practitioners should belong. Their reports, however, too often are inadequate as indicators of return on investment. Research-based reporting systems are essential to insure client understanding of results and preserve consultant-client relationships.

FIGURE 6.1.
This Weekly Personal Log Sheet is Used by Professionals in One
Counselor Practice to Assure Minimal Time Loss in the Face of
Unforeseen Delays.

THINGS TO DO   WEEK OF _____

WRITE	PHONE	SEE	DO

NEXT WEEK

WRITE	PHONE	SEE	DO

Nature of the Problem

Professional managers often have little grasp of public relations. They are unfamiliar with professional terminology. They don't understand practice strategies. They only vaguely comprehend how desired results work to their benefit. Traditional public relations approaches are inadequate to survival and prosperity in these circumstances. As practitioners once were told at a PRSA convention, "If you buy a pound of steak, you get a pound of steak from an honest butcher, and you watch the scales. You buy $100,000 worth of public relations and you get 'I'll report to you and let you know how we did.' "

If this approach ever was satisfactory, it is acceptable no longer. Sophisticated managers responsible to demanding boards of directors require more. Public relations is a major organizational investment. It no longer is a bargain-basement item in the budget. Like other investments, public relations expenditures must be justified. If public relations is to be sold and stay sold, results must be measured.

Measurement Tools

Available measurement tools have been increasing in quantity and quality. All are not applicable in every situation, but some almost always can be used to produce desired results. This is achieved only where research is incorporated into programs from their inception.

Focus groups, telephone polls, and communications audits long have been used by practitioners. In recent years, more sophisticated devices have been added. The Ketchum publicity tracking model was among the first of these. It was developed by Ketchum Public Relations, one of the nation's larger counseling firms to produce quantitative and qualitative measurement of media exposure.

The Ketchum model is more sophisticated than most. It evaluates not only exposure but audiences and relative impacts. It does not, however, measure audience responses. As Ehrenkranz and Kahn as well as a host of others have pointed out, the two are not identical.

Parallel use of focus groups, pretest-posttest techniques, and other devices add to practitioner ability to measure results. By this point, however, cost factors begin to intrude. Few clients are apt to approve budgets where the cost of analyzing outcomes approaches program costs. Research tools nevertheless must be built into program budgets, and managers must bend every effort to keep them there. Outcomes must be measured and reported to as great an extent as possible.

IN SUMMARY

Successfully managing public relations organizations requires balanced practice expansion through efficient application of human and economic resources. Efficient use of time is critical to the process. Time must be allocated to maintain service to existing clients while acquiring new clients.

Client service is the primary requirement of both organizational and counselor practice. Staff development and practice development rank second and third for organizational practitioners. Practice management and practice development are priority items for counselors. Differences arise out of counselors' more critical economic concerns. These are ameliorated by the presence of a presumably strong parent in organizational practice.

Decisions as to ultimate objectives are required of all managers before practice development begins. What should be the scale and thrust of the practice? Size is not necessarily an indicator of success.

With projected sizes established, practitioners can proceed to practice expansion. Balance through diversity of clientele is essential—diversity protects organizational and counselor practices. Administratively dependent organizational practices can suffer with changes in senior echelons. Economic cycles can endanger counselor practices confined to few business sectors.

Counselors also may experience vulnerability where they serve a few large clients, or where one "big account" comes to dominate the organization. Balance in these instances requires numerical as well as business diversity.

Human resources must be developed as organizations grow. Practice development plans provide guidelines for practitioners. They indicate prospective needs. These can be satisfied through cross-training, educational programming, or recruiting.

Human resources development also must focus on anticipated supervisory/managerial needs. Employees must be given opportunities to grow into these roles before managers look outside the organization.

Managers also must allocate economic resources to assure optimum productivity. Equally important are steps to insure that all personnel productively apply the time available to them.

Finally, the public relations manager must maintain reporting mechanisms to provide adequate evidence of performance to senior managers or clients. Without such evidence, the practice is unnecessarily vulnerable to client losses.

ADDITIONAL READING

Ehrenkranz, Lois B., and Gilbert H. Kahn. *Public Relations/Publicity: A Key Link in Communications*. New York: Fairchild, 1983.

Glueck, William F. *Organization Planning and Development.* New York: American Management Association, 1971.

Greenberger, Martin. *Electronic Publishing Plus.* White Plains, N.Y.: Knowledge Industry Publications, 1985.

Hall, Richard H. *Organizations: Structure and Process.* Englewood Cliffs, N.J.: Prentice-Hall, 1977.

Lasser, J. K., Tax Institute. *How to Run a Small Business,* 5th ed. New York: McGraw-Hill, 1983.

Pascarella, Perry. *Technology—Fire in a Dark World.* New York: Van Nostrand Reinhold, 1979.

7

Financial Management

Financial management too often is viewed by public relations managers as a necessary evil. Few are educated or trained in finance, yet all are equipped with the basic tools required for success. Financial management is a process like any other. It involves developing and executing a plan. Objectives are expressed in dollars rather than attitude and opinion. The process otherwise is identical to the public relations process.

THE MANAGEMENT PROCESS

Environments

Financial management in public relations exists in multiple environments. Managers function in counselor or organizational settings. The latter may be cast in traditional or consultant formats. In traditional situations, revenues are arbitrarily set by the organization. Expenditures may be organizationally mandated as well. The manager's responsibility is to execute programs within budgetary limits.

The Consultant Model

Different circumstances prevail where organizations use the consultant model. Managers use the counselor operational pattern. Revenues are a function of ability to develop and sell services to clients within the organization. Managers demonstrate the value of public relations in terms meaningful to senior management. The public relations unit earns a profit. The profit is earned through services sold to other managers at their discretion. Service value thus is endorsed by others in the organization.

Risks Exist

Risk of failure also exists but is unlikely to exceed that incurred where no proof of performance is available. Organizational public relations units have been among the first sacrificed in the face of economic hardship. Senior management too easily can view the function as an expensive luxury without convincing evidence of productivity.

Objectives

Profit is the primary objective of the financial management plan regardless of type of organization. Other terminology may be used in nonprofit organizations. "Net operating revenue" is a favored phrase but labels are unimportant. All describe outcomes measured in dollars. Numbers of dollars are indicators of success. Financial plans help managers control costs, monitor progress, and measure results.

Controlling Costs

Financial management processes generate revenue and expense projections. They consist of short-and long-term estimates. The short-term are based on the organization's fiscal year; the long-term most frequently cover five years.

Annual and five-year fiscal plans or budgets are used to monitor organizational progress. Monthly revenue and expense statements are primary monitoring tools. They provide managers with data for the current month, the year to date, the same month of the previous year, and the status of each item in relation to the total allocated.

Measuring Results

Data generated by financial management systems serve multiple purposes. They assist managers in controlling financial outcomes. They express outcomes in terms universally understood in business. The latter attribute is vital. Arranging loans or financing, or placing a value on a practice for sale or merger, for example, require financial data.

Total financial management consists of a great deal more. Depreciation, amortization, and tax liabilities are only a few of the factors that require attention. Most, however, can be turned over to professionals.

Getting Help

Public relations departments and counseling firms render professional services to clients. They offer knowledge and skill in a specialized discipline. Implicit in their practices is the premise that expert counsel is the best approach to public relations. This concept holds true in other disciplines. Professional services in accounting, law, insurance, and other areas are essential to success in public relations.

Counselor Practice

Counselors usually obtain accounting assistance from certified public accountants. They preferably should be experienced with public relations practices. Experience with other professionals may be an acceptable substitute.

Public relations practitioners usually require help in preparing profit and loss statements, balance sheets, and tax filings. These documents can be inexpensively prepared by accountants armed with three sets of documents from the counselor: detailed statements to clients, deposit slips, and check stubs or copies. Data also may be provided in electronic form from practitioners' computers.

For management purposes, a detailed chart of accounts is necessary as well. This is a list of categories to which expenses and revenues can be assigned for summary purposes.

Organizational Practice

Accounting assistance in organizational practice is readily available. Accountants and business managers welcome colleagues' interest, especially in achieving greater productivity.

Organizational managers' needs go beyond organizational accounting. Departmental budgets in some organizations consist of as few as a half-dozen lines or items. They are gross categories to which charges are assigned. Their all-encompassing nature makes successful monitoring and control difficult. Again, a detailed chart of accounts is necessary. While readily created, it requires more time and effort in the accounting department. The manager's first task thus may be persuading others to provide necessary tools.

Using Computers

Where accounting cooperation is not forthcoming, departmental computers may create practical alternatives. Equipped with appropriate software, they can provide all necessary data. Given compatibility with accountants' computers, they also can create significant savings for counselors. Data then are amenable to transfer via floppy disc, eliminating duplicative input procedures.

BUDGETING

Despite what Chester Burger & Company's Robert L. Ferrante described as a "phobia about budgeting among creative people," the process is a vital component of public relations practice. Managers deal with multiple budgets. Organizational, departmental, and project budgets exist in organizational and counselor practice. They vary only as to application. Project budgets in organizations are comparable to client budgets in consultant firms. Their successful use in either situation requires establishing several systems.

Preliminaries

Financial management objectives—cost control, progress monitoring, and measuring results—can be defeated by system weaknesses. They arise in human and structural areas.

Human Factors

The understanding and support of unit personnel is essential to achieve budgetary objectives. Involving them in the process helps in achieving understanding and gaining support. The process largely is educational. It produces a sense of "proprietorship" on the part of all involved. The budget becomes "our budget." Involvement produces commitment to objectives, which in turn enhance results.

Technical Factors

Budgeting systems in organizational practice may require modification. "Public relations" has been too broadly applied in the budgetary sense in some organizations. Donations, yearbook advertising, and similar items often are included in the budget. Distortion results where they are a significant portion of the total.

The process should begin with a reexamination of "public relations" expenditures. Items inappropriate to professional practice should be segregated to avoid distorting results. They preferably should be budgeted separately.

The reexamination process should include every budget component. Each item must be examined to insure the unit is being charged only for its own expenses. Supplier relationships also should be reassessed. Those that exist may not be the best available. Periodic pricing pattern audits are advisable. Obtaining competitive prices on every item or service acquired is overly time-consuming. It is equally unwise, however, to buy from any vendor over a long period without reexamining prices.

Systems

Budgeting is part of financial management and a system in and of itself; it varies in organizational settings with "parent" systems. In counseling situations, senior practitioners establish systems. A near-infinite number exist but four predominate: zero-based, modified zero-based, percentage of sales, and method-based.

Zero-Based Budgets

Funding in zero-based budgeting is based on current conditions and prospective need rather than past expenditures. It has become popular because it requires all activities to be reevaluated. Prior years' expenditures are ignored. Each program component is reexamined.

The system identifies programs that may be marginally productive. The process is time-consuming, however, and requires difficult value judgments. The abstract value of a media relations program, for example, is difficult to measure.

Modified Zero-Based Budgets

Modified zero-based budgets are hybrids. The approach is based on existing budgets and project needs in each expense area. Each is evaluated and two figures are calculated. One becomes part of a minimal budget. The other is incorporated into an optimal budget. The former shows funding needed to continue activities. The latter shows optimum funding. The process is more easily accomplished than zero-based budgeting. It assumes existing programs are worthy of continued funding. The assumption is a weakness, since some programs may not meet this criterion.

Percentage of Sales Budgets

The percentage of sales budgets are beset by several problems. Manufacturers' promotional expenditures often are expressed in this way. Public relations budgets in some organizations are calculated as a percentage of advertising budgets or sales projections. No fixed percentages exist although rules of thumb are applied in some areas. Fixed percentages would produce inconsistencies since advertising budgets are major variables across industries.

Another weakness arises out of the nature of public relations. If all expenditures were sales-oriented, the approach might be valid. Financial, employee, and community relations do not meet this criterion.

Method-Based Budgets

Method- or objective-based budgets have been popular where management by objective systems are used. Public relations objectives are established as subsets of organizational objectives. Funding then becomes a function of resources estimated as necessary to achieve objectives.

Regardless of method, budgets must be developed to a level of detail adequate to permit precise monitoring. Program timetables and budget flowcharts, as described by Voros and Alvarez, facilitate the process, which begins with planning.

The Planning Process

Budget planning processes are similar in counseling and organizational practices. Budgets in each case are the sum of resources needed to accomplish predetermined tasks. Managers' roles vary since organizational managers must comply with prescribed budgeting systems.

Learning the System

Their first task is learning the system. Mastery is essential because public relations units compete with other organizational components for funds.

Organizations use cyclical budgeting procedures. Planning usually begins three to six months prior to anticipated approval dates. Specific forms are provided. One or more approvals may be required.

Organizational accountants are a primary source of information; they may also provide assistance in preparing budgets; and at minimum they can provide instruction in accounting procedures. Accounting departments often are involved in budget review processes. Members' prior knowledge of the public relations budget and supporting data can be helpful to managers.

A Dual System

Counseling firms' managers deal with multiple budgets. Where firms are subsidiaries of larger organizations, processes similar to those in organizational practice may apply. There nevertheless remain multiple budgets with which managers must deal. They include the firm's budget and client budgets.

Counselors are governed by client budgets in projecting their own budgets for any period. Where on-going relationships exist, developing projections is an easy task. The nature of assignments is well-defined. Revenues and costs are known.

Counselor budgeting is complicated by several variables, client turnover being most significant among them. Assignments end and new ones begin. Managers use historical trends and economic forecasts to estimate results for budget periods. Close monitoring is vital to stay within budget and income limitations.

Developing the Budget

Budget development begins with income and expense projections. In counselor firms and organizations using the consultant model, documents resemble financial statements. Revenue and expense items are shown.

Revenues are not shown in traditional organizational budgets. Managers nevertheless can generate comparable data to demonstrate departmental value. They need only establish hourly rates for personnel and keep time records by project.

Revenues

Revenue sources should be specified in detail. Other than where assignments are narrowly defined, they should be specified by function. Within an employee relations program, for example, revenue items should be shown for managerial-supervisory training, publishing an organizational newsletter, and conducting organizational communication studies. Prior year's revenues from each source should be included for comparative purposes.

To facilitate planning and human resources management, timetables can be established showing project requirements by month in hours or dollars. This practice also generates project cost data helpful in subsequent budget cycles.

Expenses

On the expense side, budgets should show every cost incurred in rendering services. Overhead factors should be included where the consultant model is used. Costs of space, utilities, telephone, janitorial services, and so on, are among them. Valid profit figures can not otherwise be calculated.

Expenses or costs generally arise in two areas: administrative and functional. Administrative costs include all expenses that can not be charged to individual clients: overhead costs plus office supplies, dues and subscriptions, travel and miscellaneous expenses. The cost of person hours not charged to clients also is included.

Operational or functional costs, in contrast, consist of all elements for which clients are charged. They include personnel time, production costs, and out-of-pocket expenses that appear on client statements. As in the case of revenues, they should be expressed in detail.

In organizational units, subbudgets should be established for financial, employee, governmental, and community relations programs. Individual program budgets are established in each category. In financial public relations, these might include media relations, shareholder and analyst meetings, and preparation of annual and quarterly statements. Time and production costs should be itemized in each case.

Detailed budgeting enables managers to demonstrate performance. Reports to senior management logically would include tasks performed for other units, numbers of hours involved, estimated costs, and savings as compared with external sources.

Budget Formats

Most larger organizations require that budgets be submitted in specific formats. Extent of detail required is a variable. The most useful structure will correspond to unit operational patterns. If responsibilities include financial public relations, for example, accounting may devote a single line to this function. Public relations managers are better served by separate lines for investor relations, analyst relations, and shareholder relations. Costs in each area can be subdivided into labor, material, and overhead costs. Items such as the annual report would be allocated among operational sectors. Managers usually find their needs require more detail than is necessary in reporting to senior managers. This should not create problems where organizational and public relations budgets are prepared concurrently. The latter then becomes nothing more than a detailed version of the former.

CHARGING FOR SERVICES

Charges for public relations services traditionally are based on numbers of personnel hours involved. Value of services rendered indirectly has been a factor as well since skill and knowledge levels vary with assignments. Personnel are assigned in keeping with these requirements.

Bases for Compensation

Where the consultant model is used, organizational public relations units may employ the same rate-setting procedures used in counselor firms. Rates usually are expressed as multiples of hourly wages paid personnel. Multiples have increased over the years from 2 to 2.5 times wage rates to 3 to 3.5 times wages. The term "wage rate," however, is amenable to multiple definitions.

Hourly Variables

Most salaries in public relations practice are calculated on annualized bases and paid in monthly or bimonthly increments. Wage rates involve assumptions as to numbers of hours employees will work and/or for which they will be paid. "Normal" work weeks vary in length. Multipliers are not comparable indicators of counselor charges. The variables must be defined as well.

Several compensation systems have been used in public relations practice. They include flat fee and cost plus agreements as well as retainer versus hourly rates systems. The latter sometimes include hourly rates lower than "open" rates. The Public Relations Board's Burt Zollo also has reported use of a sliding scale approach under which rates decline as numbers of hours charged to clients increase. Regardless of "packaging," most practitioners base charges on estimated time requirements multiplied by hourly rates.

Flat Fees

Flat fee arrangements usually prove more expensive to clients. Consultants must guard against unforeseen problems by adding a "contingency factor" after multiplying estimated time requirements by hourly rates. Unsophisticated clients tend to be wary of hourly rate structures. Many prefer fixed fees. They are practical only where work can be defined with sufficient precision to permit accurate time estimates.

Cost Plus

The cost plus approach has been popularized in the construction industry. Where applied to public relations, it usually is combined with a flat fee or hourly rate structure covering time involved. The percentage override or markup is applied to out-of-pocket costs, as in the case of an annual report. Complex printing projects may require the work of graphic designers, photographers, and other specialists.

Retainers

Retainer fees most often are used in two applications. In one, they constitute guaranteed income levels, usually on monthly bases. Clients pay the fee or the sum of hourly rates, whichever is greater in any month. In the other, the fee is a fixed monthly rate covering predetermined services. Practitioners occasionally discount hourly rates where retainers are involved. Retainer fees are payable in advance. Other charges are payable monthly or at the conclusion of a project.

Establishing Rates

Hourly rates must be rationally and realistically established. They must be adequate to cover operating expenses and yield a profit yet remain competitive.

Pitfalls

Profit consists of revenue in excess of expense *after all salaries have been paid*. Salaries must include compensation for administrative support as well as direct services to clients. This principle applies in every practice situation, including the sole proprietorship.

Novice proprietors often consider they have a profit when there is "something left at the end of the month" to put in their pockets. They confuse compensation and profit. Only sums remaining after proprietors have been adequately compensated can be considered profit. Adequacy is a matter of individual iinterpretation. Hourly rates nevertheless must be established for all personnel. Their compensation is part of the organization's fixed expenses. When revenues are inadequate, proprietor compensation suffers. Shortfalls are carried on practice books as accounts payable.

Return on Investment

Perhaps the soundest approach to establishing profit objectives involves return on investment. Owners invest in their practices and are entitled to returns on those investments. Return rates should be calculated in light of two factors: prevailing interest rates and level of risk.

If funds invested in federally insured certificates of deposit yield a 10 percent annual return, business profits should be greater. Funds invested in a business are more readily lost than those in a certificate of deposit. A pretax profit of 15 to 20 percent of sales thus would not be illogical.

Bases for Dollar Estimates

Entrepreneurs in public relations make capital investments in two forms. The most obvious is cash, which includes all expenses incurred. Less obvious is "sweat equity," which consists of time invested in establishing the organization. All uncompensated time must be included. Founders' capital investments then consist of each plus the value of invested time.

Investors are entitled to a fair return based on risk involved. Profits accrue after this expense has been paid. The investment also might be viewed as borrowed funds on which interest must be paid as a part of operating expenses. Hourly rates charged to clients must yield sufficient revenue to recover interest costs, all other expenses, and profit.

Numbers of Hours

Numbers of saleable hours available to managers vary; they are fewer than those for which employees are paid. The latter include vacations, holidays, sick leave, jury duty, and such. The former consist only of hours worked. Hours worked are the best beginning point for calculating rates. All hours worked will not be sold and billed to clients. Percentages of hours sold vary from one organization to another.

Few counseling organizations consistently bill more than 80 percent of available hours. A 40-hour week would yield 32 hours if this percentage were applied ($40 \times .80 = 32$). To recover the cost of 40 hours paid in charging for 32 hours worked, the 40-hour rate would have to be multiplied by 1.25 ($32 \times 1.25 = 40$).

The 1.25 multiplier would not allow for fringe benefits or overhead factors. Fringe benefits in most organizations cost employers about 30 percent of payroll. Real cost of a 40-hour employee thus would become the equivalent of 52 wage hours ($40 \times .30 = 12; 40 + 12 = 52$). To recover fringe benefit costs with 32 hours billed would require a multiplier of about 1.63 ($32 \times 1.63 = 52.16$).

The 1.63 multiplier includes neither overhead nor profit factors. Overhead is the sum of all operating expenses, including rent, utilities, telephone, office supplies and equipment, and other items not billed to clients. They can be calculated on an hourly rate basis by dividing anticipated billable hours into estimated total overhead. The result must be added to each billable hour. Further increments must be added to cover profit and taxes.

When all has been accomplished, the hourly rate will be more than three times the wage rate.

Cautions

Contemporary trends toward higher multipliers—usually 3.5 times wage rates—are a product of necessary caution. Calculated rates are based on assumptions. Critical among them is that 80 percent of hours paid will be billed. Where this assumption proves invalid, anticipated profit can become significant loss.

TIME RECORDS

Adequate hourly rates do not assure economic success. Numbers of hours worked and numbers billed are primary determinants; however, hours billed are fewer than hours worked. A further shortfall may occur where billable hours are not accurately recorded. Time management and recording thus become critical elements to organizational success.

Success Management Systems *involve daily reports*

Little uniformity exists among public relations time management systems. Most use time cards or time sheets; few declare themselves happy with the results.

Dissatisfaction arises out of systemic and human weaknesses. The principal problem is mechanical: failure by employees to maintain accurate records. This difficulty may be compounded by poor reporting systems.

People Problems

Creative individuals have relatively little patience with paperwork. Supervisors and managers concerned with quality and quantity of creative output are hesitant to demand accurate record-keeping. Systems thus become non-systems and in some cases never are used. In a monograph prepared for the Counselor Academy of the PRSA in March 1982, Joe S. Epley, APR, president of Epley Associates, Inc., in Charlotte, N.C., quoted one member: "If I were to require timesheets, we would never get any work done. In addition, all my creative juices would dry up.... What do I want out of life? What I now have... an agency that makes money in a totally unstructured and 'loose as a goose' way."

Seeking Solutions

Others have attempted to install systems involving daily reports with varying results. Problems arise when reports are not completed each day. Employees tend to forget telephone calls and other routine matters over several days. Revenue is lost in the process. Few people attempt to "log" every telephone call. Most managers require any task consuming more than 15 minutes be recorded.

Successful systems involve daily reports. Employees are required to submit timesheets before departing for the day. When away from the office at the end of a business day, employees must submit them the following morning.

Coding Systems

Success also requires simple, easy to use forms. Coding methods determine ease of use. Two primary sets of codes are involved—one identifies clients; the other specifies the nature of work performed. A third set of codes can be included where managers want to monitor nonbillable time devoted to specific activities. These may include practice development, marketing, sales, professional development, and so on.

Many use alphabetic rather than numeric codes. The former are more readily memorable by employees. City General Hospital, for example, is more recognizable as CGH than as 763. In like manner, a telephone call is more readily coded TEL than 062. Sufficient space must be allocated for activity descriptions as extensive as managers may require.

Typical System

Typical of time recording devices in public relations is the weekly time report used by Burson-Marsteller (see Figure 7.1). The reverse side of the form provides the following instructions to users:

1. Print legibly.
2. Time sheets with inaccurate or incomplete information will be returned to originator for correction.
3. Reports must be submitted to accounting weekly on Mondays.
4. BM billing period ends 15th of mo. It cutoff falls on a week day, complete 2 time sheets—one through cutoff, and one subsequent to that date.
5. Use latest IBM client code list for correct client numbers when recording inter-company time, e.g., billing Marsteller or International.
6. Do not break time into units smaller than 0.25 hr.
7. Do not report hours for paid holidays. Report religious holidays when office is open, jury duty, etc., as absence.
8. Total each line, number of items report and hours per day; each day must total at least 7 hours.

Recording Systems

Gathering information is the first step in time management. Data then must be transformed into multiple reports. One should be used for individual employees, another provides data for monthly reports to clients, a third should be a complete activity summary for managers.

FIGURE 7.1. Burston-Marsteller Weekly Time Report.

BURSON-MARSTELLER WEEKLY TIME REPORT
(Instructions printed on back)

WEEK ENDING SUNDAY (or the 15th) ☐☐ Mo. ☐☐ Day 19 ☐☐ Year

EMPLOYEE OFFICE CODE ☐☐☐☐ OFFICE NAME ____________

EMPLOYEE NO. ☐☐☐☐☐ EMPLOYEE NAME ____________

ITEM	CLIENT CODE	CLIENT NAME	PROJECT NO.	SUB. PROJ. NO.	MON Hours	TUES Hours	WED Hours	THURS Hours	FRI Hours	SAT Hours	SUN Hours	TOTAL HOURS	OFFICE CODE
1.	–											.	
2	–											.	
3	–											.	
4	–											.	
5	–											.	
6	–											.	
7	–											.	
8	–											.	
9	–											.	
10	–											.	
11	–											.	
12	–											.	
13	–											.	
14	–											.	
15	–											.	
16	–											.	
17	–											.	
18	–											.	
19	–											.	
20	–											.	
21	–											.	
22	–											.	
23	– 3 2	New Business										.	
24	– 3 3	Administrative										.	
25	– 3 4	Company Meetings (Non-Client)										.	
26	– 3 5	Outside Meetings, Conventions, etc. (Non-Client)										.	
27	– 3 8	Company Promotion										.	
28	– 9 0	General										.	
29	– 9 1	Absence										.	
30	– 9 2	Vacation										.	

☐ TOTAL ITEMS TOTAL HOURS ☐

FORM # BM-103

Reprinted by permission.

Employee Reports

Employee reports should summarize work by client and activity. Summaries showing billable and nonbillable activities are especially important. Comparative data should be provided to inform employees of changes in productivity levels from one period to another.

Client Reports

Reporting to clients or superiors has been an area of weakness in public relations organizations. Especially in creative ranks, many assume their work is finished when tasks are completed. Detailed reporting also is vital to support billings and assure clients their interests are being pursued. Systems should generate activity summaries by project or assignment to meet these needs. Each should specify individuals involved, tasks performed, and time expended.

Management Reports

Duplicates of employee and client reports are adequate for most management purposes. They assist in monitoring activity in behalf of clients and facilitate organizational oversight.

Generating Reports

Summaries of employee reports are readily prepared by computer. The nature of hardware and software in use may dictate formats. Other than in large organizations, data input can be handled in a matter of hours by one employee. Output is even more rapid.

Input data also can be a major component of client statements where sophisticated systems are available. They consist largely of time charges. Out-of-pocket expenses can be entered separately with appropriate function codes. Markups can be calculated by the computer in many cases. Statements then can be generated promptly. Summary data can be used by accountants in preparing financial reports and tax returns.

COUNSELOR CASH MANAGEMENT

Successful cash flow management requires efficient billing, credit management, and disbursement systems. Billings must be complete and on time. Credit management requires sound credit and collection policies equitably enforced. Disbursements must be made on timely bases to obtain discounts and maintain preferred customer status with vendors.

Billing Systems

Billing efficiency accelerates revenue flows. Associated profit potential may appear small in relation to total revenues but it can be significant. Profits are realized in interest that compounds rapidly when large-balance dollars are involved.

Speed in collecting requires timely issuance of statements. Timeliness and other factors influencing prompt payment should be defined in counselor-client agreements.

Cycles, Discounts, and Penalties

Among elements that should be specified are billing cycles, prompt payment discounts, and late payment penalties. Early billing cycles tend to be most productive; they speed processing in clients' offices. Experience suggests a greater percentage of statements issued between the 20th and 25th of the month will be paid by the 10th.

Timeliness

Timeliness in billing involves more than mailing statements on predetermined dates. It should include all charges through the prior day. This is practical in most organizations only where computers are used. With a computer, complete and timely bills are produced where:

1. Daily time records are entered at the close of each day or, at latest, at the start of the following day.
2. Records of expenses to be charged to clients are submitted and entered weekly.
3. Vendor statements and invoices are submitted in keeping with organizations' billing cycles.
4. Computers are programmed automatically to add retainer fees and calculate markups in keeping with client-counselor agreements.

Prompt data entry and internal reporting permit completion of the first two steps without difficulty. The third requires cooperation from vendors and is forthcoming where two prior conditions are fulfilled. First, organizational needs must be made clear to all vendors. Second, the volume of added business should be significant. This is the case where practitioners concentrate work with few vendors.

Concentration contributes to economical operation in two other ways. Time expanded in monitoring vendors declines and paperwork tends to be reduced.

Credit and Collection

Most credit and collection problems can be avoided, but avoidance requires mutual understanding between organizations and clients on four points:

1. Billing cycles, discounts, and late payment penalties as described earlier
2. Ownership of materials created for clients
3. The point at which services will be suspended in the absence of payment
4. Responsibility for litigation costs

These conditions should be specified in consultant-client agreements. Problems seldom arise where agreements also are reviewed by principals prior to execution.

Monitoring

Practice financial status requires constant monitoring; both counselor and client finances are involved. Monitoring is readily accomplished where financial reporting systems produce frequent management reports. Clients' financial conditions are more difficult to assess.

Internal reports should contain aged receivables data by client. Payment histories should be generated when payments are more than 30 days in arrears. Client conferences are indicated when histories show lengthening payment delays.

Conferences should focus on problems at hand. Managers should seek agreements under which accounts are quickly brought current and remain current. Where clients are unable to comply, suspension of services should be considered.

Credit Reports

Commercial credit reports can be of value in monitoring. Several organizations produce such reports. Dun & Bradstreet (D&B) is best known among them. D&B reports are compiled from information provided by organizations and their customers. Where credit use is extensive, reports are relatively valuable. Content originates largely with customers rather than organizations involved. The reverse may be true where organizations use little credit. Most report content that may have been provided by the organization at D&B's request.

Guarding against Losses

Virtually every business suffers losses, and public relations is no exception. Several devices limit loss potential, one of them being a well-defined and uniformly applied credit policy. Others involve legal safeguards applied where client credit worthiness is in doubt:

Agency Relationship. Counselors in some cases limit liability by establishing agency relationships. They specify to vendors that counselors are acting as clients' agents. This relieves the agency of obligations incurred in client's behalf.

Credit Insurance. Credit insurance can be used where agency relationships are impractical. Premiums may be paid by clients, but high cost often discourages client acceptance of such arrangements.

Prepayment. Clients unwilling or unable to pay for credit insurance may agree to prepay counselors. This device often is used where retainers are involved; it also can be applied to anticipated expenses when credit is a problem. Agreements usually require periodic client deposits.

Materials Ownership. More limited protection may be obtained through client agreement provisions vesting ownership of materials in counselors until all charges are paid. Their value to the client can become insignificant in relation to mounting indebtedness, reducing effectiveness of the arrangement.

Handling Disbursements

Prompt and efficient disbursements are important to public relations organizations. They contribute to strong credit ratings and tend to induce greater-than-normal supplier loyalty. They enable organizations to take advantage of prompt payment discounts, which are offered by many vendors and often can be negotiated with others.

Credit Ratings

Public relations organizations usually work with relatively few vendors. These relationships are especially valuable in establishing credit ratings. Strong ratings help in soliciting new business, especially among credit users.

Executives of firms using credit extensively consider a good credit rating a sign of economic strength. Their perceptions may or may not be valid. To the extent they influence prospective clients and others, good credit ratings are worthy of attention.

Supplier Loyalty

Prompt payment is a hallmark of a "good customer." The nature of public relations practice makes this status important. The "good customer" is the firm for which vendors "go the extra mile" to provide products or services with unusual speed or quality.

Cost Containment

Limiting unnecessary expenditures is a vital component of management. Every dollar saved goes directly to "the bottom line." To organizations earning a 20 percent pretax profit on fees and commissions, a dollar saved is worth $5 in revenues.

Much of the cost containment effort in public relations is directed at time management. Near equal potential for economy exists in other areas.

Most significant are "overhead" items: office space, equipment, supplies, telephone, travel, and the like.

Travel

Savings in travel costs accrue to the benefit of organizations and clients. Most are readily obtained; but some require negotiation with vendors:

1. Cost of accommodations: Hotel chains offer commercial discounts and will negotiate rates for volume users.
2. Air fares: Discounts are available where travel is planned in advance. Rate changes require constant monitoring or a reliable travel agent.
3. Auto rentals: Advertised rates are beginning points for negotiation by frequent users.

Supplies

Most office supply items are offered at substantial discounts by mail-order houses. Volume purchasing is necessary but volumes are not prohibitively high. Computer supplies are offered at especially attractive prices. Continuous-form paper and ribbons often are available at 50 to 60 percent of retail prices. To take advantage of savings, managers should designate individuals as purchasing agents. They should retain current catalogs and place orders as necessary. Over time, inventory quantities and reorder levels can be established.

Equipment

The office equipment market is highly competitive. Copying machines, typewriters, computers, and other equipment often are available through mail-order houses or national distributors at huge discounts.

Acquisition options include rentals, leases, and lease-purchase agreements as well as outright purchases. Even where service is vital and a local source preferred, "shopping the deal'" can result in lower prices.

MONITORING PROGRESS

The best financial control mechanism is of little benefit unless managers monitor results. Monitoring is best accomplished by examining several documents. Financial statements and balance sheets are especially important. Several statistics, expressed as ratios, also can be helpful in monitoring the economic health of the enterprise.

Financial Statements

The term "financial statement" often conjures up statements akin to those of public companies in the minds of managers. These specters tend to courage use of management tools that need be neither complex nor frustrating.

Balance Sheets

Financial statements come in several forms. Most common is the balance sheet—a summary of what the organization owns and what it owes on a specific date. The difference between the two (net worth) belongs to the owner(s). Balance sheets are broken down into several components:

1. Current assets or items of high liquidity such as cash and accounts receivable.
2. Fixed assets, usually furnishings and equipment used to produce revenue. Fixed assets usually are depreciated or written off for tax purposes over a period of time.
3. Current liabilities, including bills to be paid in the ensuing 12 months. Included are accounts payable, taxes, short term bank loans, and such.
4. Long-term liabilities, consisting of items to be paid beyond the 12-month period covered by current liabilities. Mortgages on equipment and long-term bank loans are included.

Income Statements

Income statements cover extended periods of time, usually 12 months. They show operating income and expenses for each month. The latter are subtracted from the former to show profit or loss. Income statements help managers by providing comparative monthly data.

Cash Flow Statements

Profit is an inadequate indicator of economic health in businesses that are not strongly capitalized. Where accounting is handled on accrual rather than cash bases, profit data are less reliable. Profits earned but uncollected appear on accrual balance sheets. Cash flow and cash utilization thus must be monitored as well.

Cash flow statements show sources and applications of revenue—where it comes from and where it goes. Since they deal in cash, they are sensitive barometers of business health.

Other Reports

Title and format of financial reports are less important than content. Managers of Burson-Marsteller offices use two Budget Worksheets as monitoring devices. One is entitled "Detail of Expenses" (see Figure 7.2). The other is an "Operating Profit and Loss Statement" (see Figure 7.3).

Analytical Ratios

A number of ratios can be quickly calculated to supplement financial statements in the analytical process. Most data needed come from financial

FIGURE 7.2 Burson-Marsteller Detail of Expenses Worksheet

1982 Actual	1983 Actual		1984 Revised	Forecast
		Attendance Bonus		
		Retirement Trust & Savings		
		Employee Insurance		
		Educational Incentive		
		Total Benefits		
		Rent		
		Audio/Visual		
		Office Automation		
		Word Processing		
		Special Equipment Rental		
		Alterations & Moving		
		Repairs & Maintenance		
		Telephone		
		Stationery & Supplies		
		Copier Machine		
		Art Dept. Supplies		
		Internal Stats		
		Misc. Taxes		
		Central PR		
		Intercompany		
		Total Facilities		
		Local Advertising		
		Flowers & Gifts		
		Insurance-Operating		
		Contributions		
		Dues & Memberships		
		Subscriptions		
		Training & Meetings		
		Messenger Service		
		Employee Relocation		
		Overtime Meals		
		Express, Postage		
		New Business		
		Slide Central		
		Temporary Services		
		Employee Costs-Prof.		
		Employment Costs-Cler.		
		Information Banks		
		Miscellaneous		
		Central PR		
		Intercompany		
		Total Other Expenses		

FIGURE 7.3 Burson-Marsteller Profit and Loss Worksheet

1982 Actual	1983 Actual		1984 Budget	Revised
		Operating Income		
		PR Services		
		Production		
		Mimeo/Information Banks		
_____	_____	Interoffice Transfers	_____	_____
_____	_____	Total Operating Income	_____	_____
		Operating Expenses		
		Compensaton:		
		Payroll		
		Acct. Handling & Adm.		
		Secretarial		
		Overtime		
		Central PR		
_____	_____	Regional Fee	_____	_____
_____	_____	Total Payroll	_____	_____
		Benefits		
		Payroll Taxes		
		Central PR Benefits/Taxes		
_____	_____	Intercompany	_____	_____
_____	_____	Total Compensation	_____	_____
		Client Services:		
		Direct Client		
		—Client Dev.		
		—Travel		
		—Entertainment		
		—Unbillable		
		Other Travel		
		Other Entertainment		
		Bad Debt		
		Free Lance		
		Central PR		
_____	_____	Intercompany	_____	_____
_____	_____	Total Client Services	_____	_____
		Depreciation & Amortization		
		Facilities		
		Other Expenses		
_____	_____	Corporate Expenses	_____	_____
_____	_____	Total Operating Expenses	_____	_____
_____	_____	Profit Contribution	_____	_____
(+%)	(+%)	Percent to Operating Income	(+%)	(+%)

Reprinted by permission.

124

statements. Among the more useful are capital:income, sales:net profit, sales:gross profit, sales:net profit, debt:net worth, and assets:liabilities.

There is no magic in the resulting numbers. They are merely indicators of economic strength or weakness. Close monitoring of barometers of business health is essential, however, in minimizing potential for fiscal disaster.

IN SUMMARY

Financial management is a complex process consisting of multiple relatively simple components. The process is designed to produce maximum profit by reducing costs and enhancing revenues. It is controlled by a budget.

Budget development results in a plan by which progress can be monitored and results measured. One of several developmental systems often is used to avoid potential human and technical weaknesses. They include zero-based, modified zero-based, percentage, and method-based approaches.

Organizational and counselor budgeting processes are similar. Organizational practitioners are limited by employers' systems. They can be adapted, however, to meet departmental needs. Where the consultant practice model is employed, all other elements are identical. Revenue and expense projections are required. Revenues usually are calculated on the basis of anticipated time charges.

Hourly rates require care in calculation to insure a profit, or a surplus in the case of the organizational practice. Use of hourly rate systems requires precise reporting methods. Failure to report time expended can be costly.

Successful reporting systems involve daily time reports. They require easily applied coding systems. Where computers are available, reports can be used to generate detailed reports for employees, managers, and clients. The system also can generate statements and facilitate billing and collection processes.

Successful financial management requires careful cash flow management. The process begins with the billing system and client-consultant agreements. The latter should spell out consultant expectations as to timely payment. Discounts and late-payment penalties should be specified.

Disbursement and cost containment processes also are essential components of financial management. The former are important in generating a reputation for economic strength and vendor loyalty. The latter limit unnecessary expenditures and enhance net revenues.

ADDITIONAL READING

Buchele, Robert B. *The Management of Business and Public Organizations.* New York: McGraw-Hill, 1977.

Gardner, Herbert S., Jr. *The Advertising Agency Business,* 3rd ed. Chicago: Crain, 1980.

Holtz, Herman. *How to Succeed as an Independent Consultant.* New York: John Wiley, 1983.

Lasser, J. K., Tax Institute. *How to Run a Small Business,* 5th ed. New York: McGraw-Hill, 1983.

Meyers, Herbert S. *Minding Your Own Business: A Contemporary Guide to Small Business Success.* Homewood, Ill.: Dow Jones-Irwin, 1984.

Schall, Lawrence D., and Charles W. Haley. *Introduction to Financial Management,* 3rd ed. New York: McGraw-Hill, 1983.

Voros, Gerald J., and Paul H. Alvarez. *What Happens in Public Relations.* New York: AMACOM, 1981.

Zollo, Burt. *The Dollars and Sense of Public Relations.* New York: McGraw-Hill, 1967.

8
Marketing Public Relations

Marketing a public relations practice involves a series of steps, none of which are especially difficult. Too few managers have mastered the process, however, and their practices suffer as a result. Process components include:

1. Environmental assessment
   a. Identifying major trends
   b. Forecasting their impact on clients and prospective clients
2. Examining organizations in sufficient depth to predict their reactions with some precision
3. Determining organizations' public relations needs based on
   a. Trend projections
   b. Anticipated organizational reactions
4. Developing services that will
   a. Appeal to organizational managers
   b. Produce beneficial outcomes in terms of specific problems
   c. Create profit for public relations practitioners

Balance Vital

Public relations managers' problems in the marketing arena arise out of a logical but erroneous assumption. They too often assume that marketing's components—research and development—require equal attention. Practitioner tendencies to emphasize service rather than research compound the problem.

The reverse is necessary in marketing. Three of the four steps itemized above involve research or information-gathering. The first of them is environmental assessment, which involves the same techniques used by practitioners in developing strategic plans (See Chapter 3). Acquiring knowledge of prospect organizations and their needs are critical to the marketing process in public relations. Developing services responsive to prospect needs then is accomplished with relatively little difficulty.

Limitations

Marketing programs, like public relations programs, are not created in a vacuum. They are a function of unit strategy and structure. They are extensions of the organizational development process. Information gathered and applied in planning organizational structures also applies in marketing. Form (the organization structure) arguably might better follow function (the marketing plan)—an approach that is practical in some circumstances. It would be workable in creating a new organization, for example, assuming adequate resources are available. It also may be practical in established organizations where resources can be readily and productively redirected. Few such situations exist. Practical limitations must be considered in developing the marketing plan, according to Lovelock and Weinberg. They are imposed by the limits of existing resources or those that can be readily acquired.

ENVIRONMENTAL ASSESSMENT

Information is the dominant currency of marketing. With sufficient information to make accurate forecasts, success is virtually assured. Without adequate information, the reverse often is true.

The process begins with information-gathering or environmental assessment. A two-part process is involved: scanning and monitoring. Scanning identifies events that may contribute to trends; monitoring follows these trends—the two proceed concurrently and continuously. Episodic assessment is increasingly risky as social change accelerates.

Prospect Information

Trend data obtained through monitoring is one component of the second step in the research process. The others are results of analyses of organizational and competitor strengths and weaknesses.

Research proceeds from environmental assessment to formal data-gathering and analytical processes. These measure attitude and opinion among target groups. In research directed toward existing and prospective clients, managers seek to determine:

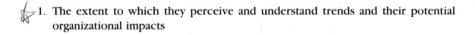

1. The extent to which they perceive and understand trends and their potential organizational impacts

2. The extent to which prospective clients and their organizations are prepared to cope with the impacts
3. Their perceptions of organizational needs in responding to trends and their implications

Responses in the latter areas are a function of prospect knowledge levels. Since these may vary radically, survey data are subject to distortion. Distortion potential is compounded since industry groups in many communities consist of relatively few organizations.

Sample Problems

With few exceptions, communities are served by a handful of banks and savings and loan associations. These conditions militate toward research through focus group interviews with customers of individual organizations rather than sample surveys. As marketing consultant Herbert S. Meyers points out, interviewers must serve as educators as well as information-gatherers. Respondents must be made familiar with trends and prospective organizational impacts if interviews are to produce valid data.

A product-oriented sample questionnaire designed for in-person interviews is shown in Figure 8.1. A similar approach can be used for services. Classification data would require modification to reflect organizational rather than individual prospects.

The value of valid research data is readily illustrated in an example well-known in marketing: Lee Iacocca's experience with Ford Motor Company's Mustang. Iacocca validated data originating in environmental assessment (auto buyers' affinity for imported models). First he showed prototype models to selected groups. With their affirmative responses, he proceeded to formal survey research. Resultant data contributed to one of the automotive industry's most successful innovations.

Prospect-oriented research is a vital component of marketing. Managers require additional information, however, before moving from environmental assessment to formal research. Organizational reactions and responses to trends vary. They are influenced by organizational environments and circumstances.

ORGANIZATIONAL REACTIONS

Success in management requires sensitivity to organizational interdependency in contemporary society. Knowledge of organizational nature and structure also is vital. These caveats apply to internal departments and counseling firms.

Many organizations are wedded to structural models proven in the industrial age but of questionable contemporary value. Others are seeking

FIGURE 8.1.

Designing a Marketing Research Questionnaire.

1. The basic information should be filled in before the interview. The questionnaire should be designed with simple, nonpersonal information first, becoming increasingly complicated and personal.

2. The earliest parts should be stated by the interviewer in his own words and should be used as a method of establishing rapport with the subject.

3. The product description should be informational. It should not be imparted in a "selling" way. The interviewer should avoid the tendency to produce product-biased answers.

4. The presumed product appeals, including price, must be tested by the questionnaire. The assumptions should be presented to the interviewee for his reaction.

5. The interviewee's buying intentions at various price points should be determined. Perhaps a demand curve can be constructed. If the interviewee's intention is not to buy, clues to his reasoning should be sought as a guide to possible product or service correction.

6. Retail outlets and advertising media should be explored.

7. Avoid specific questions relative to age and income.

Sample Questionnaire

Name of respondent _____   Name of interviewer _____
Address _____   Date _____
Phone _____   Time _____
Other (nonpersonal) relevant data _____

Good morning. My name is _____, and I am conducting a marketing study for a new product (service) called _____. The answers you give to the following questions will help determine whether or not to introduce this new product (service) idea and what features to incorporate into the product. May I have a few minutes of your time?

The name of this product is _____. It is a _____, and it functions (purposes) are _____ _____.

The benefits of this product are _____ _____.

1. What is your immediate reaction to this idea?

Positive	Negative
Great _____	So-so _____
Like it very much _____	Do not particularly like it _____
Like it somewhat _____	Do not like it at all _____

Why do you say that? Explain. _____
_____
_____

FIGURE 0.1. (continued)

2. Which of the following best expresses your feeling about buying this product if it were available to you?

Positive	Negative
I'm absolutely sure I would buy it _____	I probably would not buy it _____
I'm almost sure I would buy it _____	I'm almost sure I would not buy it _____
I probably would buy it _____	I'm absolutely sure I would not buy it _____

Why do you say that? _____

_____

_____

3. All things considered, what is there about this product idea that appeals to you most. What do you consider its most important advantages?

Appeal	Advantages
1. _____	1. _____
2. _____	2. _____
3. _____	3. _____

4. How much do you think such a product would cost? _____

5. Where would you expect to buy such a product? _____

6. Where would you expect such a product to be advertised? _____

7. Are there any suggestions you would care to make that you think might improve this product? _____

Classification data:

1. In which category does your age fall:

   Under 15 _____
   16–21 _____
   22–29 _____
   30–49 _____
   50–60 _____
   Over 60 _____

2. Please tell me where you total family income falls:

   Below $5,000 _____
   $5,000–9,999 _____
   $10,000–14,999 _____
   $15,000–20,000 _____
   Above $20,000 _____

3. Check one:

   Female: Single _____ Married _____
   Male: Single _____ Married _____

Thank you for your cooperation.

Source: From Herbert S. Meyers, *Minding Your Own Business: A Contemporary Guide to Small Business Success.* Homewood, Ill.: Dow Jones-Irwin, 1984. Reprinted with permission

to modify structures in keeping with social change. Structures in either case involve more than is shown on organizational charts. Leaders' management styles and the life cycles of their products or services also are significant. Knowledge of these elements is critical in developing and maintaining working relationships.

Organizations exist, in other words, on paper, as functions of leaders' management styles, and in context with the life cycle model described earlier. Life cycles obtain to products and services, organizations and individuals. Marketers contend that product life cycles have been accelerating at an unprecedented pace. The automobile, they point out, required decades in moving from birth to maturity. The videocassette recorder, in contrast, moved through the same stages in a matter of little more than two years. Public relations has been and will continue to be influenced by these cycles.

Organizational Life Cycles

Humans progress through infancy and adolescence to maturity and ultimately to senility and death. Organizations in parallel may be viewed as emerging, developing, maturing, and declining. The human progression is natural and irreversible. Astute organizational managers may intervene during the two latter stages to induce renewal. This usually is accomplished by providing for orderly leadership succession. The extent to which the strategy succeeds varies among organizations. Where renewal succeeds, managerial changes influence inter- and intraorganizational relationships. These relationships are formed by three factors: (1) the life cycle positions of organizations and their products or services, (2) managers' leadership styles, and (3) organizational structure. The last element is especially significant to public relations managers. Individuals' positions in organizations influence their motivations.

Organizational Structure

Six structural levels have been identified in complex organizations, each with its own objectives. At the apex of the organizational chart is the board or enterprise level dedicated to creating new wealth. Immediately below, at the corporate or chief executive officer level, are those who allocate resources to achieve board-specified objectives. Next in descending order is the sector or senior vice-president level, charged with optimal resource utilization. There then follow the business segment level (vice-president), charged with strengthening the organization; the department (manager) level, responsible for product/market development; and the section (supervisor) level, focused on unit effectiveness.

Leadership Styles

Individuals at each level vary in leadership style, which in part are products of personal preference. Two other factors are stronger determinants. They are the nature of individual responsibilities and the position of organizations and/or their products/services on life cycle continua. The following are three typical leadership styles:

Entrepreneurial. Entrepreneurial leadership styles are prevalent in emerging or developing organizations. Individuals involved can be characterized as risk-accepting, venturesome or opportunistic, effective as opposed to efficient, innovative, and minimally controlling of subordinates.

Maintaining. Maintaining leadership styles most often are found in developing or maturing organizations. Maintaining executives usually are moderately risk-accepting, moderately venturesome, effective and efficient, relatively sophisticated, and moderately participative in approaching their duties.

Conservative. Conservative leadership most often is found in maturing or declining organizations. Conservative managers tend to be autocratic, risk-avoiding, efficient rather than effective, nonparticipative, and nonventuresome.

Managerial reward criteria vary with type of organization, and at times they may outweigh individual management style preferences. More important, reward criteria and related factors tend to predispose managers toward specific public relations methods.

Entrepreneurial executives usually are rewarded on the basis of performance. Market share, gross sales volume, and relative product/service, price/quality factors are most frequently used as performance indicators. Maintaining executives usually are found in developing or maturing organizations. Their performance-based rewards most often are governed by sales-related ratios—sales:marketing expense, sales:capital investment, sales:working capital, and sales:capacity usually are among them. Conservative executives in maintaining or declining organizations usually are rewarded on the basis of different statistical indicators: return on investment, cash flow versus investment, pretax profits versus sales, and gross profit versus sales. These conditions imply special approaches to public relations.

IMPLIED PUBLIC RELATIONS NEEDS

Programmatic Variables

Organizational public relations programs vary in content and thrust. They are influenced by managers' responsibility levels, leadership styles, and organizational life cycle positions. The nature and extent of public relations programming are shaped by four factors arising out of these elements:

1. Organizational communication needs as perceived by manager(s) involved
2. Managers' communication styles
3. Media most congruent with organizational need and individual style
4. Resource allocation patterns implied by organizational life cycle position

External and internal environmental influences are felt in these areas; so are relative organizational economic positions.

Economic Implications

Developing and maintaining organizations are most likely to have resources for extensive public relations efforts. Need may be greatest among entrepreneurial organizations but resources tend to be fewer. Public relations priorities also may be higher among entrepreneurial managers but their resources are limited as well. Incentives for public relations expenditures diminish in maturing and declining organizations. Reward mechanisms discourage significant investment by conservative managers.

Communication Channels

Communication channel selection also is influenced by economic factors governing the relative importance of constituent groups to managers. In entrepreneurial or maintaining organizations, for example, high priorities attach to employee communications because product/service quality is a management reward criterion. Public relations managers thus should expect interest in employee newsletters and similar devices.

Strong capital needs also are implied in these organizations' managerial reward structures. Interest in programs to enhance stature in the eyes of the media—especially financial media—thus should be expected. Primary constituencies would include securities analysts and other components of the financial community where organizations are publicly owned. Financial public relations programs then gain high priorities.

Analytical Processes

Every organization is amenable to examination in this manner. Analyses lead public relations managers to logically deduced sets of motivational factors. They also permit deductions as to constituent groups, message content, communication channels, and economic resources. Deductions must be examined with communication needs implied by environmental assessment data. They together suggest practitioner strategies.

Assessment processes should be sensitive to the presence of five "driving technologies" futurists expect to dominate the economy for the remainder of the century: computers, factory and office automation, new materials, biotechnology, and health/medical technologies. Demographic trends also are strong predictors. Local and regional development trends may be significant as well.

Forecasting

Success in developing new public relations services is a product of managers' abilities to accomplish two objectives. They first must forecast the impact of environmental trends; then they must fashion services that will assist organizational executives in coping with resulting problems. Christopher H. Lovelock and Charles B. Weinberg outlined the process graphically in *Marketing for Public and Nonprofit Managers*. While their focus was the not-for-profit sector, the process is as applicable in for-profit organizations (see Figure 8.2).

Managers must maintain organizational perspectives to achieve these objectives. They must examine emerging issues from client viewpoints and in light of their priorities. Several examples of recent vintage serve to illustrate the process.

Identifying Needs

Two organizational needs arose in the early to mid–1980s with the crises at Three-Mile Island (Pennsylvania) and Bhopal (India). They demonstrated organizations' relative ineptitude in coping with problems. Managers were found unprepared to handle media relations under crisis conditions and inept as organizational spokespersons. Public relations practitioners responded to the first need by extending the scope of a well-established practice technique. For the second, they developed a new service that since has become a practice specialty.

Disaster Planning

The response to Bhopal and similar events was a new form of disaster planning. It consisted of three parts. First, traditional plans were reviewed and revised in keeping with contemporary conditions. Second, every organizational manager whose role ever might require emergency response was made party to the planning process. Finally, the process was extended through use of simulations.

While the first component of these disaster response programs was relatively well-established in public relations, the others were new. They proved marketable because senior managers recognized the potential for organizational damage.

FIGURE 8.2.
The Process of Market Targeting.

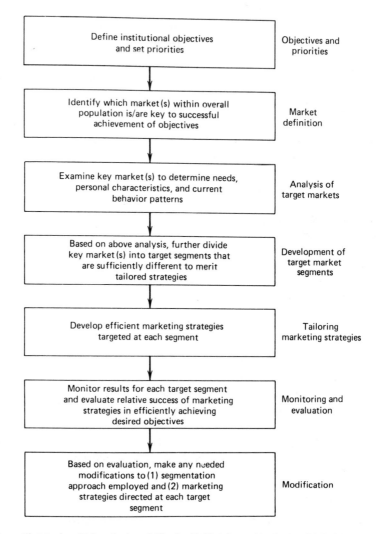

Source: From Christopher H. Lovelock and Charles B. Weinberg, *Marketing for Public and Nonprofit Managers.* © Copyright 1984, John Wiley & Sons, Inc. Reprinted by permission.

Public relations managers capitalized on these newly recognized needs. They reviewed disaster plans and expanded them beyond traditional boundaries. The process was developmental and educational. What earlier had been a plan executed by organizational practitioners was extended to multiple management levels. Extended plans recognized that contemporary disaster potential requires more than effective media handling.

Executive Preparedness

Detailed contingency plans were developed to guide every management level. Managers were rigorously trained through disaster simulations. The training included the intricacies of media relations. Special emphasis was attached to developing ability to serve as spokespersons. Demand for these services became so great that a number of specialized businesses developed. They were established in major media centers to prepare executives and managers to cope with media inquiries, interviews, and related events. Untold hundreds of thousands of dollars moved from organizational treasuries to counseling firms in the process.

Noncrisis Needs

Need for public relations skills tends to become quickly evident in crisis situations. They are equally needed in connection with slower-developing problems. A typical situation arose in the mid 1970s when Congress amended the Taft-Hartley Act to make voluntary nonprofit hospitals subject to union organizing efforts.

Unions responded with strong organizing efforts. Hospitals, on the other hand, were relatively unprepared. Their executives had not previously been required to deal with unions. Their management systems often were inadequate. Counseling firms soon found themselves involved in hospital labor relations problems. Many encountered further communication needs and another subspecialty of public relations developed.

Secondary Needs

Problems seldom come into being of their own volition; they are caused by action or inaction. In the hospital situation, inaction was responsible. Free of requirements that they engage in collective bargaining, many had permitted weaknesses to develop in management structures.

Junior managers lacked management skills. Senior technicians were apt to become supervisors and managers. Few technical disciplines provide educational or experiential backgrounds in management. Supervisory training was rare.

These weaknesses were compounded by internal and external factors. Internally, immunity from unions had engendered neglect of personnel policies and procedures. Typical systems permitted managers and supervisors near total latitude in such critical areas as discipline. Externally, pressure was developing rapidly for containment of health care costs. Many hospitals were ill-equipped to respond. Their wage/benefit programs were archaic and amenable to employee abuse.

Filling the Needs

Alert public relations practitioners—especially those initially engaged in meeting labor relations challenges—identified and responded to the underlying problems. Most responses took two forms. Managerial/supervisory training programs were developed to strengthen middle management. Personnel policies and wage/benefit programs were redesigned to eliminate abuse and improve reward systems. Hundreds of thousands of dollars again changed hands in the process.

Identifying Future Needs

Identifying situations where practitioners have responded to change is easily accomplished. Attempting to specify areas where problems may arise is another matter; nevertheless, this objective can be achieved. Managers need only look to changes occurring in society to identify opportunities.

The process involves two parts. First, managers must identify trends that will impact existing or prospective clients. Second, impacts must be defined to a point at which needs can be identified and responses developed.

General Trends

Demographic change and on-going redefinition of social responsibility ultimately will impact every organization. The former is more readily defined. Declines in numbers of workers are a function of demographic trends. Everyone who will be working in the United States for the ensuing 18 years already has been born. Nothing can be done to alter the numbers. Redefinition of social responsibility is no less pervasive but more difficult to define. Expectations of organizations are changing. So is the meaning of "good corporate citizenship." To what extent remains to be seen.

Work Force Impacts

Work force changes demand employer responses, especially in labor-intensive industries. A "seller's market" in labor will be new to most organizations. The nation has experienced occasional shortages of technical personnel but general shortages have been unknown since World War II.

What will be the organizational impacts? Highly competitive circumstances will arise; organizations may engage in "bidding wars" for employees; and the bidding will require more than dollars and cents. Research has established that workers want more from their jobs than money. Virtually every study conducted in this area places wages low on lists of employee motivators.

Logic suggests Naisbitt's concept of a "nourishing" employee environment will be critical to employer success. Creating such environments implies changes in managerial/supervisory techniques. Individuals in these roles will become mentors or counselors. Retraining needs will be a pressing management concern; so will wage and benefit plans. Worker demand for "personal growth" will require more educational benefits. Well-designed, they can be as beneficial to employers as to employees.

"Re-inventing the corporation," to use the title of one of Naisbitt's books, will become management's primary concern. Communicating details—the nature of changes and reasons they're necessary—will be a major employee relations responsibility. The need will compound as managers and supervisors are inundated by change necessary to long-term survival. Beset by organizational demands, they will tend to be less effective in transmitting information to employees.

Social Responsibility

Tomorrow's definition of "social responsibility" is difficult to forecast. Organizational managers have been attempting to come to grips with the concept for years without success. What are an organization's obligations to communities in which it operates? Fair wages, wholesome work places, and participation in United Way campaigns are common expectations. But what of urban redevelopment, community health and welfare, and the like? Are these—or should they be—exclusively governmental responsibilities?

The federal government in the mid–1980s was responding to the latter question in the negative. Greater community involvement was urged on business and industry. Whether this trend continues or abates, managements must respond. The nature of and reasons for their responses will have to be specified and communicated to stakeholder groups. New public relations needs will result.

Future Certainties

While these trends are general in nature, others of greater specificity readily can be identified. Perhaps most significant is the emergence of new "driving technologies" that futurists anticipate will alter society over several decades. Each implies multiple changes and attendant public relations needs. The technologies and their prospective impact are as follows:

Computers

The computer's impact on society is growing. In the mid–1980s, an estimated 15 percent of U.S. households were using computers. A few were used occupationally; fewer still for communication. Futurists predict these will become major computer applications.

Rapid evolution of information utilities is expected to alter the concept of libraries. Educational delivery systems may be radically changed as well. More and more individuals may work at home, linked to offices by computers. Perhaps most significant from a public relations perspective, as computers become more dominant in communication other media inevitably will be less used.

Automation and Robotics

Factories of the future exist in the United States and abroad. Manufacturing plants operating around the clock but staffed on one shift by a handful of personnel have been developed in Japan. In the United States, IBM and others are proceeding along similar lines.

This trend may trigger changes akin to those in the steel industry during the early 1980s. Competitive disadvantages then led to mammoth "rust bowls" in industrial states. From some came early calls for massive worker retraining programs but the calls never were answered, nor were several major questions they implied: Retraining by whom? At what cost? Who will pay?

IBM retrained workers while installing robots in a computer assembly plant in Lexington, Kentucky. The company presumably accepted a social responsibility to do so. But will other, less-affluent organizations do likewise? If they fail to do so, what then will occur? The questions are more than philosophical—employee relations, governmental relations, and community relations needs are implicit in alternative responses.

New Materials

Fiber optics, new plastics, and ceramics are among materials society soon will come to use extensively. Fiber optics already have been adopted on a wholesale basis in telecommunications. New plastics are beginning to replace metals. The automotive industry is looking toward using ceramics in engines.

New technologies require new skills; they also render older skills obsolete. The social impact of new materials will be similar to that of automation. Results are difficult to project but organizational public relations needs will compound.

Biotechnology

Battle lines already have been drawn in biotechnology. More will emerge as science presses its search for knowledge. Early efforts to strengthen vegetable resistance to frost brought protests over possible unforeseen consequences. The legal and medical professions continue to debate the times of birth and death. Such debates appear likely to multiply.

Similar problems appear inevitable as science learns more of genetics and acquires the ability to manipulate the characteristics of plants, animals and—ultimately—human beings. Potential for public relations is obvious.

Health and Medical Technology

Early evidence of need relative to new technologies arose in health and medical technology. So did moral and ethical issues with which society continues to wrestle. At what point does a fetus gain legal rights? How long should an individual be kept on life support systems? Who has the right to "pull the plug?"

Prospective questions are no less difficult than those already under debate. If medical care is made a right rather than a privilege in the United States, who will determine which candidates receive limited numbers of organs suitable for transplant? Who will decide whether a few months or years added to the life of a genius is more valuable than the lifetime of a teenager? Who will play God?

Public relations practitioners are unlikely to be called upon to answer such questions. Their talents and skills will be essential, however, to organizations and individuals caught up in attendant public debates.

DEVELOPING SERVICES

Neither clients nor prospective clients are essentially interested in public relations, nor are they especially enamored of communication programming. Their primary concerns are satisfaction of organizational needs—they seek practical solutions to problems.

Economics and Conflict

Their problems largely are economically oriented. They are obstacles to executing organizational strategic plans. In the case of the impending national labor shortage, they threaten an organizational resource. Changing social responsibility concepts may threaten reputations as well as sales and profits.

Telecommuting via computers and telephone lines threatens automotive industry profits. The advent of fiber optics already has eroded the copper industry. Insect- and disease-resistant crops threaten agricultural chemical products. Computers and self-diagnostic medical equipment impinge on physician practice.

For each potentially adverse impact, there are benefits: more computer sales, greater use of telephone systems, greater efficiency in telecommunications, higher crop yields at lower costs, reduced healthcare costs. The issue in many cases is a matter of whose ox is gored. A quantum increase in demand for public relations services will develop in any event.

Professional Response

Management's greatest marketing challenge involves crafting public relations programs to meet organizational needs. They must provide measurable beneficial results, preferably in economic terms.

In an era of labor shortages, for example, competition for personnel will become intense. Recruiting and training costs will increase. Public relations programs that reduce employee turnover will be in demand. They may involve restructuring of wage/benefit programs. They may require retraining of managers and supervisors. They will require communication services.

Chemical manufacturers already have invested in biotechnology in the interest of self-preservation. Further research ultimately will produce insect- and disease-resistant food crops. As that day approaches, public relations need will compound. Initial concerns will focus on neutralizing adverse public opinion. Government relations efforts also may be needed. Alert managers will find unprecedented practice opportunities in these and similar circumstances.

The nature of their responses will govern the success they enjoy. Real estate experts have found successful investing in land and buildings dependent on three variables: location, location, and location. Successful marketing of public relations programs similarly will require results, results, and results. Managers must specifically address constituent problems or needs. Approach to prospective clients must be oriented accordingly. While practitioners sell employee relations programs, clients will be buying reduced turnover rates. Where practitioners offer government relations programs, organizations will be buying acceptance of new processes or biologically altered plants.

When this rationale is firmly established—and only then—will managers be ready to begin offering public relations services to existing and prospective clients.

DESIGNING THE PLAN

Marketing plan development is governed by the nature and size of the public relations unit. In organizational situations, where single professional units predominate, practitioners undertake the effort alone. They identify needs, specify services to satisfy those needs, and call on managers to acquaint them with the services.

Organizational Context

Counseling firms develop similar plans but execution varies with organizational size and management policy. Two patterns predominate. Marketing in one is assigned as a primary responsibility to one or more individuals. Responsibility in the other is spread among senior managers or among all professionals. The latter approach is often used in smaller firms where every professional is involved in client service. Most handle multiple accounts. Size precludes specialization.

Designing the Design

Where marketing is "everyone's job," managers must insure that it does not become "no one's job." The plan must be designed for ease of monitoring. Monitoring is essential. On-going client service needs otherwise tend to make marketing a stepchild. This especially is true where personnel are not sales oriented. Many enter the profession from the "creative side." They often harbor an aversion to selling. It can be overcome, but only where monitoring creates an element of compulsion.

Goals and Strategies

Successful marketing plans focus on individual prospects of known potential within commercial, industrial, and institutional sectors. Prospect lists categorized by economic potential create primary guidelines.

Goals and strategies established as growth projections guide the effort. These are translated into minimum requirements for personnel. Requirements are specified in numbers of new business contacts in given time periods, usually a week or a month.

Programmatic Components

Marketing requires two primary components: individual selling based on the prospect list and a supporting communication program. Communication and selling can be handled separately. The former responsibilities often are assigned to personnel whose sales skills are limited. Those with stronger sales backgrounds then spend greater amounts of time on personal contacts.

Monitoring becomes the responsibility of senior managers who guide and assist others involved. Their duties may include accompanying others on sales calls when team efforts are indicated.

Practice development, marketing, and sales processes must be maintained as a cohesive whole for optimum productivity.

IN SUMMARY

Developing successful marketing programs is a lengthy process. Research and follow-through are essential. Logical deduction based on research data enables managers to plan productive programs.

The research phase of the marketing effort involves three primary components. The first consists of the information-gathering processes of environmental assessment: scanning and tracking. The former is used to identify events that may point to developing trends; the latter monitors trend development.

The second step in the process requires planners to identify commercial, industrial, and institutional groups that will be impacted by emerging trends. They then estimate the extent of prospective impacts and attendant public relations need.

In the third phase, planners specify prospective clients in commercial, industrial, and institutional groups. They are examined individually to assess potential reactions. The latter step involves reviews of organizational life cycle status and managerial leadership styles. They are indicators of prospective response to changing environments.

Near-unlimited numbers of social trends may create potential problems for organizations. Those arising out of demographic change are certain to develop.

Organizations also will be influenced by the evolution of the five "driving technologies" of the next several decades: computers, automation, new materials, biotechnology, and health/medical technologies. Directly or indirectly, they will change almost every organization.

The extent of change will vary across organizations. Public relations managers must extrapolate from data gathered in research to estimate impact potential. Projections enable managers to estimate organizational needs and develop mutually productive services to meet those needs. Marketing plans then are installed in a manner enabling senior management to monitor progress.

ADDITIONAL READING

Bachner, John P., and N. K. Khosia. *Marketing and Promotion for Design Professionals*. New York: Van Nostrand Reinhold, 1977.

Coxe, Weld. *Marketing Architectural and Engineering Services*. New York: Van Nostrand Reinhold, 1971.

DeLozier, M. Wayne. *The Marketing Communications Process*. New York: McGraw-Hill, 1976.

Fine, Seymour. *Marketing Ideas and Social Issues*. New York: Praeger, 1981.

Kotler, Philip. *Marketing for Non-Profit Organizations*. Englewood Cliffs, N.J.: Prentice-Hall, 1975.

Lovelock, Christopher H., and Charles B. Weinberg. *Marketing for Public and Non-Profit Managers*. New York: John Wiley, 1984.

Luther, William M. *The Marketing Plan: How to Prepare and Implement It*. New York: AMACOM, 1982.

Mauser, Ferdinand F. *Modern Marketing Management: An Integrated Approach*. New York: McGraw-Hill, 1961.

Meyers, Herbert S. *Minding Your Own Business: A Contemporary Guide to Small Business Success.* Homewood, Ill.: Dow Jones-Irwin, 1984.

Udell, Jon G., and Gene R. Laczniak. *Marketing in an Age of Change.* New York: John Wiley, 1981.

9
Practice Development

The primary objective of practice development is sales. Sales generate revenues essential to success. They provide resources to accomplish organizational objectives. Practice development does not involve selling in the usual sense, nor is it marketing—it encompasses these functions and more.

Practice development is the sum of steps public relations managers take to assure practice growth. Under the consultant model, the process applies to organizational and counselor units. It is limited in organizations as to prospective clientele, but this circumstance requires no change in managerial practice.

The Development Process

Practice development is a mirror image of the public relations process. Five steps are involved: environmental assessment, defining impending problems/opportunities, developing centers of influence, identifying prospect groups, and creating networks.

These are developmental efforts. They establish foundations for marketing and sales programs that some contend are components of organizational development. The processes are on-going. They are oriented to impending problems or opportunities among existing and prospective client groups. These are generators of demand for services. Opportunities are near limitless, as demonstrated by a review of organizations' external environments.

Market Orientation

Developing a market orientation comes naturally to some but with difficulty to others. It involves information-gathering and analysis. It is a process that can be managed, and sound management techniques insure its success.

Practice development often requires new skills and new discipline. Practitioner backgrounds largely are creative. Analytical abilities honed in public relations usually enable them to identify potential development areas. Thereafter, obstacles tend to arise.

Problem Areas

First among the problems is an absence of education or training in marketing and sales. Coupled with predispositions toward creative areas, this produces a tendency toward unbalanced effort. Creative functions are permitted to take precedence over marketing, marketing communication, and sales. An erratic and inefficient selling program often results. Such difficulties can be avoided, and organizational planners must assign rational priorities to the effort. It must be undertaken on a consistent basis and from a process perspective.

ENVIRONMENTAL ASSESSMENT

External Environments

Environmental trends are paramount in identifying organizations' public relations needs. The environmental assessment process ultimately deals with five factors:

1. Developing trends in the environments
2. Their anticipated impacts on the organization and its stakeholders
3. The individuals who will be controlling response mechanisms
4. Organizational technology
5. The size and scale of the organization

The first two are of primary concern at the outset. Where changes in external environments create little impact, others are of no consequence. Contingent theories of organization suggest they come into play where significant impacts are involved. In these conditions, they influence organizational responses that are of concern in public relations.

Practitioner information-gathering begins with the positioning of the public relations unit. Counselors are at a minor disadvantage relative to corporate staffers as to knowledge of personalities. This handicap is offset, however, by counselors' broader perspectives.

Scanning and Monitoring

Environmental assessment has two dimensions: scanning and monitoring. Scanning involves a superficial review of events. Scanners watch the horizon for events that may signal change. Scanning is nondirectional, covering a full 360 degrees. It is creative and intuitive. Scanners look for activity patterns providing clues to the future.

Where scanning is largely intuitive, monitoring essentially is analytical. The process involves following trends believed to be developing. It focuses on a narrow area or areas to ascertain the speed and strength with which identified trends are developing. The extent of trends' organizational impact on the organization thus can be better estimated.

Scanning and monitoring should be components of external and internal assessment. They should be planned, scheduled activities, handled on regular rather than ad hoc bases. Their scope varies with the nature of the public relations organization. Environments of clients, prospective clients, and the public relations organization are of primary concern.

Constraints

Time and economic factors limit environmental assessment. Larger and better-financed organizations often subcontract significant portions of the process to firms such as the Naisbitt Organization and SRI International. Naisbitt, like Yankelovich and others, largely are monitoring rather than scanning organizations. SRI functions in the latter area, with more than 1,500 scanners around the world.

Organization

While procedures vary, environmental assessment is vital to successful practice; it must be organized within existing resources. Few can afford the many applicable publications and research services available. Those used vary with practice and goals, strategies and action plans. For the most part they can be classified by category.

First are general-interest publications such as daily newspapers in communities where the organization is active. Local business newspapers and locally published general or special-interest magazines also might be included.

Second are national general business publications such as *The Wall Street Journal, Business Week, Industry Week, Fortune, Barron's,* and *Forbes.* The first three should be "must" reading.

The third level consists of industry or professional publications in three categories. (1) those dealing with public relations, which should be read by every practitioner; (2) those that serve the industry or industries in which the practitioner is employed; and (3) those that serve industries previously identified as harboring trends that might enhance practice potential.

In the health-care sector, for example, the second group might include *Hospitals, Healthcare Management,* the *Journal of the American Association of Healthcare Administrators,* regional publications such as *Southern Hospitals,* and the journals or newsletters of state hospital associations. The third group then would include publications dealing with legislation and regulatory matters, health-care technology, and the journals of health-care professionals.

For larger organizations dealing primarily with publicly held corporations, management professor Robert Hershey recommends the *Wall Street Transcript*, the *Official Gazette* of the U.S. Patent Office, and a clipping service.

Selectivity becomes essential as counselors approach the third level. Their reading concerning the businesses or industries of established clients should be mandatory. Beyond those industries choices are difficult.

Techniques

Some have found lists of prospective industries rather than prospective clients to be better selection guides. Lists help practitioners scan multiple industries over extended periods. Caution is necessary to prevent lists becoming inflexible. External events reported in general interest and general business publications may suggest changes. Pending legislation to deregulate the financial industry in the early 1980s, for example, should have been such a signal. Appropriate publications immediately should have been included on "must" lists for the duration of the anticipated transition.

A similar strategy is appropriate for organizational practitioners with one variation. Their employers often subscribe to general publications and those oriented toward internal constituencies. Where this is not the case, accountants, managers, human resources directors, and others usually are willing to loan copies and are flattered by inquiries. The objective here, as in the case of the counselor, is to gain insight into businesses in which prospective clients are engaged, problems they face day to day, and long-term trends that may impact their practices.

Identification

The assessment process enables practitioners to identify existing or potential needs in organizational components, organizations, or industries. They then design specific services to produce mutually beneficial results. Proposed services must be adequately productive to justify user cost and profitable to consultants.

The ability to anticipate future events is helpful in this context. The process involved is called forecasting; it requires analytical thinking. An analysis of the impact of technology developed by the World Future Society provides some insight (see Figure 9.1).

PROBLEMS AND OPPORTUNITIES

Environmental assessment processes in practice development are applied to public relations units as well as prospective clients. They are applied to practices to determine: organizational strengths and weaknesses, the nature

FIGURE 9.1.
The Effects of Three Technological Developments.

THE EFFECTS OF TECHNOLOGY

Futurists chart the possible consequences of actions or technologies in order to anticipate their possible effects. Unintended, unknown, and delayed consequences may prove even more important in the long run than the direct and intended effects.

	First-Order Consequences	Second-Order Consequences	Third-Order Consequences	Fourth-Order Consequences	Fifth-Order Consequences	Sixth-Order Consequences
Automobile	People have a means of traveling rapidly, easily, cheaply, privately, door-to-door.	People patronize stores at greater distances from their homes. These are generally bigger stores that have large clienteles.	Residents of a community do not meet so often and therefore do not know each other so well.	Strangers to each other, community members find it difficult to unite to deal with common problems. Individuals find themselves increasingly isolated and alienated from their neighbors.	Isolated from their neighbors, members of a family depend more on each other for satisfaction of most of their psychological needs.	When spouses are unable to meet heavy psychological demands that each makes on the other, frustration occurs. This may lead to divorce.
Improved Refrigeration	Food can be kept for longer periods in the home.	People stay home more because they don't need to go to stores.	Same as above; also, more free time for wife.	Same as above. (Also, additional free time increases demand for recreation and entertainment.)	Same as above.	Same as above.
Television	People have a new source of entertainment and enlightenment in their homes.	People stay home more rather than going out to local clubs and bars where they would meet their fellows.	Same as above. (Also, people become less dependent on other people for entertainment.)	Same as above.	Same as above.	Same as above.

Source: © 1986 by the World Future Society, 4916 St. Elmo Avenue, Bethesda, MD 20814 U.S.A., Telephone 301/656-8274. Reprinted by permission.

of the existing practice, the nature of competition—present and future, extent of specialization, rational geographic parameters, and realistic goals and strategies.

Strengths and Weaknesses

While often unrecognized by those involved, organizations have strengths and weaknesses. Practice development efforts capitalize on strengths and avoid weaknesses. They arise from the backgrounds of professionals in the organization—educational or experiential. Virtually any body of knowledge can be productively applied in public relations. Application requires recognizing strengths and seeking out areas of application.

Those with backgrounds in human resources management, for example, might concentrate developmental efforts in employee communications. Those with financial backgrounds might seek clients in shareholder relations.

Recent experiences also can serve as practice development springboards. Practitioners who have handled crisis situations often can market knowledge and experience gained to those anticipating similar problems. Consultants who have developed productive programs for one client find it beneficial to seek other applications. Ethical limits may require that new clients be in distant cities or different industries.

Practice Mix

Practice mix data can be used in like fashion. Practice analysis often reveals uneven client distributions. Counselors may find disproportionate volumes of work in manufacturing, distribution, or sales organizations; in nonprofit or institutional sectors. Organizational units may find their efforts overly concentrated in financial public relations or employee communications.

Balance is advisable regardless of practice type or size. Practice balance among counselors minimizes the potential impact of client attrition as a result of economic change. They seldom equally impact all segments of the economy. Organizational perspectives are similar. The greater the number of managers who view public relations units as important, the more secure their positions.

Examining practice mixes thus serves two purposes: It alerts practitioners to prospective problems and uncovers potential expansion areas. The latter indicators, no matter how strong, should be considered tentative in the early stages. Adverse competitive circumstances can neutralize perceived potential.

Competition

Other areas—existing or developing—may be neglected. In still others, the practice's internal strengths may be significantly greater than competitors'.

Greatest potential for practice development exists where strength is paired with competitor weakness. Areas in which emerging problems suggest development of new clienteles can be ranked second in potential. Third ranking then would be assigned to areas where competitor expansion is limited by ethical constraints.

Business development plans thus should catalog two sets of strengths and weaknesses: those of the public relations unit and those of competitors. With rare exceptions, they are known or can be inferred from knowledge of competitors' practices.

Pragmatically, competition exists in counselor and organizational practices. Turf problems, as they are called, arise between public relations units and other organizational components. They may involve other communication-oriented disciplines or other professional units. Among the communication disciplines are advertising, marketing, development, and sales promotion. Functions outside the communication area where conflict may arise include human resources, accounting, and law.

Specialization

Practitioner and competitor strengths and weaknesses may suggest potential for practice specialization. Specialized firms are earning the industry's highest profits, according to consultant Dan Baer. "It's better to do a few things well than to deliver mixed results across a broader front," Baer told a Spring 1986 PRSA Counselor Academy meeting in Phoenix. "The days of the pseudo-PR generalist are numbered. It is becoming increasingly difficult for a PR firm to be all things to all clients...."

Most Counselor Academy members practice in the nation's larger cities where specialization is universally feasible. In smaller communities, profitable generalized practices will continue to exist. Baer's comments nevertheless emphasize the potential in exploiting practice strengths and competitors' weaknesses. Practice specialization in smaller communities also implies greater geographic scope. This factor also must be considered in planning.

Geographic Scope

Geographic practice patterns should be factored into development equations by counselor and organizational units. Expansion through acquisition and diversification has been a major developmental trend in institutions, business, and industry. Hospitals and banks typify the former sector. Services organizational units rendered to one component of a conglomerate or multisite organization often can be provided to others. Absence of competing organizational units at remote locations also creates opportunities.

Circumstances are similar among counselors, especially in markets dominated by few firms. Dominant organizations often succumb to over-confidence. They are prone to confine developmental activity to larger firms or to smaller geographic areas. These conditions open the door to competitive incursions.

Geographic factors can be especially important. Neglected suburban communities can yield multiple profitable accounts in a relatively short time. While few may qualify as "bread and butter" accounts, numbers of smaller and medium-sized prospects make these communities worthy of exploration.

Competitive analyses also should include evaluation of potential for new and existing products or services. What services does the organization offer that are not available from competitors? What services may be wholly absent from the marketplace? Both deserve careful examination. The doors of competitors' clients are left open by ethical codes to services not being provided by those firms.

Reasonable Goals

The foregoing should not be interpreted as encouraging an expansion binge. Few would deny dreaming of doubling or tripling the size of their practices—such glowing dreams can turn into traumatic realities. No organization can manage uncontrolled growth, and too rapid expansion produces disaster as often as success. Problems arise as growth impairs ability to serve existing clients.

Reasonable growth patterns should be the practitioner's goal. What is "reasonable?" The question can be answered only in terms of individual practices. Geographic factors also may play a part. Providing services to multiple clients in a single industry requires relatively low incremental time demand. Environments are known. Assessment systems are in place. Concurrent growth in multiple industries can be demanding.

The principal pitfall is the "revolving door" syndrome. Where dissatisfied clients exit as rapidly as new clients are signed, practices suffer rather than grow. "Proceed with care" is the cardinal rule. Reasonable goals should be set and practice development organized accordingly.

Budgeting

Practice development budgeting is a difficult process. Practitioner budgets tend to be more difficult to establish. The question, "How much is enough," defies response. Little published data exist. Promotional budgets in commercial, industrial, and professional sectors range from less than 1 percent to as much as 10 percent of gross sales. Most marketing-oriented professions spend 5 to 8 percent of fee income.

Lest percentages become misleading, a word of caution is necessary.

They usually include the time of those involved. Substantial portions of the public relations organization's nonbillable time presumably may be dedicated to practice development. "Paper" cost thus would be high while incremental cost is relatively low.

Conservative budgeting and investment of human and capital resources is preferable. "Feast or famine" conditions must be avoided. Consistent, affordable development effort is essential.

CENTERS OF INFLUENCE

Centers of influence are among more neglected resources that public relations managers can apply in practice development. These are individuals in positions to refer prospective clients. They may be existing or contingent assets. They may be obtained naturally or through careful cultivation. They require continuing attention to be optimally productive.

Existing Assets

Existing centers of influence are individuals with whom managers became acquainted before attaining management rank. They often are members of earlier peer groups.

They can contribute to managers' practice development success provided relationships are not permitted to wither by neglect. Too many tend to neglect those with whom they came in regular contact in earlier occupational settings. New occupations bring new relationships. New circles are more readily accessible than old. Once-strong relationships tend to deteriorate in occupational transitions.

The burden of preventive or remedial action rests with the practitioner. It is most easily handled by maintaining social contacts through professional or other organizations. Maintaining contacts—especially among the media and in the business community—can be productive. Managers should encourage new employees accordingly, even to the extent of funding membership dues.

New Assets

Change in occupation and promotion in occupations create new contacts similarly valuable in practice development. The nature of these contacts is a function of practitioners' positions. Organizational managers' contacts will not be identical to counselors', nor will those of personnel at different organizational levels.

Organizational Assets

Peers are the most influential and knowledgeable contacts of organizational managers. Their experience in the organization equips them with knowledge of matters that earlier required public relations attention. Executives in other divisions are worthy of cultivation in the same context. The process produces insights and contacts that will be beneficial in the future—especially where the consultant practice mode is in place.

Vendors are another group requiring cultivation. Included are designers, photographers, printers, or others who provide products, services, or overload assistance. They regularly see peers, clients, prospective clients, and others. In the process, they gain knowledge of value to public relations managers.

This knowledge can range from problems such as personnel shortages to new production techniques in the graphic arts. The information can vary in value. Contacts involved nevertheless are worthy of cultivation. Salutary relationships with vendors contribute to managers' reputations in the professional community. Among counselors, they are vital referral sources.

Counselor Assets

Every counselor organization creates a latent referral network. It consists of professionals that the practice engages in banking, insurance, law, and accounting as well as vendor firms. It also includes vendors and others in public relations practice.

While selected on the basis of professional skills, the banker, insurance broker, accountant, and lawyer should be cultivated as prime sources of business referrals. Early interviews with prospective providers of such services should include several questions: Is the firm representing other communication organizations? Is it committed to refer all prospective clients to them? How can a mutually satisfactory referral system be established?

The latter question is especially important. Public relations professionals' practice development efforts position them to make referrals. The essential ingredient in productive referral networks is *mutual* benefit.

This ingredient must be present in relationships with vendors as well. Practitioners must recognize, however, that artists, designers, typographers, printers, photographers, and others deal with many counselor firms. They cannot reasonably expect to be first to hear of all new business leads, nor should they consistently be last. The two-way street principle applies here as well.

The same principle governs networks within the profession. Practitioners often are in a position to help one another. Counselors often are sources of information concerning job vacancies for organizational practitioners. members of the latter group frequently become aware of situations in which counselor assistance is needed.

Care and Feeding

Information and referrals flow to managers in proportion to their investments in cultivating centers of influence. Cultivation involves two factors:

First is the quid pro quo mechanism suggested above; the second, often neglected, involves little more than courtesy.

A simple "thank you" by mail or telephone—preferably both—goes far to assure one good turn will be followed by another. Holiday greeting cards and get-well notes are mandatory. So are letters of congratulation when appropriate. Regular but infrequent informal visits are beneficial. An occasional lunch also is helpful, especially with consultants to the practice.

Managers in large public relations firms find it helpful to apply tracking systems similar to those used in monitoring prospective clients. Centers of influence requiring attention can become too many to be entrusted to memory for regular cultivation. Very seldom, however, will they be so plentiful as to support a practice development program.

Systematic prospecting programs are necessary. They generate new business and prospects to be referred to centers of influence.

PROSPECTING

The Process

The heart of the practice development program is a three-part process sales professionals call "prospecting"—an on-going search for sales prospects. It involves finding, classifying, and tracking prospects.

Finding Prospects

Prospects for public relations services literally are everywhere. Almost no organization today can claim to be without public relations needs. Fewer will be able to do so tomorrow.

The external assessment process should be a primary generator of prospects. It should identify organizations experiencing problems and those capitalizing on opportunities. Every new business is a prospect. So are existing organizations developing new products or services.

Chambers of Commerce, industrial development organizations, and similar authorities publish lists of such businesses. Business newspapers publish lists of corporate charters. Local business directories, usually published annually, often include detailed information about community businesses.

Prospects are so plentiful that counselors experience difficulty in establishing priorities. They should be based on perceived need, economic potential, and consultant qualifications. Knowledge of the prospect's business or industrial sector is a plus; so is experience in the area in which services apparently are needed. Perhaps most important is urgency of need—pressing problems discourage prospect procrastination.

Counselors' greatest frustrations occur where initial contacts reveal that prospects recently retained counsel. Practice development efforts nevertheless must be guided by established priorities. They can best be established and managed through prospect classification systems. They insure the development effort is allocated in keeping with priorities.

Prospect Classification

Classification systems can be as simple or complex as circumstances require. Prospects usually are classified by economic potential, but they also may be categorized by sales effort and estimated time needed to close the sale. These factors correlate well in most cases. Smaller accounts usually are more readily sold and less productive.

Simple classification systems are most popular. Few involve more than three categories. They can be labeled A, B, and C or otherwise designated in sequence. Frequency and type of sales contacts are based on economic potential and time factors. Most systems specify numbers of personal calls, telephone contacts, and letters on annual bases. Total numbers of contacts usually are comparable. Those higher on priority lists receive more personal calls and fewer letters.

Managers should develop systems in keeping with individual needs. They vary with type of practice, communities involved, and other factors.

Development and use of a system is more important than mechanical factors involved. Without a system, effort tends to vary inversely with practice volume. Practitioners fall into the sort of mentality often assigned by advertising agencies to recalcitrant prospects: "When business is good they don't need it; when it's bad they can't afford it." Consistency in practice development is vital. Time from initial contact to signing a new client often is measured in months or years. Failure to act until practitioner need develops can be fatal.

Making Contact

Prospect contacts, which vary in intensity, are the first steps toward client relationships. "Intensity" refers to the extent to which contacts are designed as first steps in the sales process. At one end of this spectrum is the seemingly casual contact. It may occur socially or through activities in which practitioner and prospect are involved. At the opposite pole is a preliminary offer of professional services.

Neither is inherently good or bad; the superiority of one or another is a function of circumstances. Most practitioners have used all of them. The situation is not unlike that University of Maryland Professor James E. Grunig describes as to public relations practice models. They range from press agentry to consultancy. Practitioners tend to denigrate the former and exalt the latter but all continue to be used.

At what some contend is the "professional" end of the contact spectrum are those in social or philanthropic settings. At the other end are direct sales approaches. They are considered here in that order—from lowest to highest level of "intensity."

Social

Every human engages in social activity. In practice development, it involves consultant and prospect in activities that bring them together in social settings. Country clubs, bridge clubs, and similar environs are viewed as sources of business contacts. They may in part serve these ends. They tend to be productive to the extent that the activity is of real interest to the consultant. Those who prefer reading a book by the fire are unlikely to shine in socially oriented development efforts.

Philanthropic

Another increasingly popular technique is based on philanthropic or charitable activities. Consultant and prospect are drawn together, for example, by mutual interest in Boys Clubs and service to the organization. Commitment on the practitioner's part again is essential to the cause. The process is time-consuming and must be rewarding to participants.

Educational

Perhaps most used is an educational approach. Practitioners provide a service to organizations to gain salutary exposure to members. In most cases, education is offered through trade or professional associations of decision makers believed to need public relations services. Counselors contact associations and offer seminars at no cost. Since associations can charge members for such programs, their executives are prone to accept. Given practitioner knowledge of members' problems and professional expertise, such projects almost invariably are productive. At worst, they establish contacts with many potential clients in favorable circumstances and in a short time.

Articles and Speeches

Several other devices also have proven beneficial. They include writing for prospect groups' business or professional journals and speaking at their conventions or meetings. The first tends to be most productive. This especially is so where counselors also use the educational approach described above.

Journal article reprints can be distributed during seminars; they can be left with prospects after sales calls; and they can be used as mail advertising. At least two other attributes also commend this approach. Professional magazine reprints are less expensive and more credible than brochures. Where content is presented in "case history" format, articles create implicit third-party as well as implied editorial endorsements.

Convention-going

Relationships with clients and their associations also open doors to convention or annual meeting appearances. They create unparalleled opportunities to meet clients' colleagues under favorable circumstances: at meals, over coffee, and during social events.

Where practitioners are knowledgeable concerning industry problems, opportunities arise to engage conventiongoers in conversation. Further comments regarding public relations applications later can be presented—as implied or implicit proposals—in correspondence or otherwise.

Direct Approaches

Frontal approaches to executives of prospect organizations are neither unethical nor inappropriate; they often are among more productive techniques. Where used, however, they must be controlled to avoid waste.

Components of the direct approach process usually include letters, follow-up telephone calls, and in-person interviews. They usually occur in that order.

Letters should be relatively ambiguous. Consultants should assume prospects already have sources for professional services. They must exercise care to avoid unethical behavior.

The letter promises a follow-up telephone call, which must be made. The objective is an interview. Calls thus should be confined to generalities. Interviews are oriented to validating prospect needs, discussing potential solutions, and inducing prospects to accept formal proposals.

Neither first nor second contacts with prospective clients may produce success but the effort should not be abandoned. Consultants must exercise patience. If assessments of impending need are accurate, prospects ultimately will acquire counsel. The consultant's objective then is to maintain contact. "May I check back with you in X days/weeks/months?" The response should be duly noted, and appropriate follow-up planned.

Record-Keeping

Planning requires a prospect tracking or record-keeping system. Record-keeping is a burdensome but essential part of practice development. The burden too often is ill-handled out of aversion to detail, but this can be corrected by applying one of several systems.

Systems may be simple or complex. Many successful practitioners use nothing more than a desk calendar and copies of correspondence. This approach is adequate provided correspondence follows every prospect contact.

Where letters follow telephone calls or meetings—which tends to impress in any event—copies can be filed and follow-up dates penciled on calendars. Letters presumably contain sufficient detail to permit appropriate follow-up.

Such informal systems tend to become overburdened under pressure of organized practice development efforts. More formal techniques then become necessary. Most begin with a "contact worksheet" containing information about the prospect. Others use index cards or computer files. Systems should be as simple as possible, emphasizing function rather than form.

NETWORKING

Most techniques described have been used from time to time and with varying degrees of success by many if not most counselors. They succeed or fail based on thoroughness and consistency in application. Another approach—networking—also is often used. It is more significant in organizational practice, however, than in consulting.

In Organizational Practice

The term "networking" typically is used in job hunting rather than sales and marketing contexts. It applies since respect for practitioners is vital to professional success.

Networking in professional development takes varying courses. Organizational practitioners experience little difficulty with the process, an essential component of consultant model practice. It requires practitioners to develop a body of knowledge concerning the needs of other organizational components. The ways in which public relations techniques may be applied become evident in the process.

System

The effort should be undertaken systematically, with priorities established on the basis of perceived need. As marketing executives find the productivity of advertising declining, for example, they should become primary targets for public relations staff members. Objectives should include: becoming familiar with marketing personnel and problems, gaining the confidence of individuals involved, identifying potentially productive applications for public relations techniques, and clearing the way for mutually beneficial relationships.

Analysis

In larger organizations, public relations' constituencies include most staff managers and may include line managers. Where diversified organizations or holding companies are involved, divisional executives also may be included in a list of prospective clients. Functional areas worthy of the practitioner attention at minimum include the following: marketing, advertising, sales promotion, personnel, sales, planning/development, legal services, and accounting.

In Counselor Practice

When counselors establish client relationships, these areas also are worthy of attention. At minimum, bases for working relationships should be established. Need for professional services one day may extend beyond the original assignment.

Networking in counselor practice also should involve requests to clients for new business leads: "Do you know of any others in the community who might benefit from this service?" Most businessmen are well-acquainted with their peers and not reluctant to make suggestions.

CLIENT APPLICATIONS

Practice development is designed to enhance productivity. It focuses primarily on prospects and the ways they may be contacted and induced to become clients. Optimum profit arises where the system is applied to existing clients. Their neglect because of practice growth is a potential problem that can be avoided.

Client Classification

Managers often proceed with practice development on the assumption that existing client relationships are in all ways satisfactory, but this is not necessarily the case. Some relationships are more productive than others. Clients vary as to fees paid, services required, potential for expansion of services, timeliness in making remittances, and so forth. Their value should be monitored on these bases.

Monitoring

Monitoring is most readily handled through classification systems similar to those used with prospects. Only the criteria vary. The product should be a listing of clients by category. In the preferred category will be relationships in which:

1. The consultant is providing comprehensive public relations services
2. Services are mutually profitable
3. Ancillary factors such as client prestige and referral processes are productive
4. Significant growth potential exists

At the opposite end of the spectrum are relationships in which the reverse is true or collection problems may exist. Between the extremes are several other categories. More or less routine "bread and butter" accounts generally are classified below the prime clientele. Next in order come clients less attractive but perceived as having developmental potential. Finally come the "problem children."

Enhancement

Part of the developmental effort must be directed toward practice enhancement, which involves moving clients up the classification system ladder or off the client list. The former is preferable to the latter, but problem children are a practice liability. The "up or out" rule eventually must prevail.

IN SUMMARY

Suprasystems and subsystems in which organizations function are changing so rapidly that "status quo" is nonexistent. Organizations are progressing or retrogressing. They must progress merely to maintain relative stability. Practice development programs thus are essential to survival.

Complex environmental assessment programs are necessary in practice development. They must deal concurrently with multiple subsystems and suprasystems: those of the public relations practice, its clientele and prospective clients. From the latter environments come the events, trends, and issues that generate needs for services.

The complexities of environmental assessment, especially for counselors, may suggest external assistance, which is available from several trend-watching organizations. Practitioners also find it necessary to develop internal and individual systems to assure optimum results.

Assessment processes equip managers with information necessary to identify areas of practice potential. These must be examined with relative strengths and weaknesses in the practice and among competitors. The data together enable managers to establish development goals and necessary budgets.

Centers of influence are the most valuable and productive components of practice development programs, but they require continuing cultivation. Systematic prospecting is equally necessary. This is a three-part process involving identifying, classifying, and tracking prospects.

Prospect development also is necessary. It may involve one or more of several approaches, all designed to produce sales. Contacts can be made through social, philanthropic, or professional activities. Direct solicitation may be used. Networking techniques compound effectiveness, especially for organizational units.

Prospects should be categorized by potential to focus the practice development effort on those that show greatest promise. As prospects are identified and contacts developed, an efficient record-keeping system also becomes necessary.

A client classification system also should be developed. The practice development effort here is directed toward enhancing the productivity of existing relationships. Where these can not be brought to acceptable levels, resignation of accounts may be in order.

ADDITIONAL READING

Bachner, John P., and N. K. Khosia. *Marketing and Promotion for Design Professionals*. New York: Van Nostrand Reinhold, 1977.

Blake, Gary, and Robert W. Bly. *How to Promote Your Own Business*. New York: New American Library, 1983.

Coxe, Weld. *Marketing Architectural and Engineering Services*. New York: Van Nostrand Reinhold, 1971.

DeLozier, M. Wayne. *The Marketing Communications Process*. New York: Mc-Graw-Hill, 1976.

Fine, Seymour. *Marketing Ideas and Social Issues*. New York: Praeger, 1981.

Grunig, James E., and Todd Hunt. *Managing Public Relations*. New York: Holt, Rinehart and Winston, 1984.

Kotler, Philip. *Marketing for Non-Profit Organizations*. Englewood Cliffs, N.J.: Prentice-Hall, 1975.

Luther, William M. *The Marketing Plan: Hot to Prepare and Implement It*. New York: AMACOM, 1982.

Mauser, Ferdinand F. *Modern Marketing Management: An Integrated Approach*. New York: McGraw-Hill, 1961.

Nickels, William. *Marketing Communication and Promotion*. Englewood Cliffs, N.J.: Prentice-Hall, 1982.

Udell, Jon G., and Gene R. Laczniak. *Marketing in an Age of Change*. New York: John Wiley, 1981.

Wilson, Aubrey. *The Marketing of Professional Services*. Maidenhead, England: McGraw-Hill (UK), 1972.

10

The Sales System

Selling professional services consistently and successfully is a complex undertaking. It is based in the practice development program and requires substantial marketing effort. Other than in rare instances, neither is productive in the absence of on-going sales effort.

Exceptions may exist in organizational public relations. Where constituent relationships have been developed to optimum levels, additional work may come to the public relations unit unsolicited. Pragmatically, this seldom is the case. Additional work does indeed develop; it is stimulated, however, by senior managers' respect for practitioners' professional abilities. New assignments seldom are forthcoming where public relations personnel fail to develop strong working relationships and educate constituents to their capabilities.

To a lesser extent, counselor practices may grow on the strength of organizational size and reputation. Such development is more apparent than real. A Burson-Marsteller or a Hill & Knowlton (the world's largest counselor firms) may attract clients by virtue of size and qualifications. Knowledge of these and other premier organizations is pervasive in the business community. It did not, however, develop spontaneously. It was and is a product of continuing effort in two areas: practice development and superior service to clients.

Practice growth is a product of consistent effort for most managers. Consistency is more important than brilliance. Well-designed and dutifully followed, practice development, marketing, and sales produce results. More crudely put in one counselor's words, "The law of averages takes care of darn fools and sorry salesmen."

While systematic approaches put the law of averages on the salesperson's side, more is involved. Criteria often used by executives in selecting consultants are shown in Figure 10.1. Also shown are recommended procedures in selection of public relations agencies. From a practitioner's standpoint, they imply a set of commonly used standards that professionals are expected to meet.

THE SALES PROGRAM

Practice development programs are designed to create professional exposure for the consultant. Marketing identifies needs among clients and prospective clients and enables practitioners to develop saleable services. Sales programs add clients and expand services to existing clients. Most components are applicable in counselor and organizational settings but applications differ to some extent.

Primary Components

Sales processes are directed toward one objective: productive interviews with qualified prospects. The effort begins before the interview and continues beyond the close of the conversation. Months or years may elapse between initial contact and ultimate sale but the process remains unchanged. It consists of a series of steps:

1. A first contact, usually by mail
2. One or more follow-ups, almost invariably by telephone
3. The initial interview
4. Interview follow-up, consisting of one or more of the following:
   a. Further interviews
   b. Additional telephone contacts
   c. Submission of a formal proposal
   d. Development and delivery of a formal presentation
5. Closing the sale
6. After-the sale procedures

The steps constitute a process; they are interdependent. Results are a product of the process rather than any single step. No step is more or less important than any other. They are presented in chronological order to induce understanding rather than emphasize one or another.

Differences in Application

Prospect identification by counselors is more difficult than in organizational practice. Initial contacts are more readily made by organizational practitioners. Components of the sales process otherwise are uniformly applied.

FIGURE 10.1.
Choosing a Public Relations Consultant.

Choosing a Public Relations Consultant	Assigned to	Date/Time Assigned	Date/Time Completed
I. Meet or correspond, if necessary, with the managing news editors of these publications and electronic media; ask for the names of six public relations consultants who are considered to be outstanding in your area of concern: 1. *Public Relations Journal.* 2. *Advertising Age.* 3. American Management Association. 4. *Wall St. Journal.* 5. *New York Times.* 6. Local metropolitan dailies. 7. AP and UPI. 8. Local NBC, CBS, ABC, and PBS outlets. 9. Your industry's official publication.	_____	_____	_____
II. Be certain that each of these editors knows the field of concern to you: 1. Financial. 2. Labor. 3. Product. 4. Legislative. 5. Scientific/Technical. 6. Special fields peculiar to your company.	_____	_____	_____
III. Assure each editor that his or her response will be held in strict confidence.	_____	_____	_____
IV. Stress no concern for: 1. Proximity to your headquarters. 2. Budget size. 3. Size of consulting firm.	_____	_____	_____
V. With CEO, Executive Vice President, and Treasurer, determine need for: 1. Continuous service with annual retainer. 2. Spot task or "one shot" for a stated fixed fee. 3. Combination of both.	_____	_____	_____

continued

FIGURE 10.1. (continued)

Choosing a Public Relations Consultant	Assigned to	Date/Time Assigned	Date/Time Completed
VI. Determine budget by: 1. Estimating the time needed by an account executive to accomplish desired work. 2. Reviewing salaries offered to PR account executives in "help wanted" ads in *Wall St. Journal*, and striking average of top figures. 3. For full-time work by AE, multiply that figure by 4. This will give manpower cost. 4. Add 25 percent of the total for normal expenses, travel, entertainment, photography, etc. 5. If desired work will take only one-half of AE's time, multiply one-half the average salary by 4, but keep the expense figure the same as for a full-time level.	——	——	——
VII. Pick three PR counseling firms from among all the names suggested by choosing the three most common.	——	——	——
VIII. Invite each of the three firms to a pre-presentation visit. 1. Ask each to prepare a pitch, allowing a decent interval of time for preparation. 2. After outlining task, ask each to bring in a suggested budget, manpower needs, time needed, and costs. 3. Ask for a rough idea of the approach to the recommended problem solution.	——	——	——
IX. Include in your selection committee: 1. CEO. 2. Executive VP. 3. Operations VP. 4. PR Director.	——	——	——

(continued)

FIGURE 10.1. (continued)

	Choosing a Public Relations Consultant	Assigned to	Date/Time Assigned	Date/Time Completed
	5. Advertising manager.			
	6. Marketing VP.			
	7. Treasurer.			
X.	Following the pre-presentation meeting, ask each for personality reactions and attitudes.	____	____	____
XI.	Schedule the presentations for one each day, and a day apart. Allow not more than three hours for each presentation.	____	____	____
XII.	Consider the following:	____	____	____
	1. Qualifications of all those who will work on your account:			
	a. Account executives.			
	b. Account supervisor.			
	c. Implementers.			
	2. Estimated time needed to complete task.			
	3. Budget required.			
	4. Estimate of expenses.			
	5. Approach to problems.			
	6. Homework done (or its lack).			
	7. Track record of counsulting firm in allied or pertinent fields.			
	8. References.			
	9. Financial status of consulting firm.			
	10. Creativeness.			
	11. Grasp of your organization's financial, market position, and future.			
	12. Depth of knowledge of your company's products or services.			
	13. Aggressiveness.			
	14. Credibility.			
XIII.	Check out references and submit copies to selection committee.	____	____	____
XIV.	Allow two days for consideration and set up a meeting of the committee for a vote.	____	____	____

(continued)

FIGURE 10.1. (continued)

Choosing a Public Relations Consultant	Assigned to	Date/Time Assigned	Date/Time Completed

XV. After selection, notify those who were not chosen immediately, and set up a procedural meeting with your new PR consulting firm to establish:
  1. Ground rules for working.
  2. Relationship with internal PR staff member.
  3. Relationship to other executives.
  4. Frequency of visits.
  5. Reporting of responsibility.
  6. Payment schedule for retainer, fee, and expenses.
  7. Demands and requirements:
    a. Counseling only.
    b. Counseling and implementation.
    c. Availability of other external manpower when needed.
  8. Definition and description of tasks.
  9. Limitation of authority and responsibility, internally and externally.
  10. Confidentiality policy.
	———	———	———

XVI. Contractual factor:
  1. Length of contract.
  2. Termination terms.
  3. Re-negotiation.
  4. Renewal terms.
  5. Trial period:
    a. Long term.
    b. Short term.
	———	———	———

Source: From Nathaniel H. Sperber and Otto Lerbinger, *Manager's Public Relations Handbook*, © 1982, Addison-Wesley Publishing Company, Reading, Massachusetts. Reprinted with permission.

IDENTIFYING PROSPECTS

Few public relations professionals encounter difficulty in identifying commercial, industrial, and institutional sectors that may be impacted by environmental trends. Identifying specific prospects in these sectors is more difficult.

Several prospect sources are available to most practitioners. They range from daily newspapers to sales information services. Generally they can be categorized as daily newspapers, other newspapers, magazines, governmental publications, directories, commercial services, and other sources.

Daily Newspapers

All daily newspapers within the practice area should be scanned for prospects. They vary in number by locality. Scanning is time consuming but can be delegated to others. Considerable precision in definition is necessary in assigning the work. Support personnel should be instructed to clip or mark any information concerning: new or expanding organizations in the area; new products or services they are offering or preparing to offer; and changes in key personnel, especially chief executive officers.

Where publications include metropolitan dailies, scanners also should gather "trend" articles. These are analytical or "think pieces" regularly found in publications such as the New York *Times*. They often are valuable in environmental assessment.

Other Newspapers

Similar articles appear in nationally circulated newspapers such as *The Wall Street Journal* and the *Christian Science Monitor*. They also should be monitored for information concerning publicly held companies operating in the area.

Legal and business newspapers are of equal importance. They often publish lists of new corporate charters. Published names of incorporators may not be helpful—they frequently are attorneys but most law firms will forward correspondence. .

Business newspapers began appearing in significant numbers in the mid to late 1980s. They contain business information in greater detail than the dailies provide. Other newspapers worthy of preliminary examination include the *Journal of Commerce*, published in New York City, and newspaper-like periodicals published by the federal government listing requests for bids or proposals.

Magazines

Few magazines are of sufficient interest to be added to a prospecting list. In most states, however, there are business magazines managers should consider after examining sample copies. Most content is feature-oriented but occasional worthwhile news items are published. Scanning procedures in the environmental assessment process usually include magazines such as *Business Week* and *Industry Week*. These may be used in prospect scanning but seldom are productive.

Governmental Publications

Few publications of governmental origin are of interest to most practitioners. Managers interested in this area should ask governmental agencies to add their firms' names to bid or request for proposal lists.

The volume of material published by government makes their publications marginal prospect sources. This especially is so where counselors are averse to time-consuming bid/proposal practices and usually slow payment procedures.

The federal government has been prodded by congressional action to expedite vendor payments. States, counties, and municipalities remain notoriously slow. Where large contracts are involved, this can be troublesome for smaller firms.

Managers also should be wary of governmental tendencies to write ambiguous specifications and "buy price." This practice puts conscientious professionals at the mercy of "low-ballers." They tend to base proposals on inferior quality standards and raise contract prices through change orders.

Directories

Directories vary in value because of obsolescence; nevertheless, they can be assets in identifying prospects. Directories are most valuable where managers seek an overview of an industry group or geographic area. Most are organized geographically and list firms by Standard Industrial Code (SIC) number. Some name multiple officers and key personnel.

Most suffer from obsolescence. Directories usually are published annually, but data are several months old on publication dates. Many listings are out of date before new editions appear. Companies continue to exist but personnel will have changed.

Directory value also varies with practice geography. State business and industrial directories often are helpful. They usually are published by or for chambers of commerce or industrial development authorities.

City directories can be helpful but the percentage of obsolete information tends to be high. Privately published city directories are apt to be more current and accurate.

The directory category also includes membership directories, which are published annually by business and professional organizations. Listings are limited to members and are likely to be incomplete, except in the cases of bar or medical associations. Membership in these groups is a virtual necessity for practitioners.

Commercial Services

Multiple commercial information services also are available. They include construction industry activity reports and publications listing organizational expansion plans.

A relatively expensive but helpful service is available from Dun & Bradstreet, whose system generates credit reports on most businesses. They include relatively complete business descriptions as well as officers' names.

Dun & Bradstreet also sells mailing lists. They are available on 3 × 5 index cards, pressure-sensitive labels, and floppy discs for computer use. Buyers specify information needs geographically and by SIC number. Sales volumes, numbers of employees, and identities of key officers are provided.

Other

Other useful information sources range from specialized magazines, such as *Yachting*, to relatively complete directories such as that of the American Hospital Association (AHA). The AHA directory lists hospitals by location, by size, and by type of ownership. It also provides chief executive officers' names and lists of services offered.

With the help of a librarian at a local or, preferably, college or university library, public relations managers can obtain information on almost any industry from these sources.

INITIAL CONTACTS

Counselors who diligently pursue practice development and marketing strategies make significant numbers of initial prospect contacts. They often lead to sales opportunities: appointments with executives in their offices to discuss public relations services. They usually are too few to support a sales program.

Organized efforts are designed to generate predetermined numbers of new contacts on weekly or monthly bases. They consistently yield interviews that produce sales in predictable numbers. One small counseling firm that tracked results over a period of years found that five contacts with qualified prospects ultimately produce three interviews and 1.3 sales.

In organizational practices, prospects usually are known to consultants and initial steps in the sale process are handled informally.

Letter Contacts

Individually typed and signed form letters have been successful avenues to interviews for many counselors. Letters vary primarily as to ambiguity. Some contend they should serve as "bait" to pique the interest of recipients. Others become quite specific. A stronger case can be made for the former approach. Initial interviews clarify prospect and practitioner perceptions of organizational need. Consultants attempt to sell services that meet clients needs. They ultimately sell services prospective clients want to buy.

Sales problems are compounded where prospects are unfamiliar with public relations services. Letters oriented to specific services may encourage refusal of interviews on the assumption that no others are available.

Letter Content

Letter content nevertheless may be specific or general. Where specific, letters usually cite identified needs prevalent in recipients' industries. Crisis planning doubtless was the subject of many such letters in the wake of the Bhopal and Three-Mile Island chemical and nuclear accidents.

In the alternative, content may be quite general, merely suggesting that writers have a new approach to a generic business problem. Alternatively, they may offer information of interest to the prospect.

Follow-up Options

As in content, a number of follow-up options exist for letter writers. Replies can be awaited but seldom are forthcoming. Postage prepaid reply cards may produce a better response. Follow-up telephone calls are preferable.

Need for public relations services often is neglected by organizational executives. They are no different than most in responding first to each day's pressing problems. They seldom include latent or contingent difficulties public relations practitioners seek to avoid.

Telephone Contacts

Telephone contacts are appropriate in two situations: as follow-ups to letters or as initial approaches to individuals with whom practitioners are acquainted. "Cold" telephone calls tend to trigger negative emotional responses no matter how great the prospect's needs and how potentially productive the service.

Sales letters—well-written, accurately typed, and delivered on attractive letterheads—introduce the organization and the writer. They seldom produce direct responses but provide bases for telephone follow-up. Experimentation indicates that ambiguous letters encourage respondents to accept calls.

Focusing the Call

Callers must direct conversations toward a single objective: obtaining an interview. This requires delicate conversational balance. Prospect questions should be answered—denying information can be fatal. Responses should be general in nature, however, and appointment requests should be restated if necessary.

Example: "We offer a broad range of services to meet any communication need. My limited knowledge of your organization makes it difficult for me to be more specific. It will take only a few moments of your time to determine which—if any—of our services might be profitable for you. Would this week or next be more convenient for a meeting?"

Setting the Hook

The first call may not produce an interview. The minimum acceptable outcome is prospect agreement to accept a second call. When prospect schedules are crowded, caller might respond: "When might it be convenient for me to call again. I believe we might be of assistance and would appreciate an opportunity to meet you in any event."

Outright rejection is rare; postponement is common; delay is not necessarily bad. Repeated delay tends to make prospects feel obligated ultimately to grant interviews: "I'll make a note to contact you again in X weeks/months and will look forward to meeting you at that time."

Record-keeping

Notes on letter copies and calendars usually are sufficient to prompt follow-up calls. Where practice development/marketing/sales systems are complex, more detailed records are advisable.

The Appointment

Three elements are significant in arranging appointments: time, place, and participants. Other than where prospects prefer otherwise, interviews are best conducted on Tuesdays, Wednesdays, or Thursdays between 10 a.m. and 4 p.m. Interruptions and distractions are more frequent at other times.

Interviews are best scheduled in prospects' offices. Lunches should be avoided, since many executives work through lunch hours and value the time involved. Moreover, luncheons lack formality; they may encourage idle discussion when consultants are seeking to establish business relationships.

Numbers of interview participants vary. Organizations preferably should be equally represented. Consultants who prefer to call in pairs should indicate this will be the case. Prospective clients usually are similarly courteous, asking whether consultants object if others are present. The question invites a response indicating the consultant will not be alone.

INTERVIEW PREPARATIONS

Sales success is a function of the sellers' knowledge of prospect organizations and environments. This principle applies to organizational practitioners as well as counselors. Interview preparations can be time-consuming. Many familiarize themselves with prospect endeavors before making initial contacts. Research is essential prior to interviews where it has not been undertaken earlier. Productive sales efforts are based on knowledge. Interviews are no different. Success is governed by knowledge of organizations, operations, and decision makers.

The Research Process

More information concerning prospects is available than many believe. Detailed data are contained in required Securities and Exchange Commission (SEC) filings where organizations are publicly owned. Alternative sources also exist. Information sources vary with organizations. Practitioner needs govern the extent to which they should be explored. Knowledge of information availability nevertheless is helpful.

Business Data

Considerable information often is available from regulatory bodies under the Freedom of Information Act. The SEC is one of many. Similar information is available where organizations are regulated in any way.

Complete operating information on hospitals, for example, can be obtained through Medicare program administrators. Data on expansion plans are available through agencies that issue certificates of need. They are prerequisite to major construction projects and equipment acquisition.

State and federal agencies regulate banking, public utilities, transportation, broadcasting, and other endeavors. All are required to provide copies of organizational filings. Agencies such as the Occupational Safety and Health Administration and the National Transportation Safety Board can be helpful. So can the Food and Drug Administration, the Department of Agriculture, and others. The list could continue at length. Practitioners first must ascertain the nature of the business or businesses in which prospects are engaged. Where organizations under study are subsidiaries of others, data on parents may be illuminating.

Executive Data

Dun & Bradstreet reports are logical points of departure for information on organizational decision makers. Reports contain names and titles of key executives; *Who's Who* directories provide biographical information. Financial data often can be obtained through consultant banking connections.

Supplemental Information

Additional information on individuals and organizations can be gleaned from multiple sources. Newspaper files may be most helpful. They contain information published about organizations and their personnel. Access to this information once usually was restricted to newspaper personnel. Microcomputers and subscriptions to information utilities today provide access for others. Practitioners are using these resources in increasing numbers.

In organizational practice, comparable information can be obtained from colleagues or direct from prospects. Most individuals require little encouragement to talk about themselves, their careers, and their problems.

From Data to Interests

The information-gathering process produces insights into organizations and individuals. It enables practitioners to identify problems and needs. The next step is extrapolation from data to interests and needs. The process is a matter of logical thinking best illustrated through a series of questions.

The Organization

What businesses is the organization in? Over how broad a geographic area? What problems have been prevalent in the area in recent months or years? To what extent have they been resolved? What trends identified through environmental assessment processes threaten problems for the industry? For the individual firm? Which are amenable to resolution through public relations programming?

The Individual

What are decision makers' backgrounds—personal, educational, business, avocational? What do histories of former employers suggest as to experience? Predispositions? What is the individual's reputation in the community? Among peers? Among subordinates?

Responses, while seemingly minor in nature, enable practitioners to establish rapport with prospects, a condition essential to productive interviews. Practitioners should be especially alert to information indicative of shared avocational interests. Durable relationships often have been based on mutual interests in golf, flying, or other pursuits. The principle applies for both counselors and organizational practitioners. Interview and record-keeping techniques also apply uniformly.

THE INTERVIEW

The Preliminaries

The first—and briefest—portion of a successful interview is devoted to establishing rapport. This can be accomplished through mutual business or individual interests. The latter in no circumstances should be feigned—deception inevitably returns to haunt deceivers. Knowledge of the individual's business or industry will suffice. It can be used to pose questions about issues understood by both parties. Most executives enjoy talking about their businesses; they should be encouraged to do so.

At an appropriate point, conversation should be turned to the business at hand. Before discussing prospect needs, brief introductory statements describing consultant organizations and services are appropriate. Prospects should not be assumed to have read and remembered earlier correspondence.

Descriptions should include references to clients served in the prospect's industry or related industries. Services to organizations with which prospective clients may be involved also should be mentioned. These may be business, professional, civic, or philanthropic groups.

The introductory phase of the conversation can be closed with one of two statements. One invites prospect comment on services mentioned. The other suggests applying a service to meet a problem indigenous to the prospect's industry. From a sales perspective, the interview begins at this point.

The Sales Interview

Prospect needs should be the focal point of the interview. Consultant services and prospect needs are not identical. Services are a means to an end. Clients buy benefits services create.

These circumstances surround every purchasing decision. The homebuilder may be selling houses. Buyers are acquiring shelter, comfort, security, and status. Auto dealers are selling cars. Buyers seek transportation, convenience, and, again, status. Organizations and executives are no different. Consultants sell services. Executives buy more customers, community stature, contented employees, and similar outcomes or benefits.

Interviews must induce prospects to identify needs amenable to satisfaction through consultant services. Unsatisfied needs—real or perceived—are primary purchase motivators. They must be defined and understood by both parties if consultant-client relationships are to develop.

Interview Techniques

Understanding industries, organizations, and prospects arm consultants to apply an often-used questioning technique. Called "the funnel approach," it proceeds from the general to the specific.

General questions should be open ended in nature. They should not be amenable to "yes" or "no" responses. They should induce executives to talk. This objective is achieved where consultants control any tendency to speak at length.

At prospects identify needs and concerns, doors open to consultant responses. They may include ideas, suggestions, and helpful information that need not relate to public relations services. The process establishes consultant interest in prospect problems.

As conversations "wind down" or drift into trivialities, consultants should move to questions about identified needs. Is the absentee problem significant? Would better employee understanding help correct the situation? Has the company considered an employee publication? A suggestion system? An incentive program? Which is of greatest potential?

The discussion has shifted not once but twice. The first was from general questions requiring lengthy responses to specific inquiries encouraging "yes" or "no" answers. The second was from a series of questions to a point of decision: "Which of the solutions do you prefer?" This was tantamount to "asking for the order." Potential for negative response was limited by the manner in which questions were posed.

Avoiding Pitfalls

Consultants at this point are tempted to extol the virtues of their organizations, personnel, knowledge, skills, and techniques. This temptation must be resisted for further obstacles are in sight. Consultants now must compete with managers for organizational resources. Each seeks more for his or her unit or pet project; all cannot win. The consultant's approach to closing the sale probably will determine the outcome.

A "bottom line" approach is indicated. Services offered must be positioned as contributors to organizational success. They should be presented as making the enterprise more competitive, more profitable, or both. Consultants must emphasize benefits rather than services.

Competition and Ethics

Sales efforts occasionally will cross the paths of competing consultants. These circumstances need not be fatal to the effort, but two conditions must be met to avoid potential problems.

When told prospects retain public relations counsel, consultants immediately must ask the extent of the assignment. Any reference to services involved thereafter must be avoided. Consultants are free under most ethical codes to tell prospective clients they may assign work to any number of vendors. Consultants than should guide the discussion to areas of need *not* addressed under previously existing assignments.

Closing the Interview

Interviews are points of beginning. Other than where crises compel immediate decisions, they seldom end in closed sales. In 20 years of counselor practice, the author has only once come away from an initial sales call with a new client. Few interviews lead to sales in less than 30 to 45 days. Some require a year or more to close.

Management Needs

Consultants should be sensitive to executive needs. Most want written agreements in contract or letter form. They more frequently require time to sell projects or concepts to colleagues. This may produce a request for a written proposal or formal presentation.

The latter development occurs even where executives have the power to make and impose decisions. Most avoid such tactics. Consensual approaches benefit consultants and executives. Early meetings may involve only members of client administrative staffs. Implementing programs requires support from others. Their prior commitments ultimately serve consultants well.

Early contact with these individuals is advisable. Consultants preferably should meet with them before presenting proposals. Where access is limited, as much information as possible should be obtained concerning parties to the decision-making process. The proposal or presentation then can be designed to minimize potential conflict. Under any conditions, consultants should seek to close initial meetings with commitments from prospects to further discussion.

Consultant Needs

These commitments are the minimum results sought in initial interviews. Conversations also may produce requests for proposals or presentations. Least encouraging is the response, "Let me think about it."

In the latter case, a simple tactic can be helpful: "When would you like me to check back with you?" Note the phraseology: not "would you..." but "when would you...." The question presupposes an affirmative response. Prospects in most cases will respond accordingly.

Should they hesitate, another device can bring the desired result: "Let me give you a call in 60 to 90 days." Consultants should retain the initiative throughout the selling process by assuming responsibility for follow-up.

Prospects are not prone to punctuality in follow-up. Conversations and proposals often are forgotten amidst day-to-day problems. Managers may procrastinate until problems become crises. Seldom are they swayed by suggestions that problems are less expensively solved before reaching crisis proportions.

When prospects request proposals, another strategy is appropriate: "Let me discuss your situation at length with our staff before responding in writing. We'll have a proposal on your desk in about _____days." The specified time span should be at least double consultants' estimates of time required. Prospects at best will be impressed by earlier delivery. At worst, the consultant will have ample time to complete the work.

RECORD-KEEPING

Some consultants experience no difficulty in taking notes during interviews. They handle the process unobtrusively and without disturbing the flow of information and interchange of ideas. Others find the process distracting and take no notes.

In the latter circumstances, information pertinent to future contacts should be recorded *immediately* after the meeting. Thank-you letters also should be written to prospects for the time devoted to the interview. They should confirm any agreement as to follow-up.

Sales interviews end only when these tasks and one other have been accomplished: follow-up dates must be noted to insure further action at appropriate times. Prospects should not be abandoned even where interview outcomes preclude short-term follow-up. Notes should be made to remind consultants to make second approaches in 6 to 18 months.

Chicago-based counselors Ruder Finn & Rotman manage the process through periodic sales summaries (see Figure 10.2). The summaries deal with the total sales process. Components include new accounts and internal growth (expansion of services to existing accounts). Organizations to which proposals have been made are listed, as are those for which proposals are being prepared. Initial meetings, sales letters, and solicitation mailings are listed as well.

The range of indicated follow-up times is considerable. Specific dates should be set based on estimates of effective timing. Change in organizations is inevitable. Needs change with environments. Personnel change in any event. Call-back time factors are best estimated in context with environmental trends. Prospects never should be abandoned in the face of a first refusal where environmental assessment indicates that potential organizational problems may develop.

IN SUMMARY

Other than where size and reputation attract a continuing flow of new clients, public relations organizations must rely upon practice development,

FIGURE 10.2.
Ruder Finn & Rotman Sales Summary.

 memo

to: MORRY ROTMAN

from: RICHARD ROTMAN

subject: CHICAGO OFFICE SALES SUMMARY

date: FEBRUARY 13, 1986

cc: Hal Bergen
    Kathy Bloomgarden/NY
    Nick Biro
    Mike Donnell
    David Finn/NY
    Peter Finn/NY
    Carl Oldberg
    Sharon Peters
    Paula Waters
    Dave Witkov
    Dukes Wooters/NY

NEW ACCOUNTS

Cort Furniture/Hands Across America	- Kaye/Bergen
Gastro-Intestinal Research Foundation	- Rotman/Oldberg/Waters
New Zealand Consulate/Te Maori Exhibit	- Rotman
Paslode	- Healy
Rehabilitation Institute	- MBR/Oldberg/Waters
American Rehabilitation Network, Inc.	- Oldberg/Waters
Quaker Oats/Dog Food	- Rotman/Gray
Wornick	- Bergen

INTERNAL GROWTH

Abbott/Aids	- Oldberg/Waters	Barton/Corona Extra Beer	- Rotman/McClintock
Abbott/Core	- Oldberg/Waters	Barton/Glenfarclas Scotch	- Rotman/McClintock
Abbott/Vision Test	- Oldberg/Waters	Dremel/Video	- Gray

PROGRAM DECISIONS PENDING

Bethesda Hospital	- Joseph	Sam Spiro & Associates	- Peters/Palmer
Dow Chemical	- Kaye/Bergen	U.S. Ameribancs	- Healy/Oldberg/Waters
National Fluid Power	- Bergen	Arthur Young/Executive Search	
			- Reiners/Donnell

PROPOSALS IN WORKS

Abbott/Blood Donation Program	- Oldberg/Waters
Citicorp Services, Inc.	- Healy/Oldberg/Waters
Ralston Purina/Wonder Bread	- Rotman/Gray

FIGURE 10.2. (continued)

CHICAGO OFFICE SALES SUMMARY -- Page Two

CAPABILITIES/INITIAL MEETINGS

Company	RF&R Contact	Status
Acco	Bergen	Meeting to discuss adding marketing program to be set for late Feb.
American Society of Real Estate Counselors	Bergen/Peters	Initial presentation made Oct. 3 Final made Nov. 8. Awaiting word.
Bromenn Healthcare Corp.	Healy/Waters	Capabilities to be presented in Feb.
Chicago Theatre Project	Rotman	Capabilities letter sent Feb. 3.
Dai-Ichi Kangyo Bank	Rotman	Recommendations presented Feb. 10.
Farmhouse Foods	Bergen/Peters	Initial meeting held July 29. Next meeting with CEO set for Feb. 17.
First National Bank	Rotman/Waters	Meeting held Nov. 14. Capabilities letter sent Nov. 22. Not chosen.
Gundlach Products	Bergen	Meeting set for Feb. 17.
Kemper Group	Nachman	Meeting set for Feb. 17; result of mlng.
Madison Gas & Electric	Bergen/Peters	Presenting employee communications and market services programs.
Meridien Computer Leasing	Biro/Bergen	Made capabilities, audit presentation. Awaiting word.
Ralston Purina/Wonder Bread	Rotman/Gray	Capabilities presentation Feb. 7.
Wallace Computer Services	Nachman	Meeting to be set re marketing program.

SALES LETTERS

American Oil Chemists Society	Bergen/Peters
American Society of Furniture Designers	Kaye/Bergen
Belmont Computer Company	Nachman
Beneficial Finance	Bergen
Barr Company	Rotman
Corrs Natural Beverages	Bergen
Jack-in-the-Box	Gray
Lotte, USA	Rotman
Gerber Products	Bergen
Horticultural Gardens	Bergen/Kaye
Institute of Food Technologists	Bergen
International Minerals & Chemicals	Bergen
Lightner Associates, Inc.	Bergen
Market Facts	Bergen
McDonalds	Rotman/Gray
Nightingale-Conant	Rotman

FIGURE 10.2. (continued)

```
CHICAGO OFFICE SALES SUMMARY -- Page Three


SALES LETTERS (cont.)

    Pratt & Whitney                             Bergen
    2-V Industries                              Rotman
    The Washingtonian                           MBR
    Wilson Sporting Goods                       Donnell
    Virtual Network                             Nachman
    VMS Realty                                  Nachman


MAILINGS

    Furniture Industry                          Biro
    Annual report survey proposal letter        Biro/Nachman
      to 200 corporate executives
    82 to Associations                          Bergen
    69 to Banking Institutions                  Bergen
    75 to Forbes 500 Companies                  Bergen
    53 to Privately-held firms and              Bergen
      Wisconsin corporations
    48 to U.S. State Funeral Directors          Healy/Oldberg
      Associations
```

marketing, and sales efforts for growth. Consistency is the key to successful selling. It enables consultants to reap the benefits of time and effort invested in practice development and marketing.

The sales effort is an organized process. Its primary components are initial and follow-up contacts, interviews, closings, and after-the-sale procedures. These elements are interdependent. Sales are a product of the process rather than any single item.

The beginning point is prospect identification. This component involves research. Data are obtained through multiple sources. They include newspapers, governmental publications, directories, and commercial services. The data provide insights into commercial, industrial, and institutional areas, into individual organizations within those areas, and into the nature of their decision makers.

Initial contacts are made by mail, telephone, or both. Letters are pref-

Reprinted by permission.

erable to telephone calls. They may be ambiguous or specific as practitioners prefer, provided they achieve their primary objective: a face-to-face interview.

Interview success is a product of practitioner knowledge of organizations and their decision makers. Detailed information is available from multiple sources. These include published information on publicly held companies and data from regulatory agencies. Information on decision makers can be obtained from one or more directories as well as financial reporting services.

Information concerning decision makers' interests is the basis for interview preliminaries. They are an exercise in establishing rapport. The body of the interview is dedicated to obtaining information concerning organization and individual.

Information obtained enables practitioners to identify unsatisfied needs—the foundations of successful sales efforts. Sales presentations must focus on benefits rather than public relations programs. Individuals and organizations seek gratification of their needs. The methods or vehicles through which this is accomplished from their standpoints are secondary.

Interviews at minimum should result in agreements for follow-up contacts. They may take the form of further meetings, subsequent telephone contacts, or formal proposals or presentations. After interviews, detailed records of content should be made for future reference. Follow-up procedures, whether they require preparation of proposals or telephone calls months after initial interviews, must be strictly observed.

ADDITIONAL READING

Bachner, John P., and N. K. Khosia. *Marketing and Promotion for Design Professionals*. New York: Van Nostrand Reinhold, 1977.

Blake, Gary, and Robert W. Bly. *How to Promote Your Own Business*. New York: New American Library, 1983.

Coxe, Weld. *Marketing Architectural and Engineering Services*. New York: Van Nostrand Reinhold, 1971.

DeLozier, M. Wayne. *The Marketing Communications Process*. New York: McGraw-Hill, 1976.

Greiner, Larry E., and Robert O. Metzger. *Consulting to Management: Insights to Building and Managing a Successful Practice*. Englewood Cliffs, N.J.: Prentice-Hall, 1983.

Mauser, Ferdinand F. *Modern Marketing Management: An Integrated Approach*. New York: McGraw-Hill, 1961.

Meyer, John W., and W. Richard Scott. *Organizational Environments: Ritual and Rationality*. Beverly Hills, Calif: Sage, 1983.

11

Proposals, Presentations, and Agreements

Sales presentations rarely lead immediately to new business for public relations units, counselor or organizational. Consultants often are asked to put ideas in writing. Formal presentations occasionally are requested.

When prospects agree to become clients, relationships often are reduced to writing in one of several forms. Letters of agreement are the least formal of several documents used. Standardized contracts are used in many situations. Individually written contracts are used in others. Occasionally, and most often where government agencies are involved, more complex contracts are necessary.

CONTRACTUAL CONCERNS

Proposals, presentations, and agreements are as important in organizational as counselor practice. They may be less formal but are increasingly common, especially in large organizations.

As agreements are concluded, successful consultants initiate another process: an organized effort to establish functional interorganizational relationships. The process involves 60 to 90 days and includes developing a strong communications network.

Legalities

Contracts exist legally in business relationships whether or not they are reduced to writing. Some public relations professionals have an aversion to formal contracts. Their attitudes stem from the partnership nature of consultant-client relationships. They are based on mutual trust, confidence, and understanding. Significant deterioration erodes practitioner ability to perform.

Many professionals terminate relationships under these conditions even where clients are bound by contract. "Life is too short for this sort of thing," says one of them. "If the chemistry is wrong, I'm not interested in continuing. I do what is necessary to see client interests are protected in the transition, but the relationship must be terminated."

Contractual Boundaries

While many have applied this philosophy for years without difficulty, potential problems remain. They develop from written or implied contracts and associated documents including proposals and presentations. They may be legally binding where no formal agreement specifies the parties' obligations.

PROPOSALS

Components

Proposal format and content can take many forms. They range from single-page letters to elaborate bound documents. In any form, proposals should include at least eight components: (1) background information, (2) description of the problem, (3) methods to be used, (4) scope of the project, (5) expected results, (6) resources to be applied, (7) cost factors, and (8) consultant background. Each component can be expressed concisely or in detail. Extent of detail should be governed by circumstances. Special care is necessary where proposals later may be legally binding. Most importantly, as underscored by Richard A. Connor, Jr. and Jeffrey P. Davidson, the proposal must be client- rather than consultant-oriented.

Content Determinants

Proposals range from concise summaries of agreements reached in conversation to sales documents. The latter condition applies where decision makers are required or feel it necessary to obtain the concurrence of others. Practitioners may or may not be party to subsequent discussions. Proposals must present the practitioner's case in its entirety where direct contact with other parties is impossible or impractical.

Problems Compounded

Before preparing proposals, consultants must consider carefully the individuals by whom they will be read. Several factors deserve special attention. They include the positions, backgrounds, implied interests, and potential reactions of those involved. These factors together govern development of proposal content, style, and format.

Content

Consultant's work in most cases produces benefits for multiple organizational components. Administrators are relieved of burdens that otherwise would accrue. Department managers in communication disciplines gain professional advice and counsel. Directors' economic interests are better served.

Benefits should be addressed in preparing proposals. They should deal with results clients seek rather than techniques through which they will be achieved. Anticipated outcomes should be related to interests of those involved. Employee relations proposal content, for example, should indicate the benefits of anticipated reductions in turnover rates. They accrue in the form of time as well as dollars. Work loads are reduced in personnel departments and among those handling orientation and training. Managers and supervisors gain through improved efficiency levels.

Proposals also should respond to any recipient concerns. Organizational practitioners, for example, might feel threatened by counselors' presence and concerned over the long-term security. Proposals then should specify assistance counselors will render to internal units. They also should describe how any responsibility temporarily assigned to consultants will be restored to departments when assignments are complete.

Consultant access to organizational personnel for diagnostic purposes varies from one situation to another. Prospective clients usually provide considerable information where proposals or presentations are invited. They also may permit consultants to meet preliminarily with staff members. Where proposals originate with consultants, access should be requested.

Style

Several writing styles can be used in proposals. The style selected should be determined by readers' needs. Where backgrounds are diverse, this objective is not easily achieved.

Senior managers and directors may be assumed to be relatively well-educated. Multisyllable words will not trouble them. Junior managers may experience difficulties, however, and verbiage should be adjusted accordingly.

Those not involved in initial discussions may require information presented earlier to senior managers. Their interests may suggest a need for variation in detail. Senior managers and directors focus primarily on financial matters. Others are concerned with departmental impacts.

Format

Diverse needs tend to produce more verbiage than prospective readers can manage. This problem can best be solved by producing a document in sentence outline form with a detailed table of contents. This format enhances access to specific components for each reader.

PREPARING CONTENTS

Variables

Format and length are major variables in preparing proposals. Balance is the consultant's primary challenge. Each component must contain all information readers require within reasonable length limitations. Readers' needs should be paramount at all times. Burying vital information in torrents of unnecessary prose defeats consultant objectives as readily as failure to provide adequate detail.

Background Information

Two varieties of background information usually are presented. The first relates to the problem at hand; the second to the proposing organization. The former is mandatory in the introductory section of the proposal; the latter can be deferred to the section dealing with consultant background.

Brevity Essential

Organizational information preferably is placed toward the end of the proposal. This technique enables writers to be brief in developing early proposal components and encourages readers to continue.

Background information should be presented in three parts. First should be a brief description of needs the proposal addresses. Writers then should specify problem origins. Finally, long-term implications should be identified.

Pertinent Data

Information about problem origins should be readily extracted from environmental assessment data. A brief "worst case" depiction of difficulties that may arise if the problem is not solved then may be added.

Problem Statement

Problem statements usually are presented in three parts. They include a brief history of the need or problem, a summary of events or occurrences that led to existing conditions, and objectives of the public relations problem.

History. Historical description should begin with a summary of environmental assessment data. Repetition should be avoided. The bulk of the statement should deal with impact of identified trends on the organization.

Descriptions of diagnostic processes applied by consultants also are appropriate. Similar situations in which consultants have been involved also may be described.

Events. Events or occurrences indicative of the impact of external trends on the organization should be summarized. Brevity is appropriate. Readers usually can be assumed to be knowledgeable; where this is not the case, however, necessary detail should be included.

Objectives. Problem statements should conclude with lists of objectives to be achieved. These must be expressed from a management rather than a public relations perspective.

If the problem involves employee morale as evidenced in excessive absenteeism and tardiness, objectives should be expressed in economic terms. Cost-sensitive managers abhor absenteeism and tardiness. Their attention, understanding, and support are more readily gained where programs relate to organizational economic objectives.

Objectives ideally are presented in tabular form. "Our objectives in undertaking this assignment are": Objectives then are specified in numerical order.

Methods and Techniques

In listing methods and techniques proposed in resolving the problems, consultants seek to: present a rationale for the proposed activities, and gain reader comprehension and agreement as to proposed methods.

Importance

The importance of this proposal section cannot be understated. The document is designed to induce acceptance. Approval is unlikely if readers fail to understand and support methods proposed. They must be described in detail and related to resolving organizational difficulties and improved economic results. Counselor Patrick Jackson's "Eight Ways Public Relations Contributes to the Bottom Line," reprinted as Figure 11.1 from *pr reporter*, constitutes an ideal starting point.

Description

Rather than dealing first with the problem and then with solution and benefits, the proposal should deal first with desired results, then with changes necessary to achieve them, and finally with methods through which change will be achieved.

In the absenteeism and tardiness example mentioned earlier, writers first would specify potential savings if existing patterns are modified. These should be reduced to dollars and cents by applying percentage ranges to historical data. Writers then would identify morale levels prerequisite to change. Finally, they would list techniques to be applied.

FIGURE 11.1
"Eight Ways Public Relations Contributes to the Bottom Line"

Process	Principal Activity	Outcome
1. Awareness & Information	Publicity, promotion, audience targeting	Pave the way for sales, fundraising, stock offerings, et al.
2. Organizational Motivation	Internal relations & communications	Build morale, teamwork, productivity, corporate culture; work toward One Clear Voice
3. Issue Anticipation	Research; liaison with all publics	Early warning of issues, social-political change, constituency unrest
4. Opportunity Identification	Interaction with internal/ external audiences	Discover new markets, products, methods, allies, positive issues
5. Crisis Management	Respond to or blanket issues, disasters, attacks; coalition-building	Protect position, retain allies & constituents, keep normal operations going despite battles
6. Overcoming Executive Isolation	Counseling senior managers about what's really happening; research	Realistic, competitive, enlightened decisions
7. Change Agentry	Organizational development, Quality of Work Life, corporate culture, similar techniques; research	Ease resistance to change, promote smooth transition, reassure affected constituencies
8. Social Responsibility	Social accountancy, research, mount public interest projects & tie-ins	Create reputation, enhance economic success through "double bottom line"

Source: By Patrick Jackson from *pr reporter*, January 7, 1985. Reprinted with permission.

Project Scope

Defining project scope requires substantial detail. This especially is so where responsibilities are divided among counselors, organizational public relations units, and, perhaps, other organizational components.

Specifying Responsibility

Descriptions must delineate responsibility and define interrelationships. Prerequisites to completing program components should be specified to avoid responsibility for delays caused by others. A calendar or program evaluation and review technique (PERT) chart may be included to clarify time factors. Such charts can reflect variation in responsibility.

Time Factors

Every proposal should provide projected sequences of events. Projected starting and completion dates should be included. They can be expressed in numbers of days or in fixed dates.

Two desirable results are obtained in specifying days required for task completion. First, risk of client misunderstanding is eliminated. This can occur where clients delay authorizing work but rely on originally specified dates. Second, listing numbers of days encourages early decisions.

Expected Results

Caution is necessary in developing "expected results" sections. They traditionally are brief. They itemize outcomes clients can expect when projects are complete, thus eliminating potential misconceptions. They must be carefully prepared because intervening factors beyond consultant control can distort or delay outcomes. Assumptions on which outcomes are contingent therefore must be specified.

Potential Distortants

Distortion potential occurs in two areas: external and internal environments. External events are beyond client and consultant control. Resultant delays usually produce no misunderstandings.

Internal environments are another matter. Managerial and supervisory failure to support employee relations programs, for example, can be disastrous. Programs can become ineffective or counterproductive no matter how well conceived and executed.

Preventive Steps

Consultants must guard against such problems and blame that may be attached. *All* contingent sources of difficulty should be specified. Every outcome beyond consultant ability to control should be identified.

If correction of absenteeism/tardiness problems depends in part on timely personnel department delivery of new policies, this should be specified. Where retraining managers and supervisors is essential, this must be cited as a precondition to success.

In the absence of such caveats, decision makers may assume consultants are accepting total responsibility for outcomes. This can lead to client dissatisfaction and loss of future assignments.

Consultant Resources

Resources that consultants anticipate applying should be described in detail. Several benefits accrue: Detail supports what otherwise might appear unnecessarily high fees; it also identifies personnel and their responsibilities.

Describing Resources

Since resources largely are human in form, descriptions consist primarily of lists of personnel. They should be identified by name, title, and responsibility. If organizational background information is to be provided in this section, an additional sentence or two concerning each individual is appropriate.

Defining Duties

Titles are not necessarily reflective of duties; definitions are necessary. Project directors responsible for work must be identified. Managers who have day-to-day responsibility also must be named. Those who occasionally may be assigned in support roles also may be listed.

Some specifics are necessary in addition to names, titles, and general responsibilities. The proposal should specify which team members will be responsible for major programmatic components. Those who will have overall control and handle day-to-day liaison also should be named.

Costs

While brevity is the essence of other proposal components, cost data should be provided in as exhaustive detail as practical. Practicality is limited by types of compensation arrangements, which may include fixed fees, retainer plus hourly rates, and other arrangements. Out-of-pocket costs are additional in most cases with or without markup.

Detail

Where hourly rates are involved, estimates should be provided as to rates and numbers of hours. These should be given for each major task and the project as a whole.

Out-of-pocket expense estimates should be handled in the same way. They should be itemized by task and identified as to origin. Data provided should be identified as estimated or "not to exceed" figures to avoid misunderstandings. Consultants benefit by being overly liberal rather than unduly conservative where estimates are used. Clients tend to be unhappy with "overruns" and delighted by "savings" regardless of estimates.

Summaries

Summary cost data should be included for each task. Where projects are broken down into phases or tasks, costs should be specified accordingly. The summary also should specify billing methods and expectations as to payment. Early-payment discounts or late-payment penalties should be noted.

DELIVERY METHODS

Proposals can be presented in any of several ways: They can be delivered by hand or by mail; they can be presented in meetings; they can be handled as verbal presentations; and they can be distributed in written form after formal presentations.

No data exist as to which approach may be most productive. Prospective clients appear to prefer whichever method will be least demanding of their time. Most are willing to express preferences, and consultants should request guidance.

Personal Delivery

The ultimate in speed and service can be accomplished by personal delivery. Such efforts at best produce little benefit. At worst, they can be counterproductive.

Without benefit of appointment, practitioners delivering proposals are unlikely to have opportunities to hand them to prospects. Where appointments are made, practitioners' judgment may come into question. Why do they have time to spend on such mundane matters?

Attempts to restate proposal content verbally are apt to produce negative results. This especially is so where practitioners try to "talk prospects through the proposal" page by page. Prospects presumably are able to read and may resent lengthy verbal restatements.

Where short-term follow-up is necessary, cover letters can close along these lines: "I'll call for an appointment in a week to ten days to answer any questions that may arise."

Mail and Messenger

Impersonal delivery usually is adequate to consultants' needs. The U.S. Postal Service suffices where time is not a factor. Delivery services, however, offer more than speed.

Many use Federal Express or similar services to deliver news releases.

Why? "It gets the attention of the recipient," says counselor Andrew Edson. "If it comes by FedEx or Emery, it appears important. It's likely to be opened immediately and read more thoroughly. The added attention is worth the expense."

Presentations

Practitioners sometimes are asked to present recommendations to management staffs or organizational directors. The presentations vary in formality and content. They should be well-rehearsed, says consultant Jack Matthews, and should be designed to present fresh ideas and stimulate dialogue with those present.

Less formality usually is appropriate where management staffs are involved. Consultants presumably became acquainted with those present during fact-finding processes. The presentation should summarize findings and recommendations contained in the proposal. Ample time should be allowed for questions and answers. The primary objective is to eliminate potential objections.

Other factors are of primary concern when consultants are asked to present recommendations to boards of directors. Executive motives are most important. Is he or she merely keeping his board informed? Is the final decision theirs? Is the executive seeking to share responsibility?

Consultants should consider these "selling" occasions unless motives are apparent. A summary of findings and recommendations is in order. The chief executive should be asked to prescribe a time frame for the session. The presentation should be developed to allow adequate time for questions.

Proposal copies should be left with managers or directors. They should not be provided, however, until after verbal presentations. They tend to be distracting when distributed earlier.

St. Louis advertising executive Herbert S. Gardner, Jr., prescribed six guidelines for presentations—competitive or noncompetitive—that apply equally to public relations:

1. Presentations should be made in consultants' offices where possible.
2. The individual who will be the prospective client's principal contact should be among major presenters.
3. Consultants should attempt to be first or last in a series of competitive presentations.
4. Case histories of consultant solutions to similar problems should be a major component.
5. Level of sophistication should be based on prospect preferences.
6. Follow-up is essential, even for those who fail to win accounts. At minimum, they need to know why they failed.

Competitive Presentations

Invitations to compete for a public relations account renew long-standing debates among public relations managers. Should the invitation be accepted? If so, under what conditions? How much should be invested in the presentation? How shall the presentation be made? Unfortunately, there are no "pat" answers to any of these questions.

Washington counselor Paul Forbes suggests avoiding full program presentations in competitive circumstances. Most agencies prefer this approach, he says, "but in competition, they give away an awful lot." The Forbes organization attempts to avoid the problem by marketing diagnostic audits. Results provide bases for subsequent proposals.

Handling Invitations

Significant numbers of practitioners simply decline invitations. Others accept only where those issuing invitations are prepared to pay all or part of the costs involved. They can be considerable. Preparing presentations and accompanying proposals requires extensive research. Costs escalate where preliminary graphic design work is included or audio-visual materials are required.

How Much To Spend

The question of whether to compete is compounded where no compensation is offered. These conditions favor larger or better-funded firms. They usually have more professional time available for developmental purposes. They often have greater in-house production capabilities. Competition tends to favor the affluent rather than the best qualified.

These conditions also may prevail where limited compensation is offered. Consultant decisions then are best made by comparing compensation offered with estimates of "what it will take to do a good job." Caution is indicated when figures are far apart.

Presentation Methods

Some organizations inviting competitive presentations provide lists of those invited to prospective participants. Knowledge of competitors' past presentation patterns then can be helpful. Information often can be obtained from clients who have worked with multiple firms. Those who recently invited presentations from firms involved probably are the best sources.

Information concerning competitors' presentation "styles" can be most helpful. Were audio-visuals used? Were graphic designs presented? How "finished" were these materials? What presentation segments were most impressive? Which were least impressive? How many competitor representatives participated? With all available information in hand, a decision must be made. If the invitation is accepted, work must begin immediately.

Preparing the Presentation

Preparing for formal competition differs little from preparing a proposal. The document must be prepared in any event. Content then must be modified for verbal delivery.

Variables

Two variables arise in presentations. One is the extent to which audiovisuals will be used. The other is the number of individuals involved—those speaking and those otherwise present.

A simple yardstick will resolve audio-visual problems: Excessive "window dressing" can be as much a detriment as a help.

Numbers of participants is another matter. Room size and seating availability should be considered. More important are presentation design and content. It must be organized to accommodate prospective presenters. Change in speakers and delivery styles otherwise is obtrusive and may limit audience ability to assimilate content.

Too Many Presenters

Audiences also can be distracted rather than impressed by numbers of attendees. Those neither needed to respond to questions nor among prospective account personnel should be excluded. Professional knowledge and skill are not functions of numbers, as most audiences recognize.

Most consultants prefer to make presentations in their own offices. Preparatory steps should include site and equipment inspections regardless of location. Equipment must be suitable to the room and backups must be available in case of malfunction.

Most also prefer to be first or last on presenter lists. This especially is so if presentations are to be heard in a single day. The first becomes a standard for comparison. The last may be best remembered. No data are available, however, that suggest "position" influences results.

CONTRACTS AND AGREEMENTS

Types of Contracts

Most consultant-client agreements fall in one or more of five categories: (1) verbal agreements, (2) printed forms, (3) typed contracts, (4) letters of appointment, and (5) printed conditions or standards. For organizational practitioners, a sixth form might be added: memorandum of understanding. This is merely a memo setting out basic elements of an agreement between the public relations unit and another organizational component.

The relative inexperience of nonprofessionals with public relations makes memoranda advisable. Clear understandings are vital to client satisfaction. They are no less necessary in organizational settings, especially where the consultant model is used and subsequent assignments are at stake.

Verbal agreements. Oral or verbal contracts are as binding as documents. They are weak in that they are dependent on the parties' memories. Where linked to proposals (as opposed to agreements) they are especially sensitive to misunderstanding.

Printed forms. Many consultants use printed forms, although little uniformity exists. They may provide space for supplemental conditions. Content includes information concerning operations, charges, personnel assignments, and the like.

Typed contracts. Typed contracts often are assumed to be "custom-designed." While this once may have been the case, little custom drafting exists today. Most documents are maintained on attorneys' word processors. Minor modifications are made to meet individual needs. Content may or may not differ from printed forms.

Appointment letters. Appointment letters usually are prepared by consultants but may originate with clients. They may be lengthy, containing all terms and conditions of the agreement, or quite short. In the latter case, they often are supplemented by printed forms.

Printed conditions. Printed conditions function for public relations consultants in much the same manner that "trade customs" govern printers' relationships with customers. They set out detailed conditions of employment. They usually are appended to appointment letters and made part of those letters by reference.

Contract Content

Considerable variation exists from one consultant contract to another. Most cover at least seven general areas: scope of services to be rendered, compensation, duration, client control, personnel assignment, record requirements, and termination provisions. Other areas may be covered as well, and some of those listed above may be omitted. Consultant contracts usually are products of individual experience, evolving over a period of years.

Scope of services. As the words indicate, this section lists agreed-upon services. A provision for addition or deletion of services by mutual consent usually is included.

Compensation. Compensation sections spell out amounts of retainer fees, hourly rates, and markups on out-of-pocket expenses. The latter usually are handled as separate items. Billing and payment requirements usually are included.

Duration. The time period covered by the agreement is specified.

Periodic review dates also may be established. Reviews often constitute bases for change in compensation levels.

Client control. This section usually specifies client representatives to whom consultants can turn for decisions and approvals. The extent to which these will be required also should be stated.

Personnel assignment. Names of individuals assigned by consultants to handle the work may be specified. Prior client approval often is made a condition for personnel changes.

Record requirements. Most agreements require consultants to maintain detailed records. Time expended and expenses reimbursed by the client often are mentioned specifically.

Termination requirements. This section specifies consultant responsibilities when the contract is terminated. It usually deals with ownership of records, artwork, and the like. A confidentiality provision often is inserted as well.

Sample Contract

One of the profession's better-written client agreements (reprinted below by permission) is used by Burson-Marsteller:

Gentlemen:

This letter will confirm the agreement entered into by and between ("Client") and Burson-Marsteller ("B-M") as follows:

1. *Services*

    a. *Basic services.* B-M will render such professional services ("Basic Services") as the Client shall from time to time request. Such Basic Services may include:

        i. counseling;

        ii. formulating public relations plans;

        iii. preparing news releases, feature articles, public announcements and background information for magazines, newspapers, periodicals, radio and television stations and other media;

        iv. representing and counseling Client with various publics;

        v. writing and producing films, direct mail materials, video tapes, flip charts, booklets and other promotional materials; and

        vi. staging and conducting meetings, conferences and other gatherings.

    b. *Special services.* In addition to the Basic services, B-M is prepared to provide additional services for such projects and products as Client shall from time to time request. Before B-M begins any such Special Services, Client and B-M shall agree upon B-M's compensation therefore.

2. *Compensation*

    Client agrees to pay B-M for its services as follows:

a. Each month during the term of this Agreement, Client shall pay B-M an amount estimated to cover the time-input charges and out-of-pocket expenses (as more specifically described in this Section) which are expected to be incurred during the current Billing Month. On or about the first of each month B-M shall determine such amount for the current Billing Month by reviewing (i) its actual experience during the preceding Billing Month and the current Billing Month to date and (ii) Client's projected requirements on projects for the current Billing Month and the costs thereof. A Billing Month begins on the 16th of a month and runs through the 15th day of the next month.

b. Client agrees to pay B-M for the actual time spent by its account, creative, communications and other personnel in providing Client with services hereunder as determined by applying B-M's hourly rates in effect at the time.

c. Where B-M uses services of an outside supplier in providing services to Client, Client shall pay B-M the cost of such services together with a 17.65 percent markup. Such costs shall include items such as mechanical and art costs (including typography, artwork and comprehensive layouts) and audio-visual production costs (including talent, props, scenery, sound and lighting effects, rights, license fees and producers' fees).

d. Client shall reimburse B-M (without markup) for the out-of-pocket expenses not listed in Section 2c hereof. Such expenses shall include travel expenses of B-M personnel, long distance telephone calls, telexes, postage, deliveries, hotel accommodations for meetings, and travel and entertainment of editorial and other parties whom Client has requested B-M to entertain.

e. To cover B-M's cost of miscellaneous items, such as local telephone calls and photocopies that are required to service Client, B-M charges three percent (3%) of the fee billed to Client for time-input pursuant to Section 2b above.

3. *Billing Procedures*

a. On or about the first of each month, B-M will send Client an invoice reflecting (i) the charge for the current Billing Month as described in Section 2a above and (ii) a reconciliation of the sum of the actual time-input charges and out-of-pocket expenses incurred during the previous Billing Month to the payment made by Client for that Billing Month. The reconciliation shall constitute either a charge for any amount still owing to B-M or a credit for any excess paid by Client.

b. All invoices shall be due fifteen (15) days after the date of issue.

c. If Client fails to make any payment due hereunder within thirty (30) days after the same falls due, Client shall pay, in addition to the amount due, interest thereon at the prime rate of interest charged by Manufacturers Hanover Trust Company as of the due date of such payment.

4. *Term and Termination*

a. The term of this Agreement shall commence as of   , and continue until terminated by either party giving the other party sixty (60) days' prior written notice. Client shall pay all time input charges and out-of-pocket expenses incurred up to the effective date of such termination.

b. Upon the effective date of the termination of this Agreement, all property inB-

M's possession belonging to Client pursuant to the terms of Section 5 hereof and all contracts for services and materials entered into by B-M for Client shall be turned over and/or assigned to Client.

5. *Ownership*

All slogans and publicity materials submitted or developed by B-M for Client during the term of this agreement and paid for by Client and which Client uses at least once prior to the termination hereof or which Client indicates in writing to B-M during the term hereof as being specifically within the designated plans for adoption and exploitation by Client, shall be, as between B-M and Client, Client's property exclusively. All such materials not so used or designated shall be, as between B-M and Client, B-M's property exclusively.

6. *Indemnification*

a. Client shall be responsible for the accuracy, completeness and propriety of information concerning its organization, products, industry and services which it furnishes to B-M. It will be Client's responsibility to review all advertising, promotional, publicity and other materials prepared by B-M under this agreement to confirm that representations, direct or implied, with respect to Client's products and services are supportable by competent and reliable tests or other objective data then possessed by Client, as well as to confirm the accuracy and legality of the descriptions and depictions of Client's products and services and/or competitive products or services described or depicted. Accordingly, Client shall indemnify and hold B-M harmless from and against any and all losses, damages, liabilities, claims, demands, suits and expenses (including reasonable attorney's fees) that B-M may incur or be liable for as a result of any claim, suit or proceeding made or brought against B-M based upon or arising out of (a) any descriptions or depictions of Client's or competitive products or services contained in advertising, publicity, promotion and public relations created, placed, prepared or produced by B-M or other services performed by B-M for Client; (b) any alleged or actual defects in Client's products or services; (c) allegations that the manufacture, sale, distribution or use of any of Client's products or services violates or infringes upon the copyright, trademark, patent or other rights of any third party, and (d) allegations that the advertising of any of Client's products or services induces, promotes or encourages the violation or infringement upon the copyright, trademark or other rights of any third party.

b. After material has been issued by B-M to the press or to another third party, its use is no longer under B-M's control. B-M can therefore not assure the use of its press materials by any publication, nor, if published, that it will be accurate.

7. *Agency/Client*

In purchasing material or services on Client's behalf, B-M will be acting as Client's agent, and all orders placed and contracts entered into by B-M for such purposes with its suppliers and other persons may so state.

8. *Entire Agreement*

This agreement constitutes the entire agreement with respect to the subject matter hereof, and may only be modified or amended in writing signed by the party to be charged.

9. *Construction*

This agreement shall be construed in accordance with and governed by the laws of the State of New York.

10.*Titles*

Titles are for reference only. In the event of a conflict between a title and the content of a section, the content of the section shall control.

B-M and Client have indicated their acceptance and approval of the foregoing by signing in the spaces provided below.

Very truly yours,

BURSON-MARSTELLER

By: _____
Title:

CLIENT

Accepted and agreed by: _____
Title:

Concluding a Contract

Contracts are as valuable to practitioners as to any other professionals. They are not, however, without limitations. The greatest value of the contract is derived by discussing its content with prospective clients. Discussion creates understanding; potential for disagreement is reduced.

Where problems later arise, few practitioners resort to contract enforcement. Most prefer amicable parting to litigation. Most also subscribe to a preventive strategy in launching client relationships. Some are more formal than others. All involve strong interorganizational linkages.

Sales Follow-Up

The months following conclusion of consultant-client agreements are critical to both parties. Success or failure may depend on what is accomplished during this period. Consultants emphasize five points: (1) adhering to the agreed-upon program, (2) establishing strong communication networks, (3) establishing reporting procedures, (4) continuing client education, and (5) watching for potential problems.

Working the plan. Adherence to agreed-upon programs is essential. Achieving stated goals ultimately determines consultant success. This does not mean plans are "cast in concrete." It does mean substantive changes must be agreed upon in advance. They must be communicated to all involved in both organizations; and they must be documented.

The essential guideline, then, is "no unpleasant surprises." Environmental changes may require modifying plans or strategies. New ideas or concepts may arise that will better serve clients. They should not be rejected out of hand. Neither should they be implemented without prior advice and assent.

Communication networks. Interorganizational communication channels may be specified in consulting agreements. Designated client contact persons then are responsible for transmitting consultant reports within their organizations. Delicate reminders of this obligation are in order. They can best be handled by providing multiple copies of reports for distribution by contact persons.

Where no limitations exist, multilevel communication channels should be created. These prove most beneficial when established on peer bases: CEO to CEO, account supervisor to general manager, account executive to public relations manager. Initial meetings should be held as soon as possible. Schedules for periodic service meetings, progress review sessions, and formal reporting procedures should be set at these meetings.

Formal reporting. Interorganizational communication systems should include several components. Periodic reporting meetings are essential. Written reports are advisable. Verbal briefings may be appropriate but should not supplant documents.

Review (as opposed to reporting) sessions also may be made part of the formal process. Written summaries should be prepared and distributed after all meetings. Distribution lists should be created for these and other written reports.

Client education. Consultant personnel should assume ignorance on the part of client organizations as to public relations procedures. Steps involved in brochure production, for example, may be common knowledge to practitioners. Without such knowledge, members of client organizations may harbor unrealistic expectations as to production costs, time factors, and such. The same assumption should apply especially to any changes in the plan.

Changes should be discussed in context with plans. Reasons should be clearly stated. Strategy changes should be explained. Where consultants maintain continuing education programs, client personnel might be invited to attend. Their problem potential declines as knowledge levels increase.

Potential problems. "Is the chemistry right?" The question is ambiguous, nevertheless it illustrates the level of sensitivity required of consultants. It is especially important in the early weeks and months of the relationship.

Are members of the client organization expressing annoyance? Are copy approvals received promptly? Are telephone calls being returned? Does mutual commitment pervade working meetings?

If the answer to any of these or similar questions is "no," or if uncertainty exists, problems may be developing. Mutual confidence and understanding are essential to success. They are produced by communication. As presumed experts, consultants must assume the communication burden.

IN SUMMARY

When marketing efforts succeed, more critical work begins. The period encompassing presentation, agreement, and implementation is critical in establishing consultant-client relationships. Three major developments occur during this time: The consultant makes a presentation that the client accepts; an agreement is concluded; and the foundations of a relationship are established.

The relationship is defined by a proposal, formal or informal. It may be delivered verbally in an informal setting, as a document, or in a formal presentation. The latter often includes verbal and written components. In any form, proposals generally contain eight components. They deal with the background and nature of the public relations problem, methods to be used by practitioners, the scope of their work, anticipated results, resources involved, and costs. Content is prepared in keeping with delivery method.

When proposals are accepted, the parties enter into agreements. They range from verbal commitments to formal legal documents. Regardless of format, contracts contain several key elements. They include descriptions of services to be provided, compensation, duration, client control provisions, descriptions of consultant personnel involved, record-keeping requirements, and termination provisions.

After contracts are concluded, it is incumbent on consultants to establish functional interorganizational working relationships. They are developed through strong communication and reporting systems and continuing client education. Consultants must conform to originally proposed plans. They must be alert to potential problems and prepared to take immediate remedial action to insure continued strength of client-consultant relationships.

ADDITIONAL READING

Abelson, Herbert, and Marvin Karlins. *Persuasion*. New York: Springer, 1970.

Conner, Richard A., Jr., and Jeffrey P. Davidson. *Marketing Your Consulting and Professional Services*. New York: John Wiley, 1985.

Gardner, Herbert S., Jr. *The Advertising Agency Business*, 3rd ed. Chicago: Crain, 1980.

Greiner, Larry E., and Robert O. Metzger. *Consulting to Management: Insights to Building and Managing a Successful Practice*. Englewood Cliffs, N.J.: Prentice-Hall, 1983.

Kakabadse, Andrew, and Christopher Parker, eds. *Power, Politics and Organizations: A Behavioural Science View*. New York: John Wiley, 1984.

Katz, Daniel, and Robert L. Kahn. *The Social Psychology of Organizations*, 2d ed. New York: John Wiley, 1978.

Larson, Charles U. *Persuasion: Reception and Responsibility*. New York: Wadsworth, 1983.

Meyer, John W., and W. Richard Scott. *Organizational Environments: Ritual and Rationality*. Beverly Hills, Calif: Sage, 1983.

Organ, Dennis W., and W. Clay Hamner. *Organizational Behavior: An Applied Psychological Approach*. Plano, Tex.: Business Publications, 1982.

12

Developing Constituent Relationships

The life cycle concept applicable in analyzing organizations applies to organizational relationships. Relationships are born and proceed through adolescence to maturity. Unless nurtured and maintained, they are prone to wither and die. Survival potential, according to Amelia Lobsenz of Lobsenz-Stevens, Inc., is a function of efforts undertaken during the first 60 days of the relationship.

RELATIONAL BEGINNINGS

Gestation of interorganizational relationships begins during marketing and sales processes. They are born as prospects become clients. Extraordinary care is necessary to avoid diseases of infancy and early childhood. Nurturing processes must continue if mature and durable relationships are to be developed and maintained. Neglect rapidly produces senility and death.

Maintenance burdens fall upon consultants. From client viewpoints, they are the newcomers. Client organizations seldom are adequately informed as to public relations practices. They require education and training. Practitioners' backgrounds equip them to perform in educational and nurturing roles.

Establishing Foundations

Foundations for strong client-constituent relationships are created for counselor and organizational practitioners through mutual understanding. Proposals and agreements on which relationships are based should spell out project requirements in detail. Uncertainties must be quickly resolved.

A definition of good performance is essential, says consultant David H.

Maister. Client satisfaction is determined at the beginning of a relationship when the term "good performance" is defined. In essence, he told the Spring 1986 meeting of the PRSA Counselor Academy in Phoenix, "quality must be negotiated." Standards may be qualitative or quantitative, but benchmarks must exist. Where they have not been established through proposals or agreements, they must be determined as work begins.

Building Relationships

Interorganizational relationships are complex: They involve multiple individuals, and they are influenced by individual relationships within and between organizations. Within organizations, individuals are influenced by superiors and subordinates as well as peers. Between organizations, peer relationships are most significant.

The strengths of the relationships vary; so do their abilities to influence decision making. In specific situations, predominant variables may include individual agendas. Professional and personal agendas come into play. Motivations that influence decision making originate in these agendas.

Understanding motivational factors is prerequisite to developing strong interpersonal relationships. These, in turn, are essential in developing and maintaining mature interorganizational relationships. They are no less important within organizations where they govern the success of organizational practitioners.

Individual Motivators

Maslow proposed a five-level hierarchy of individual needs. From lowest to highest they were

1. Physiological, including food and water, sleep and other bodily or biological needs
2. Safety, including security, protection, and related factors
3. Belonging, including group membership, acceptance, and love and affection
4. Self-esteem, as generated through recognition, prestige, competence, and confidence
5. Self-actualization or self-achievement; realizing one's potential; achieving goals for their own sake

Individual attention thus is engaged primarily on the basis of self-interest, responding to psychic or physical needs.

Organizational Motivators

While Maslow's theory dealt with basic individual motivators, Herzberg focused on factors that influence their behavior in organizations. His hygiene theory suggested that positive and negative motivators in organizations are not opposite sides of the same coin.

While poor compensation, for example, may be a negative motivator, good compensation is not necessarily a positive motivator. There exist, Herzberg concluded, positive and negative motivators that collectively determine satisfaction.

Mutual Support

In application, Herzberg's theory supports Maslow's approach. Herzberg suggested the same motivators that influence individual human behavior function in organizations. Individuals are motivated by "self-interest." Quotation marks are used in that the term is somewhat misleading; it requires interpretation in context with Maslow. Self-interest for individuals more influenced by Maslow's lower level motivators may be tantamount to selfishness. Self-interest at other levels may focus on community or philanthropic activities. They involve individuals at Maslow's self-esteem or self-actualization levels.

Neither Maslow's nor Herzberg's constructs can be viewed simplistically. Both are models. They suggest the multiplicity of motivators that stimulate human activity. Virtually all are operable at any given time although in varying degree.

A Basic Principle

The basic principle nevertheless applies. Bluntly put, it might be expressed in this fashion: Every individual examines every proposition in light of a single question, "What's in it for me?" Pure altruism seldom governs human behavior. While some find this distasteful, it remains mankind's primary behavioral determinant.

In maintaining client relationships, successful managers recognize and act on these factors. Rather than assuming human frailties can be suppressed, they create circumstances that conform to organizational and individual agendas for client and consultant.

Multiple Environments

Behaviors and predispositions of organizations and those who populate them are products of multiple sets of environmental pressures. One set is readily identifiable; another of equal importance is less easily recognized.

The primary environments in interorganizational relationships are those internal and external to the organizations involved. Each creates pressures on organizations and individuals within them. If either is a parent or subsidiary, the environments of related organizations also must be considered.

Primary Environments

Internal and external environments of public relations and client organizations require most attention. Assignments may require attention to one or another client environment. Where assignments deal with financial public relations, the external environment will be paramount. If employee relations work is involved, the internal environment will be of primary concern. Both require attention, however, in that both influence organization members.

Problems originating in external environments may distract managers to a point at which employee relations programs suffer benign neglect. Alternatively, difficulties arising internally may produce similar problems in financial public relations. Managers must consider organizations holistically. The principle involved is identical to that with which physicians contend. Potential for successful treatment suffers where physical problems are addressed while psychological ones are ignored.

To assure success, managers must adopt a similar approach in their own organizations. Difficulties arising out of internal or external environments too easily can impact clients. They need not be problems in the usual sense. A surge in new business can be a mixed blessing. While adding to organizational profits, it may create difficulties in maintaining service levels. Equally trying circumstances can arise through personnel turnover, which can disrupt communication networks as well as client service.

Secondary Environments

Where primary organizations are parents or subsidiaries, managers must be sensitive to their environments. No organization directly related to another has all the self-governing attributes of free-standing units. The destinies of parent and subsidiary are inextricably interlocked short of divestiture or merger.

Recurrent spates of corporate mergers and acquisitions tend to be unsettling. They superficially may involve only members of organizations directly involved, but this seldom is the case. Significant personnel changes may occur in parent or subsidiary organizations. They inevitably impact interorganizational relationships. Communication and reporting networks are apt to be disturbed in the process.

In the extreme, conflicts may arise that require ending consultant-client relationships. New organizational linkages may create conflicts in client products or services. New parent organizations may extend assignments of other counselor firms to encompass new subsidiaries.

Human Environments

Uncertainties attendant to these events also produce changes in individual priorities. Public relations personnel in recently merged or acquired organizations may decide that their career objectives can be better achieved elsewhere. Those in acquiring firms who had been preparing to depart for greener pastures might reconsider.

Internal change can produce equivalent results. When key executive posts change hands, protégés of both parties reassess their positions and may alter plans. Potential for such changes requires continuing attention from managers. So must any other event that disrupts interorganizational communication or reporting networks.

On-Going Support

Successful public relations organizations should be supportive of clients and client personnel. Supportiveness implies interest and assistance, which are readily expressed by providing information obtained through environmental assessment.

Supportiveness

For client organizations, information may range beyond that pertinent to the public relations function. A crisis or disaster in another industry of a sort that might occur in the client's field of endeavor constitutes professionally pertinent information. Data indicating development of a potential area of client expansion is beyond normative boundaries.

A new "damage control" technique in disaster planning in similar fashion might be imparted to an organizational colleague as a matter of professional obligation. Information about educational programs that might be of personal benefit would extend beyond such obligation.

Ethical Limitations

Limits of supportiveness are established in part by ethical constraints for counselors. Many will not accept employment applications from client personnel as a matter of policy. This would not preclude a consultant's mentioning a vacancy in a third organization to a client employee who had evidenced interest in a change.

USING ENVIRONMENTAL ASSESSMENT DATA

Operational Parameters

Environmental assessment processes should be expanded in developing client relationships. Prospective client environments are a primary concern during practice development, marketing, and sales processes. After the sale, the process must be extended to client constituencies. Customers, vendors, and employees are of special concern. Events, occurrences, or trends impacting any of them concern clients.

Systems Approach

Those unaccustomed to environmental assessment can use a systems approach to list constituencies. Suprasystems and subsystems are more readily visualized when client organizations are viewed as systems.

Client organizational characteristics must be examined in establishing systemic linkages. If clients are holding company subsidiaries, their situations differ from those of free-standing organizations. They are vulnerable to parent company problems as well as those of direct concern. Counselors thus may monitor parent as well as subsidiary environments.

The extended process adds to counselor burdens but is necessary if consultant and client needs are to be adequately served. Data are an asset in maintaining client relationships.

Use of Data

Environmental assessment systems produce on-going information flows. The manner in which they are conveyed to clients can be helpful. Information involved relates to client needs and opportunities; it often implies needs for further public relations services. Assistance to clients thus becomes a sort of "counselor selling."

The latter term was used some years ago in commercial banking. It referred to applying banking services to solve customer problems. Personnel were taught to be alert to customer needs amenable to satisfaction through banking services. Counselor selling became a matter of helping customer and bank. "Cross selling" today is used in the same way. The concept by any name applies in public relations.

Like most humans, public relations practitioners tend to become habit-bound. Successful execution of existing assignments is perceived as "doing a good job." This perspective limits any tendency to sell additional services. Continuous discussion of contemporary circumstances, problems, and opportunities, on the other hand, encourages sales activities.

ESTABLISHING NETWORKS

Multilevel Communication

Interorganizational relationships are delicate, says William M. Weilbacher. Their survival requires substantial and continuing effort, especially in communication.

Any number of communication problems can produce difficulties. Most prevalent are those arising where communication channels are limited. Where one individual is charged with maintaining communication, problems are almost inevitable. Difficulties occur when contact persons are ill or on vacation. Temporary replacements work with strangers in new environments. These handicaps compound problem potential.

How Problems Start

Where contact persons resign unexpectedly, potential is even greater. Replacements must be trained in days or weeks. Few can acquire necessary information and develop working relationships in so short a time. Personality conflicts can create similar problems. Where interorganizational contact is maintained at only one level, damage potential is considerable. Extensive interorganizational relationships thus are essential; they can be forged by several individuals at multiple levels.

How many levels does "multilevel" imply? No formula exists. Systems should vary with circumstances. They can involve individual or multiple client offices. They may involve multiple individuals within offices. From consultant viewpoints, systems should be sufficient to protect the interorganizational relationships. Absence of individual staff members on either side should go all but unnoticed. Established linkages should be sufficient to maintain the integrity of communication and reporting channels.

Application

The multilevel strategy is applicable wherever public relations organizations consist of more than an individual practitioner. If two are involved, one should maintain contact with client chief executives while the other handles day-to-day contact at lower levels. Where more than two practitioners are involved, lower level client personnel should be acquainted with at least two of them.

Appropriate frequency of contact varies with levels involved and with organizational size. In small to medium-sized public relations units, managers or chief executives should see their counterparts as frequently as quarterly. In larger organizations meetings may be less frequent. Their sessions preferably should be conducted as review and reporting meetings. If those involved know each other well, luncheons may be appropriate. Telephone calls may suffice in rare instances. All are aimed at one objective: avoidance of the "forgotten client" syndrome.

More often than necessary, consultant-client relationships deteriorate and business is lost because clients believe they've been forgotten or have become unimportant to consultants. This often occurs where consultant organizations experience rapid growth. The phase "they got too big for me" is a clear sign of client neglect. Many consultants have heard these words from new business prospects. Continuing effort is necessary to prevent their being used again.

Satisfactory Service

Clients most often consider themselves "forgotten" or unimportant when service deteriorates. Neither quality nor quantity of results need decline, however, for the problem to arise. Client perception is sufficient. It is a reality with which practitioners must deal.

Problem Origins

The nature of public relations practice tends to encourage perceptions of deteriorating service. Organizations usually seek counsel only when pressing needs arise. They often require substantial early attention. Needs become less pressing as problems are contained and resolved. Volume of time spent with clients or on client premises declines. The decline is perceived as deterioration.

Difficulties can be avoided when practitioners compensate for declining in-person or on-site contact. This can be done through meetings reinforced with mail and telephone contacts. They are most helpful when supported by regular progress reports and supplemented by environmental assessment data.

Progress report formats vary from one organization to another. At Burson-Marsteller, monthly reports begin with a brief summary of highlights. Where a product publicity campaign is involved, the report then might list articles published, articles accepted for publication, articles submitted for publication, articles approved by the client, case histories covered, news releases submitted to the client, and listing of special and future projects.

The latter are especially amenable to use at the chief executive level. They enable managers to discuss contingent difficulties and potential solutions with client executives. The process assures clients of consultants' continuing interest and paves the road to additional assignments.

Other Techniques

Several other techniques can be applied to reduce potential discontent. One involves promptness of service. Many a professional continuously impresses clients by exaggerating lead times in program execution. Keeping consistently "ahead of schedule" tends to be impressive. The technique also serves consultants well. It protects against occasional overload situations when work indeed is completed later than expected.

Another technique involves "paper trails." Every consultant organization should maintain records of client contacts, decisions made, and follow-up required. They can as easily be summarized in letters or memos to those involved as in file documents.

In larger organizations consultants should consider "cross-pollination" in conjunction with multilevel relationships. The procedure is simple: It requires members of groups at each level to attend meetings quarterly or semiannually at levels above and below. Only one member of each group need attend, thereby sharing the responsibility so it does become burdensome.

IN SUMMARY

The life cycle concept useful in analyzing organizations also applies to consultant-client relationships. Considerable effort is necessary in their development and maintenance.

Maslow's hierarchy of needs and Herzberg's hygiene theory provide insights into the ways humans function individually and in organizations. They react to motivational factors specified by these theorists and respond to environmental pressures.

Consultants engage the interests of all involved in interorganizational relationships to assure success. This objective best can be accomplished by understanding and being supportive of those involved.

Information produced by the environmental assessment process can be beneficial in developing and maintaining both individual understanding and salutary relationships. It should be shared liberally with all involved.

Multilevel informational and reporting systems also are helpful. This is especially so where systematic "cross-pollinating" techniques are applied to further understanding across organizational levels.

ADDITIONAL READING

Abelson, Herbert, and Marvin Karlins. *Persuasion*. New York: Springer, 1970.

Aldrich, Howard E. *Organizations & Environments*. Englewood Cliffs, N.J.: Prentice-Hall, 1979.

Baird, John E., Jr. *The Dynamics of Organizational Communication*. New York: Harper & Row, 1977.

Evan, William M., ed. *Interorganizational Relations*. New York: Penguin, 1976.

Fulmer, Robert M. *Practical Human Relations*. Homewood, Ill.: Richard D. Irwin, 1983.

Hall, Richard H. *Organizations: Structure and Process*. Englewood Cliffs, N.J.: Prentice-Hall, 1977.

Hall, Richard H., ed. *The Formal Organization*. New York: Basic Books, 1972.

Katz, Daniel, and Robert L. Kahn. *The Social Psychology of Organizations*, 2nd ed. New York: John Wiley, 1978.

Meyer, John W., and W. Richard Scott. *Organizational Environments: Ritual and Rationality*. Beverly Hills, Calif: Sage, 1983.

Weilbacher, William M. *Auditing Productivity: Advertiser-Agency Relationships Can Be Improved*. New York: Association of National Advertisers, 1981.

Zander, Alvin. *Making Groups Effective*. San Francisco: Jossey-Bass, 1985.

13
Managing the Public Relations Process

Success in public relations begins in human resources management: Seeds are planted in the orientation process, their growth begins in planning and budgeting, and the objective ultimately is achieved in the public relations process.

Success is a product of the collective effort of personnel. Where they are committed to organizational objectives, most will be achieved. In the absence of commitment, results are less salutary. Commitment requires personnel be involved in strategic planning and budgeting as well as program development.

PROCESS APPLICATIONS

The processes involved apply in organizational and counselor practices. They also apply equally to client and public relations unit budgets. All parallel the contemporary public relations process model.

The process begins with environmental assessment. Assessment results lead to constituency identification and alternative strategies designed to produce predetermined behavioral results. These steps then lead to message design and delivery channel selection.

Managerial Attributes

Several personal attributes are necessary in managers if these processes are to succeed. Integrity and openness are most important among them. Integrity means trustworthiness. It means honest dealing with employees as well as clients. It implies conscientious effort to avoid overselling the job during the employment process. It requires total compliance with every promise—implied or implicit—made during employment, orientation, and thereafter.

Skepticism and cynicism arguably have been built into much of the work force through ineptitude or neglect on the part of managers and supervisors. Personnel have learned to discount if not ignore the too casual promises often made to them:

"Do a good job and you'll go a long way."
"You have a bright future here."
"We're growing fast and promotions and raises come quickly."

Managers are better served by candor:

"Public relations is a team effort and success means team play."

"We're planning on growing X percent in the next Y months, primarily in the _____ and _____ industries. You can help us achieve these objectives, and your rewards will be commensurate with your efforts and our success."

Information Required

The organization's mission, goals, and strategies should be clearly stated. So should individuals' roles in achieving them. Managerial openness in subsequent weeks and months contributes to the maturation process.

Organizational commitment to performance must be demonstrated. Success must be measured in economic as well as creative contexts. Employees must be equipped with sufficient information to understand linkages between individual performance and organizational success.

They must understand, for example, the impact of cost overruns on client relationships and organizational profits, or revenue in excess of expenditures. They must understand clients' public relations plans and relationships between those plans and their duties. Acquisition of appropriate insights is best accomplished through participation in planning and budgeting processes. Two of each are involved.

The first are planning and budgeting in the public relations organization. The second involve clients (see Chapter 11). Most managers involve personnel in the latter processes but neglect the former. Practitioner personnel need not be privy to the organization's financial statements, but familiarity with profit and loss factors relating to specific projects is essential. Only with this information will individuals perceive relationships between their actions and organizational outcomes. Their ability to relate, to identify community of interest, renders them more amenable to managerial guidance than otherwise would be the case.

The underlying concept is not complex: Individuals given directions respond more readily when they understand why required tasks are necessary and how results concern them individually. Problems arise in the absence of such understanding.

STRATEGIC PLANNING

"Need to know" historically has governed access to information in organizations. Individuals at each organizational level have been privy only to data that senior managers presumed necessary in performing their duties. This approach proved productive in a less egalitarian age. Society has changed, however, and so have employees.

Managerial Problems

Considerable effort often is required to meet employee needs. General Motors Corporation, for example, in 1986 launched a massive corporation-wide effort to open channels of communication. The effort focused not on traditional devices such as newsletters but on managers themselves. Long-term success, the organization had determined, required new human as well as technological systems.

Successful leaders must share their visions of the future to gain employee commitment. Organizational strategic plans no longer can be—nor do they need to be—"state secrets." Most are cast in three parts: formulation, implementation, and evaluation/control. They might be developed along the following lines for a public relations counseling firm:

I. Strategy formulation
    A. Mission statement
        1. Broad: Provide public relations services to the technology, health care, and international markets.
        2. Narrow: To develop and market services that will enhance the abilities of organizations in these sectors to achieve accommodation with their customers, employees, and financial stakeholders.
    B. Organizational objectives
        1. To achieve a return on investment of 10 percent for the ensuing fiscal year.
        2. To increase sales in each primary market area by 20 percent.
    C. Strategies
        1. Open new offices on the West Coast.
        2. Develop and introduce new environmental assessment services.
    D. Policies
        1. Emphasize environmental assessment as a tool to anticipate and avoid organizational problems.
        2. Install performance-based compensation systems for all employees.
        3. Emphasize speed, efficiency, and economy of computer-based communicaton and production facilities.
II. Strategy Implementation

A. Programs
  1. Complete installation of CompuScan monitoring and reporting systems for environmental assessment.
  2. Offer new organizational assessment program to all clients.
  3. Increase market penetration in Western and Midwestern states with new and existing services.
  4. Complete affiliation arrangements with overseas counselors.
B. Budgets: Prepare budgets showing cost-benefit analysis of each planned program.
C. Procedures
  1. Develop and implement marketing program for CompuScan system.
  2. Orient all professional personnel in the environmental assessment area.
  3. Lease offices in Los Angeles; transfer three New York Staff members; recruit three others; recruit three replacements in New York.
  4. Conclude affiliation agreements in Great Britain, Europe, and Canada by mid-year.
III. Evaluation and Control
  A. Require monthly status reports on the following:
    1. Actual versus projected costs.
    2. Actual versus projected sales.
    3. Progress toward opening/staffing in Los Angeles.
    4. Progress toward completion of CompuScan system.
    5. Progress in installing.
      a. Performance-based compensation system.
      b. Environmental assessment programs.

Informational Needs

A review of the foregoing suggests little need for secretiveness. Mission statements and objectives should be common knowledge among employees. Strategies and policies may be shared exclusive of proprietary information that might be prematurely revealed. Implementation plans should be made known at the earliest possible moment. This should be done prior to public disclosure in any event. Monitoring procedures should be common knowledge within the organization.

Strategic planning can be applied with equal productivity in organizational public relations units. In counselor and organizational settings, strategic plans then become foundations for public relations plans. Strategic plans become points of departure for organizational development programs in public relations organizations. Client strategic plans similarly are the bases from which their public relations plans are developed.

Control Data Corporation's Quentin J. Heitpas suggests a planning model similar to the public relations process model (see Figure 13.1). It differs only in focus, addressing organizational needs rather than behavioral change in stakeholder groups. His structural overview parallels environmental assessment. The other steps he proposes are similar other than in

FIGURE 13.1.
The Public Relations Planning Model.

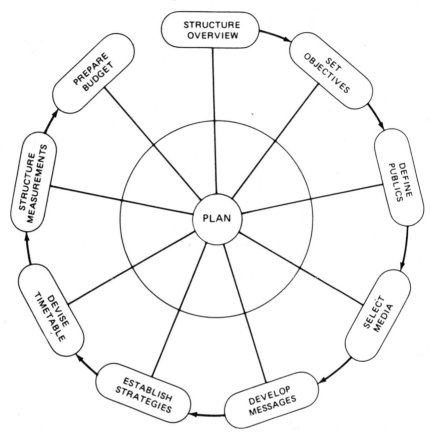

Source: From *Inside Public Relations: Experts in Action*, by Bill Cantor edited by Chester
Burger, Copyright © 1984 by Longman, Inc. All rights reserved.

terminology. "Strategies," as he uses the word, are the terms in which
messages will be conveyed.

As in the case of the strategic plan, there is little in the public relations
plan that need be held confidential within the organization. The reverse
should be true where managers seek optimum employee performance.
Knowledge of overall plans necessarily produces superior component
designs.

Budgeting processes should be similarly handled. Employees must be
familiar with budgetary components governing their activities. The information gives them direction to meet economic objectives.

Knowledge of revenue and expense expectations provides similar
guidelines for all involved. It also provides a set of objectives toward which

personnel can work and by which they can measure their progress. Need to know "where I stand" is concurrently satisfied.

BUDGETING

Budgeting, like other critical processes, must be managed. Before work can begin, practitioners must set aside an aversion to budgeting, which among some has approached phobia proportions. This can be achieved with ease where managers understand that:

1. Budgeting is as creative a process as any other.
2. Budgets are mirror images of public relations programs cast in numbers rather than words.
3. The budget process creates opportunities for practitioners to sell programs to management and demonstrate their successes in terms managers understand.

Budgets are requests for resources to achieve predetermined goals. They must convince managers that functions to be funded are necessary and will contribute to organizational objectives.

Preferably, says Illinois Bell Telephone Company Vice-President John A. Koten, components should be presented in order of importance. Prospective impacts arising out of failure to fund each component should be provided. (see Figure 13.2)

Budget presentations and periodic reviews are opportunities to demonstrate accomplishments. They also serve to educate senior managers as to how resources are used and why they are needed. They are part of a process through which managers present evidence of accomplishments and obtain resources to achieve new goals and objectives.

The Public Relations Budget

Like public relations plans, budgets initially are cast as selling documents. They usually consist of six to seven elements:

1. An executive overview summarizing principal points. Amounts requested, variation from prior patterns, anticipated results, tasks necessary to achieve them, and cost summaries usually are included.
2. A summary of behavioral objectives.
3. A summary of communication strategies, including messages to be delivered.
4. A message distribution plan indicating primary constituent groups as well as communication channels.
5. The formal budget statement, itemizing communication channels to be used and associated costs.
6. A summary that usually expands on the executive overview and may be supplemented by explanatory notes.

FIGURE 13.2.
Illinois Bell Budget Decision Packages.

Rank	Program	Impact If Not Funded	Staff
EMPLOYEE INFORMATION RANKING			
3	Information support of personnel policies and 2-way discussion programs.	Less employee understanding of personnel policies and lack of 2-way communications.	4
2	Employee magazine	Reduced understanding of complex corporate issues; no regular medium to reach retired employees.	5
1	Employee bulletins and phone-in newsline.	No timely employee information on company developments; outside media and rumor mill become primary information sources.	3
MEDIA RELATIONS RANKING			
2	Issue press information on technology advances; respond to media queries on service.	Low-technology image, more competitive losses, more service complaints to regulatory agencies, more adverse coverage on service.	1
1	Provide press information on rates and legal matters; act as spokesperson and coordinate press information.	Poor media representation and less favorable regulatory decisions.	2
ADVERTISING RANKING			
2	Bill inserts to specific customer groups on service matters and dialing changes.	No efficient way to get local service information to customers; more use of 1st class mail; lost sales opportunity.	2
1	Twelve issues of bill insert newsletter to 3.6 million customers.	No recurring way to inform customers statewide of rates, service developments, and new products/services. Lower sales, reduced revenue.	2

FIGURE 13.2. (continued)

Rank	Program	Impact If Not Funded	Staff
DEPARTMENTAL RANKING			
7	Information support of personnel policies and 2-way discussion programs.	Loss of employee understanding of personnel policies and lack of 2-way communications.	4
6	Bill inserts to specific customer groups on service matters and dialing changes.	No efficient way to get local service information to customers; more use of 1st class mail; lost sales opportunity.	2
5	Twelve issues of bill insert newsletter to 3.6 million customers.	No recurring way to inform customers statewide of rates, service developments, and new products/services. Lower sales, reduced revenue.	2
4	Employee magazine	Reduced understanding of complex corporate issues; no regular medium to reach retired employees.	5
3	Issue press information on technology advances, respond to media queries on service.	Low-technology image, more competitive losses, more service complaints to regulatory agencies, more adverse coverage on service.	1
2	Provide press information on rates and legal matters; act as spokesperson and coordinate press information.	Poor media representation and less favorable regulatory decisions.	2
1	Employee bulletins and phone-in newsline.	No timely employee information on company developments; outside media and rumor mill become primary information sources.	3

Source: From *Inside Public Relations: Experts in Action*, by Bill Cantor edited by Chester Burger, Copyright © 1984 by Longman, Inc. All rights reserved.

Development of budget figures begins with the public relations program. Components of the program are assembled chronologically (see Figure 13.3), usually listed by month of completion. Costs involved then are

FIGURE 13.3.
Program Timetable.

Exhibit 1. Program timetable.

Project	January	February	March	April	May	June
1. Financial Communications	Sales projection announcement	Quarterly statement		Publish annual report	Annual meeting	
2. Employee Communications		Income tax clinic	Publish newsletter		Fitness clinic	Publish newsletter
3. Community Relations	Prepare for auction	Fund-raising auction	Branch opening reception	Branch opening reception		

Source: Reprinted, by permission of the publisher, from *What Happens in Public Relations*, by Gerald J. Voros and Paul H. Alvarez, p. 28, © 1981 AMACOM, a division of American Management Association, New York. All rights reserved.

broken down by months in which they will be incurred (see Figure 13.4). Later, these data will be shown together with actual expenditures on monthly report sheets.

Where handled by organizational public relations units, data from the flowchart then would be summarized as a unit budget for incorporation in the organizational budget (Figure 13.5). Unit managers would work from more detailed breakdowns. These at minimum would reflect budget totals by project. Ideally the project totals would be broken down into cost items. Under employee communications, for example, the unit budget might list an employee newsletter. Cost factors would include staff time, photography, other illustrations, typography, composition, printing, and distribution. Counselors would maintain similar data by project for each client as well as the counseling firm.

The budget process is cyclical in public relations and client organizations and consists of four parts: development, presentation, control, and evaluation.

Budget Development

Preliminary compilation of budget data begins with public relations or business plans. The latter govern client budgeting; the former guide the process in public relations organizations. The costs of each component of the work must be specified. The preliminary document is a working paper, and refinement is necessary before presentation.

First, each component and attendant cost must be examined in light

FIGURE 13.4.
Budget Flowchart.

Exhibit 3. Budget flowchart.

Function	Annual Budget	January Costs	Balance	February Costs	Balance
1. Financial Communications	$250,000	$10,000	$240,000	$20,000	$220,000
2. Employee Communications	75,000	5,000	70,000	2,000	68,000
3. Community Relations	145,000	15,000	130,000	25,000	105,000
4. Product Publicity	50,000	2,000	48,000	3,000	45,000
5. Government Relations	90,000	10,000	80,000	5,000	75,000
Total	$610,000	$42,000	$568,000	$55,000	$513,000

Source: Reprinted, by permission of the publisher, from *What Happens in Public Relations*, by Gerald J. Voros and Paul H. Alvarez, p. 33, © 1981 AMACOM, a division of American Management Association, New York. All rights reserved.

of a single question: Is it absolutely necessary? Will a lesser expenditure accomplish the same results? Second, components must be arranged in priority order. Relative importance of budgetary components must be known. This information guides senior managers where expenditures must be reduced.

Research Needed

Research is necessary to determine which techniques will best meet organizational needs. This usually involves examining similar projects undertaken earlier. Related budgets and expenditures are especially worthy of review.

Cost breakdowns must be provided for each activity in the budget. If a brochure is planned, for example, costs of copywriting, graphic design, photography, typography, color separations, printing, binding, and distribution must be included. Where appropriate, even more precise breakdowns should be provided. If the copywriting estimate includes a draft, one major rewrite, and three sets of minor revisions, the cost of each should be given.

Multiple Objectives

Detail in budgeting accomplishes several objectives. It demonstrates that public relations managers know their business. It shows clients or employers

FIGURE 13.5.
Internal Public Relations Budget.

Administrative Costs

Salaries	$130,000
Office Supplies	15,000
Overhead	30,000
Travel, Miscellaneous Expenses	25,000
Subtotal	$200,000

Functional Costs

Financial Communications	$250,000
Employee Communications	75,000
Community Relations	145,000
Product Publicity	50,000
Government Relations	90,000
Subtotal	$610,000

Contingency	$ 90,000
TOTAL	$900,000

Source: Reprinted, by permission of the publisher, from *What Happens in Public Relations*, by Gerald J. Voros and Paul H. Alvarez, p. 30, © 1981 AMACOM, a division of American Management Association, New York. All rights reserved.

their economic concerns have been heeded. Most important, it established bases for revisions should they become necessary. If the brochure text requires three complete rewrites, the manager will be able to cite the previously approved budget in requesting a revision.

Budget developers also should be mindful of this concept in overall terms. As statistical projections of public relations plans, budgets should reflect professionals' best thinking as to cost and efficiency. When revision is necessary, managers can indicate where results will suffer.

Goals and strategies occasionally may have to be altered to meet economic limitations. This is preferable from the practitioners' standpoints to proceeding with inadequate resources in the face of inflated management expectations.

Other Factors

Several other factors also require attention. Budgets must be complete. They should show markups, taxes, and all out-of-pocket costs. Nothing should be omitted. They also should anticipate inflation. Costs inevitably go up rather than down. Where budgets cover extended time periods, an inflation factor should be included. All data should be based on facts rather than guesses.

This especially is true where those drafting documents are not thoroughly familiar with costs. Multiple estimates are advisable on printing, multimedia productions, and so forth. Where vendor figures are far apart, they should be rechecked to insure accuracy.

Finally, ambiguities should be clarified. These usually occur in two contexts. First, projects may not be sufficiently developed to permit precise cost calculations. Second, budgets can include assumptions that may or may not prove valid. Preliminary estimates should be identified as such. Supplementary budgets should be promised—and delivered for approval—before projects involved are undertaken. Any assumptions, such as the number of ink colors to be used in a brochure, should be specified. Here, again, bases are established for revisions that later may be necessary.

Budget Presentations

Recipients should be guided through budget presentations, which should be made in person. They should be written in comprehensible English, but not read to recipients. Documents should not be presented until verbal presentations are complete, because those who are reading will pay no attention to the presentation.

Adequate detail should be provided in the verbal presentation as well as the accompanying document. Program components should be concisely restated even if in part repetitive of earlier presentations.

Presentations should be handled as sales efforts. They should demonstrate the value of work to be undertaken. So must proposals, which also require sufficient detail to stand alone should some decision makers not be present.

At the conclusion of the presentation or afterward, approvals must be obtained in writing. There is no other way to prevent subsequent misunderstandings. Clients seldom object and objections usually are abandoned in the face of candid responses.

Budget Monitoring

The budget process ends only when work involved is complete. Like public relations programs, budgets must be implemented and controlled from inception to completion. Three systemic components are essential whether client or public relations unit budgets are involved: (1) confirming documentation for decisions and changes; (2) confirmation or approval for expenditures over predetermined amounts; and (3) internal monitoring of time and dollar expenditures.

Program Avoidance

Some have attempted to monitor public relations budgets by entering vendor costs as bills are received; however, this approach is risky and unnecessary. Risk arises since items ordered but not billed can involve substantial amounts. Small budgets readily can be overexpended in a short time. Risk in the past has been controlled through purchase order systems. While effective they are tedious to maintain and have been rendered obsolete by the advent of the computer.

With or without computers, current records must be maintained. Many recommend time sheets and purchase orders be routed through one individual or department. This technique can eliminate potential problems but computer data accomplishes the same objective. Day-to-day summaries can be generated as long as data input is handled on a timely basis.

Periodic Updates

Periodically—at least monthly but preferably weekly—revised budgets should be produced by computer or otherwise. They should show the status of each project. Amounts allocated and expended should be shown. So should percentages of work completed and dollars committed.

Updated budgets should be matched with plans and reviewed with clients or senior managers. Public relations unit members should be responsible and accountable for expenditures.

Where unforeseen delays or changes occur or are proposed, managers or clients immediately should be made aware of prospective economic impacts. Where they can not be handled within existing budgets, appropriate revisions should be prepared and submitted for approval. Public relations practice by its nature is fluid. Practitioners must respond to problems and opportunities. Where budgets are amended accordingly and all involved are kept abreast of developments, the cardinal rule of budget management can remain inviolate: no unpleasant surprises.

Multiple monitoring devices are available to generate performance data. Among the more sophisticated are several developed by AT&T Information Systems and described by Rudolph Marzano in Bill Cantor's *Inside Public Relations*. They are designed to produce qualitative as well as quantitative indicators of performance. They monitor numbers and types of media mentions, for example, as well as trends involved.

Budget Evaluation

Like initial presentations, periodic budget evaluations are sales opportunities for public relations managers. They should review budget and plan performance in detail with all involved.

Were objectives met? Were projected results achieved? Were expenditures within prescribed limits, as originally specified or subsequently modified? Did the results justify the expenditures involved? Where budgets were modified, did results improve?

Presentations should begin with restatements of objectives. Results then should be specified. Cost data should be reviewed. Finally, new programmatic plans can be presented for management consideration. The process thus comes full circle. The past provides a springboard to the future.

PROCESS MANAGEMENT

Organizational problems may persist even where strategic plans and budgets are understood. These difficulties relate primarily to process control. They often are expressed by managers in complaints concerning employee behavior:

> "He's forgotten his audience."
> "She has no sense of costs."
> "This can't be done in the time allowed."
> "That would go way over budget."

Such comments are symptomatic of lack of managerial control. In some cases they arise indirectly out of reluctance to attempt to impose constraints on "creative people."

Questionable Alternatives

Several negative guidelines applicable in managing creative individuals were suggested by Frank J. Wemhoff in an undated PRSA Counselor Academy monograph, *Mystiques of Motivating and Retaining Creative Talent.* "You can't pander to them. You can't inhibit them. You can't give them full rein. Neither can you breathe down their necks."

For those who agree, alternatives exist. Collegial or team approaches may prove productive; but apparently irreconcilable disputes occasionally arise. Here, as Wemhoff suggests, a "buck stopper" is essential. Managers must assume that role.

More often, they attempt to limit problem potential through closer monitoring or oversight. This approach tends to produce negative reactions from creative personnel. They often resent being "treated like children" and declare, "It's impossible to be creative in an atmosphere like this."

They may be right. Atmosphere is a function of corporate or organizational culture and this, in turn, is within management's ability to establish and change. Where personnel have been made parties to planning and budgeting processes, change is accomplished with relative ease.

Toward a Solution

Where those who produce components of public relations programs are involved from the outset, they tend to harbor proprietary attitudes toward resulting projects. Plans and budgets become "our" plans and budgets rather than "their plans and budgets." Emphases tend to shift from reasons why "it can't be done" to "ways to get it done."

Individuals involved are challenged to exercise creativity within constraints they helped to establish. Managers then need only install systems that assure those involved remain sensitive to audience, cost, and time as well as creative factors.

A SYSTEMS APPROACH

Virtually every public relations organization monitors the progress of specific projects with work or job orders. They invariably include client names and job descriptions. Occasionally, audiences or objectives are specified as well. Further information readily can be included to provide detailed guidance for all involved.

Process Control

Process control can be established in many ways; forms are used in most of them. Empirical evidence suggests there are almost as many forms in use as there are public relations organizations. Form design is a matter of practitioner preference. Few of those in use resemble systems. They are readily established through forms given earlier practitioner involvement in planning and budgeting.

Systems are designed to keep work flowing smoothly through the organization. Where overly rigid or complex, they can be obstructions rather than facilitators. Managers' efforts must be directed toward developing systemic control while maintaining sufficient flexibility to generate desired results.

Guidance and control can be provided on consistent bases. Weyerhauser Company creative services manager Richard E. Londgren suggests using an unusual work order format. It requires users to specify objectives and audiences as well as job specifications. A more comprehensive approach along the lines Londgren proposes is illustrated in Figure 13.6.

The Project Plan form was designed for medium-sized counseling firms; it is amenable to modification for use in firms of other sizes as well as organizational practices. The Project Plan was created to serve in lieu of the traditional job ticket. It was developed to focus staff members' attention on objectives as well as products. Similar forms are used for electronic media and other projects.

Project Plan Components

While some document components are self-explanatory, others require elaboration. Client, due date, and description fall into the former category. Other factors are more complex. They collectively focus user attention sequentially on the several components of the public relations process.

Audience

Users are required to specify audiences for each project. Multiple audience specifications are encouraged to prompt diverse product applications. Unit costs decline as printing quantities increase. Cost/efficiency factors improve where multiple applications can be productively developed. A report to shareholders, for example, may be used in whole or part for employee communication as well.

Data required in audience descriptions also encourage continuing awareness of a basic concept: Media audiences and public relations constituencies seldom are identical. An office equipment vendor, for example, may value exposure on a newspaper's business page. Business page readership may consist largely of businessmen but they represent a small percentage of total readership. Hundreds of thousands of individuals presumably may be exposed to the message. Fewer than 10 percent may be part of the business audience the vendor seeks to reach.

Practitioners must be sensitive to the differences. This especially is so where "per prospect" costs may be low while audience or media costs appear high. Merchandising specialized medical equipment at physicians' convention trade shows can be expensive. It may be considerably less costly on a per prospect basis than alternative efforts to reach a large percentage of practitioners in any given medical specialty.

Project planners become more sensitive to these differences where they are required to deal with stakeholder groups as well as media audiences. Required examination of alternative communication channels and their ability to reach target groups assists as well.

Audience Parameters

Descriptions of audience characteristics induce refinement in planning processes. Potential for successful development of communication projects is limited by developers' knowledge of those involved.

The specification process also tends to clarify planner information needs. Where major shortfalls occur, research may be necessary to equip planners to meet systemic requirements adequately.

Users are required to specify geographic areas and delivery mechanisms to assure proposed projects produce desired results. This is unlikely to be

FIGURE 13.6.
Project Plan Form Designed to Keep Creative Efforts Oriented to Program's Behavioral Objectives.

Project Plan (Print)

Client _____ Date _____

Scheduled Delivery Date _____

DESCRIPTION: (Provide complete information for estimator. Quantity, page size, number of ink colors, types and estimated number of illustrations. Any specialized production techniques must be specified.): _____

_____

_____

_____

AUDIENCE(S): (Identify target groups. Estimate numbers of individuals in each and percentage of total which this project/product will reach.):

	Group	Number	Percentage To Be Reached
A.	_____	_____	_____
B.	_____	_____	_____
C.	_____	_____	_____

AUDIENCE PARAMETERS:

	Group A	Group B	Group C
Age	_____	_____	_____
Sex	_____	_____	_____
Education Level	_____	_____	_____
Income Level	_____	_____	_____
Geographic Areas	_____	_____	_____
Shared Interests	_____	_____	_____

BEHAVIORAL OBJECTIVES: (Describe behaviors which message(s) are to be designed to induce):

Group A _____

Group B _____

Group C _____

MEASURES OF SUCCESS: (How will the success of this project be measured in terms of each group?):

Group A _____

Group B _____

Group C _____

MOTIVATIONAL FACTORS: (What positive and/or negative motivators or appeals might induce the desired audience reaction?):

Group A _____

Group B _____

Group C _____

FIGURE 13.6. (continued)

Cost Factors

Project Component	Budget Amount	Vendor Bids/Estimates			Actual Cost	Work Days Required
		Vendor A	Vendor B	Vendor C		
Concept/Copy						
Sketches						
Photos						
Other Illustrations						
Typography						
Mechanicals						
Separations						
Printing						
Envelopes						
Add/Mail						
Postage						
Totals						

ALTERNATIVE COMMUNICATION CHANNELS:

Medium	Numbers of Receivers	Percentage of Population	Total Cost	Cost/Audience Member	Production Days Required

Approved _____ _____ _____
       Account Executive   **Account Manager**   **For Client**

the case where, in the extreme, a brochure is developed for mail distribution but no appropriate mailing list is readily available.

Behavioral Objectives

Behavioral change on the part of message recipients is the primary objective of public relations. Where desired behaviors are not specified in advance it is unlikely they will be induced through the communication process.

Messages developed in the absence of specified behavioral outcomes also are apt to be ill-conceived and/or poorly designed. Specifying desired audience reactions focuses planner attention on relationships between messages and objectives.

Measures of Success

Successful public relations projects by definition must yield demonstrable results. Success in this context applies to practitioners and clients. Satisfaction of both parties' needs requires results be measurable.

The approach used is similar to that employed in requiring definition of audience parameters. In specifying measures of success, planners must consider the needs of both public relations unit and client before work begins. Research may be necessary to establish baseline data from which results can be measured.

Audience Motivators

This portion of the document requires planners to consider motivational factors for use in developing message content. If the product involved is an industrial boiler, for example, planners here would consider factors that might induce message recipients to specify the brand in question.

Decisions of this kind seldom are made on the basis of technical literature of the sort popular with manufacturers. Buying decisions are made on the basis of benefits a product will generate. The fact that the great-great-grandfather of the boiler manufacturing company president made the first unit by hand in 1908 is of no concern to the prospect.

Cost Factors

Cost data are included in the planning process to assure projects remain within established budgets. In this case, traditionally required data must be supplemented with budget data and figures from multiple bids or estimates.

Two objectives are involved. First, the process links projects to the budgeting and program development in which planners presumably were earlier involved. Second, it establishes a near competitive situation since bids or estimates are immediately comparable to budget figures. Their presence creates an implied challenge to project developers. They are encouraged to meet budgetary totals if not line-item figures.

Alternatives

The planning document requires provision of cost/effectiveness data for alternative media that might be substituted for the device at hand. This is a sort of "fail safe" mechanism. It demands a final examination of comparative cost/effectiveness figures in light of firm bids or vendor estimates. Should these exceed budgets, planners may find alternatives worthy of reconsideration.

Information generated by the plan and insights into ways in which individuals handle information tend to induce salutary results.

Multiple Processes

Successful process application requires knowledge of several other processes and systems. These include: (1) The adoption process, through which individuals evaluate and may act upon information. (2) The diffusion process, through which individuals receive and may act upon information. (3) The human organism and its idiosyncrasies.

Adoption Process

The adoption process concept suggests that ideas are assimilated in five stages. The first is awareness, in which the individual becomes aware of an idea. The second is interest, during which more information is sought. The third is evaluation or examination in context with needs. The fourth is trial or experimental use, and the fifth is adoption.

A similar process is involved, according to University of Maryland Professor James E. Grunig, in individuals' reactions to public relations campaigns. Their first response is problem identification. They then must be convinced the problem affects them, a process Grunig calls personalization. They will act, he says, only after they are shown that they have an opportunity to do so and the concept is socially acceptable.

Diffusion Process

Diffusion of ideas among humans is a function of their varying predispositions toward acceptance of innovation. A very small portion of any population—perhaps as little as 2 percent—can be categorized as innovators. These are ego-driven individuals who require little reinforcement. They want to be first in everything. A somewhat larger group consists of early adopters. They want new ideas but don't want to be pioneers.

Beyond the innovators and early adopters are the majority, sometimes subdivided as "early" or "late" in the overall scheme. These are individuals characterized by counselor Patrick Jackson as having "a Coors in one hand and a channel flipper in the other," and who "can be stirred to action about once a decade." Finally come the laggards. They adhere to older values and are all but impervious to new ideas.

Human Nature

Least recognized and arguably most important in viewing organizational relationships is the nature of the human organism. Its importance in public relations varies inversely with the extent to which it is understood.

Most managers, and most clients or employers, expect humans to respond logically to information. They assume information equals communication. Unfortunately, this seldom is the case. Humans are prone to illogical decision making.

So-called impulse buying is symptomatic of this condition. So is the "curb appeal" factor in real estate, as Jackson also pointed out. Research shows initial impressions outweigh virtually every other factor in home buying. Perhaps the ultimate in illogical decision making involves selecting a mate. Emotion, intuition, and mothers' opinions are among primary determinants.

PROCESS MONITORING

When public relations planning has been completed and the process begins, managers' tasks have just begun. Like the budget, the process requires ongoing monitoring: the plan must be implemented, deadlines must be met, expenditures must remain within budgetary limitations. The plan and the budget thus are managers' primary monitoring devices. In practical terms, they are virtually one and the same. The budget is a numerical reflection of the plan, and vice versa.

Planning in public relations is identical to that undertaken in any organization. More is needed, however, in managing the public relations process. The process in most cases is complex because the plan usually involves multiple strategies. Each may be implemented through multiple programmatic components. Each component may involve several techniques.

Coordination Necessary

The planner must coordinate all activities involved in development and implementation. Complexity and timing are major potential sources of difficulty.

Most managers use one or more of the planning methods developed during the World War II era. The critical path (CPM) and PERT approaches are typical. They involve establishing time requirements for each programmatic component. Critical dates are plotted and the lines are ordered in calendar fashion, creating flow charts for monitoring purposes.

Research Needs

Where extended programs are involved, as in the case of national presidential campaigns, research data are required as well. Planners constantly must be abreast of turns in voter attitude and opinion. Where changes are other than as anticipated in the planning process, campaign efforts may require modification.

Finally, ex post facto research is essential after every public relations program and project has been completed. Programs can and should add to practitioner knowledge and ability and consistently improve their performance.

This requires extensive "postmortem" examinations. They are necessary whether or not project or programmatic goals are accomplished. Success or failure are important, but the reasons why either occurred are more important. These must be cataloged and analyzed for future reference. Factors that contributed to success can be used again. Those that produced failure or limited success must be avoided.

IN SUMMARY

Successful management of public relations processes can be achieved only through human resources development. Predispositions among many managers toward secretiveness must be overcome. Personnel must be informed of organizational missions and goals. They must be made party to developing and maintaining strategic plans and budgets through which they are funded.

Where these objectives are achieved, those involved will respond to guidance in program and project development. They will be responsive to implied or implicit challenges to meet budgets; to focus efforts on producing measurable results; and to thereby meet organizational and public relations objectives.

The process is applicable in counselor and organizational practices alike. It also should be used in client planning, budgeting, and programming.

Linkages must be established between programs and budgets and the specific projects with which practitioners deal. A simple Project Plan form can be used to provide guidance. It leads practitioners to consider the impact of variables on program and project objectives.

Monitoring processes begin as programs and projects are implemented. Where carried out over extended periods, monitoring should include ongoing research to permit change in direction in keeping with interim results.

Postmortem examinations finally should be conducted after programs or projects are completed. Elements contributing to success or failure should be identified to enhance future practitioner performance.

ADDITIONAL READING

Albers, Henry H. *Organizational Executive Action: Decision-Making, Communication and Leadership.* New York: John Wiley, 1961.

Berkman, Harold W. *The Human Relations of Management*. Encino, Calif.: Dickenson, 1974.

Bradford, David L., and Allen K. Cohen. *Managing for Excellence: The Guide to Developing Higher Performance in Contemporary Organizations*. New York: John Wiley, 1984.

Burger, Chester, ed. *Inside Public Relations: Experts in Action*. New York: Longman, 1984.

Carkhuff, Robert R. *Sources of Human Productivity*. Amhearst, Pa.: Chilton, 1984.

Cascio, Wayne F. *Managing Human Resources: Productivity, Quality of Work Life, Profits*. New York: McGraw-Hill, 1986.

Dowling, William F., Jr., and Leonard R. Sayles. *How Managers Motivate: The Imperatives of Supervision*. New York: McGraw-Hill, 1971.

Gordon, William L., and Roger Howe. *Team Dynamics in Developing Organizations*. Dubuque, Iowa: Kendall/Hunt, 1977.

Grunig, James E., and Todd Hunt. *Managing Public Relations*. New York: Holt, Rinehart and Winston, 1984.

Heitpas, Quentin J., "Planning," in Cantor, Bill. *Inside Public Relations: Experts in Action*. Edited by Chester Burger. New York: Longman, 1984.

Hickman, Craig R., and Michael A. Silva. *Creating Excellence: Managing Corporate Culture, Strategy and Change in the New Age*. New York: New American Library, 1984.

Kopelman, Richard E. *Managing Productivity in Organizations: A Practical, People-Oriented Perspective*. New York: McGraw-Hill, 1986.

Londgren, Richard E. *Communication by Objectives: A Guide to Productive & Cost Effective Public Relations & Marketing*. Englewood Cliffs, N.J.: Prentice-Hall, 1981.

Marzano, Rudolph. "Evaluating," in Cantor, Bill, *Inside Public Relations: Experts in Action*, edited by Chester Burger, New York: Longman, 1984.

Pascarella, Perry. *The New Achievers*. New York: The Free Press, 1984.

Stanton, Erwin S. *Reality-Centered People Management: Key to Improved Productivity*. New York: AMACOM, 1982.

14

Managing Human Resources: The Employment Process

CHANGING CONDITIONS

People are the most volatile component of the contemporary organization. Beset by accelerating social and technological pressures, they increasingly are prone to vent frustrations in the work place. Managerial failure to recognize the impact of environmental factors on employees has compounded resulting problems. Employees are part of organizational psychological, social, and political subsystems and are linked directly to the technological. They are also part of and impacted by organizational suprasystems. By monitoring systemic events and trends, managers can anticipate developing pressures on employees and their potential reactions.

Public relations professionals enjoy advantages and disadvantages in managing human resources. They are people oriented by education and background. Those they are called upon to manage, however, include disproportionate numbers of creative individuals. They are bright, restless, and individualistic—men and women of the sort who "give managers fits." Those who succeed as managers learn to grant creative personnel considerable latitude while still keeping them "on the track."

Seller's Market Developing

How is all this to be accomplished? Not without difficulty in a "seller's market." Public relations is a labor-intensive industry, and this will continue to be the case. It also will cause many if not most management problems through the early years of the twenty-first century.

While only recently called to popular attention by Naisbitt and Aburdene, the nation is entering an era of human resource shortages. Demographic data are beyond argument. As the baby bust generation moves into the work force in the late 1980s, increases in the national work force will turn to declines—18- to 24-year-old entry-level workers will number 4.5 million fewer in 1990 than in 1980.

Shortages Begin

First indications of shortages of public relations practitioners appeared in the mid–1980s. Practicing professionals were making substantial offers to college students before graduation. Others, such as Art Stevens, president of Lobsenz-Stevens, Inc., were urging expansion of enrollments in public relations curricula.

Where human resources managers applied strategic planning methods, these signals were clear. A major change was in progress in one of the organization's suprasystems. It inevitably will impact public relations practice.

Responses

Successful managers are responding to changing circumstances by delegating responsibility and authority in equal parts. They see credit is given where credit is due. Creative personnel are given greater latitude to exercise creativity and feel they're making significant contributions to organizations.

The "open door" remains a major asset. So is readiness to listen, although listeners often hear more than they would like. Managers must keep employees informed, handle criticism diplomatically, and provide career paths for those who want to progress without moving into management.

Meeting Challenges

These challenges are not easily handled but can be met. One approach involves creating a new kind of job. Senior communicator or senior advisor positions would be appropriate. Compensation packages involved would be similar to those granted managers. Talented, experienced individuals thus could move up in organizations rather than look elsewhere for job satisfaction.

Quid Pro Quo

In response, managers should expect considerable qualities from their personnel. Organizational loyalty should be the first expectation. Initiative—idea generation—should closely follow. Where career ladders are created, those climbing them should be expected to make superior contributions; to look for "ways to get it done" rather than reasons why "it can't be done."

They also should be expected to display maturity; to produce well-researched ideas with alternatives considered and details worked out; to accept the fact that clients occasionally reject the best ideas, preferring to "play it safe." Managers should expect to receive staff work ready for approval. Where such work is provided, they should grant appropriate rewards.

Environmental Factors

Human resource systems are linked to four external environments. Three are of primary concern to management: economic conditions, labor market conditions, and governmental requirements. The fourth is created by organized labor, seldom a factor in public relations.

Organizations that recognize these linkages are responding with attention to four elements that influence employee satisfaction: organizational objectives, quality of work life, work group relationships, and supervisory relationships.

Those that create "the most nourishing environments for personal growth will attract the most talented people" in competitive markets, according to Naisbitt and Aburdene. Managers' primary roles will involve cultivating and maintaining these environments. Authoritarian management styles will yield to "networking" systems and companies will become "confederations of entrepreneurs."

Accommodation Essential

Implicit in the writings of these and other trend-watchers is a simple truth: Organizations that accommodate to change will flourish; others will be at risk. Accommodation processes need not be difficult. Managers have necessary tools at their disposal, which are embodied in public relations practice and strategic management. The issues management concept that developed in the early 1980s is an amalgamation of the two. It varies only in focusing on matters amenable to governmental action. As strategic management recognizes, social and demographic trends defy legislation. Accommodation or adaptation instead is necessary. Public relations and strategic planning techniques thus are appropriate.

Assessment Processes

In human resources, as elsewhere, the process begins with internal and external assessment. Data flowing from the process equip managers to deal with the five components of the human resources system: planning, intake and termination, compensation, evaluation, and career development programs. Each is composed of multiple parts applicable in counselor and organizational settings. Each must be carried out, as consultant Bill Cantor points out, with considerable care.

PLANNING

The planning function subdivides into three parts. The first is strategic planning, which involves shaping human resource functions to coincide with organizational strategies. The second is employment planning, which includes specifying quantitative and qualitative parameters for workers in keeping with management plans. The third is job analysis and design—shaping sets of tasks to create jobs.

Strategic Planning

Strategic planning in human resources requires that managers conform unit activities to organizational plans. The process is far-sighted. It extends beyond immediate requirements to forecast intermediate and long-range needs based on organizational direction.

Potential growth areas specified for early organizational exploitation imply parallel work force changes for human resources managers. No immediate change in primary employment criteria necessarily results. Secondary knowledge, skill, and background criteria should be modified early. Soon-to-be-hired personnel one day may be involved in projected growth areas.

Employment Planning

Employment planning differs from human resources planning in dealing with more immediate personnel requirements. It is designed to enhance effectiveness and efficiency in using human resources. It also must engender employee development and satisfaction while fostering compliance with equal employment opportunity and other legal requirements. Managers in this process specify numbers of employees necessary to maintain services to clients. Their qualifications must be specified.

Managers' most critical problem arises in smaller organizations where addition or loss of a single client can produce quantum workload changes. Declining loads quickly can create budgetary stress. Sudden increases quickly overburden workers. Every public relations unit strives to keep billable hours as close as possible to hours paid. Success exacts a price. Given equal growth rates, smaller units have fewer hours available for new clients.

No management can afford extended periods of overstaffing or overload. The monitoring component of personnel planning thus is difficult, especially where multiple offices are involved.

Strategic Personnel Plan

Strategic personnel plans look three to five years into the future. They are based on organizational strategic plans, goals, and strategies. Organizational plans must provide data adequate to permit accurate demand projections. Planners then can project human resource needs with relative accuracy.

Adequacy of human resources in specialized practice areas also should be a planning objective. Where members of specialized groups are near the same age and approaching retirement, successors must be hired and trained before their seniors retire.

Employment Plan

Forecasting is the essence of employment planning. The process is based on the strategic plan and forecasts of demand and supply. The latter require internal as well as external assessments. The internal are based in part on skill and qualification inventory records for all employees. Summary data from these documents provide information invaluable in employment planning. Replacement or succession charts also are necessary. They show logical promotional sequences in the event of personnel changes. They enable managers to calculate depth of resources in skill or knowledge areas—tasks usually handled by unit managers in smaller organizations. Elsewhere, they are delegated to human resource departments. Managers' primary challenge in either case is to bridge anticipated gaps between supply and demand.

JOB DESIGN AND ANALYSIS

Managers in the United States historically have taken an engineering approach to job design. They have attempted to break down jobs into their simplest components to reduce skill levels required. They made job content as repetitive as possible, seeking more and more specialization.

Personnel managers concurrently took job content as a given. They analyzed content to establish wage rates and recruited, selected, and trained workers for jobs. Contemporary managers find this approach inadequate. While the system was logical, results were not. Jobs became simplistic, repetitive, and inflexible. What made sense from an engineering standpoint produced frustration and poor performance.

New Approaches

New design approaches have been based on job enrichment. Research has shown that achievement, recognition, responsibility, personal growth, and job content are primary motivators. Job enrichment began by adding planning and controlling tasks to traditional designs.

The next step was job enlargement, in which more and different tasks were incorporated. Autonomy finally was added. Individuals and groups were granted responsibility for complete production cycles. They participated in setting goals and in evaluating performance.

Job Analysis

Job design alone will not produce optimum results in applying human resources toward specific objectives. Detailed information about necessary knowledge and skill levels also is needed. This information is obtained through job analysis, essentially a data-gathering procedure.

Job analysis results are contained in two documents: job descriptions and job specifications. The former detail the title, location, duties, equipment used, supervision given and received, working conditions, and hazards of the job. The latter specify necessary qualifications, including education, experience, training, judgment, and initiative. Physical, communication, and other skills also may be specified. This information is used in several areas:

- Organization and manpower planning, which involve dividing work into jobs at all organizational levels
- Recruiting, selecting, and placing personnel
- Establishing compensation rates
- Design and redesign of jobs
- Employee training and development program design
- Performance appraisal

Employment Processes

Recruiting and selecting are separate components of human resources management. Both are processes rather than functions. Each contributes to efficiency. They can be undertaken systematically, as in larger organizations, or as vacancies develop. Needs are generated by turnover, growth, and suitability of work forces to changing organizations.

Both processes begin with job descriptions and specifications. Analysis of these documents in context with time requirements permits development of need estimates. The planning process is relatively simple in organizations with established time standards for each type of work. The creative nature of public relations makes standards difficult if not impossible to prescribe.

Recruiting and employment in "buyer's" markets create minimal organizational risk. Ample numbers of applicants are available. Employers risk little in mishandling either process. The reverse will be true in the developing seller's market. Recruiting costs will rise. Hiring individuals who prove incompatible may create expensive disruptions. Employment and termination processes will require more care and precision.

RECRUITING

Recruiting is evolving from task to process. The change is being driven by external pressures from socioeconomic and market environments. Internal pressures also are being created by the social and psychological environments. The market environment demands improved organizational productivity. The socioeconomic environment requires that organizations compete more strongly for personnel. Internal pressures arise out of need to create nurturing environments and enhance "quality of work life."

Resulting recruiting processes involve several phases. No one is more important than another. They must be equally successful if those employed are to become productive.

The Preliminaries

Two preliminary steps are advisable regardless of search strategy: a review of attributes of existing personnel and an audit of services acquired from independent sources.

Qualification Inventories

Near-limitless numbers of skills, talents, and bodies of knowledge are applicable in public relations practice. Those available in organizations at any time are not necessarily apparent. "Best" job candidates thus may not be selected. Managers avoid this pitfall by comparing employment plans with capabilities summarized in skill and qualification inventories. These are detailed profiles of existing personnel. They enable managers to maintain constant oversight in an era of rapid change.

Organizations periodically make basic changes in services, which should result in parallel changes in employment and staffing plans. Managers' grasp of existing knowledge, skill, and expertise within their organizations is vital in these circumstances but few are well-prepared.

Poor Assumptions

Managers are prone to two tenuous assumptions, which create waste and unnecessary turnover. They first assume employees are equipped only to handle positions they occupy. Then they assume employees are happy in their positions. In the absence of formal qualifications inventories, managers' priorities should include reviews of personnel records. Other than among entry-level personnel, diverse sets of skills, talents, and bodies of knowledge are apt to be found. This knowledge better equips managers to assign personnel in keeping with talent and ability. Individual and unit productivity improve as a result.

After personnel records reviews, employee interviews may be advisable. Two primary questions should be addressed: are employees happy in their situations and would they be better-satisfied in other assignments? Humans are most productive when assigned to duties they prefer. These also are duties they invariably perform most skillfully.

Qualifications inventories should be reviewed at least annually. Reviews can be components of employee performance evaluations where formal inventories are not maintained. They also are appropriate in advance of organizational expansion. They produce "ideal candidate" profiles for use in applicant screening when compared with skills, talents, and abilities needed to achieve new organizational goals.

External Source Review

Candidate profiles should be complemented by reviews of services provided by external vendors. Their extensive use over protracted periods may imply a need for internal staffing. External source reviews also can be helpful where candidates differ little except in collateral abilities. A writer whose avocation is photography, for example, may be preferable to a candidate with no knowledge of the subject if organizational photo needs are growing.

Inventory results and external source reviews then should be examined in context with employment and strategic personnel plans. The process enables managers to establish skill, talent, and ability priorities for use in recruiting.

Total organizational needs rather than existing job or position descriptions govern the process. Job and position descriptions can and often should be changed, especially in smaller public relations units. Traditional approaches are practical only where personnel number in dozens or hundreds.

Selection Criteria

Candidate screening is the most demanding of selection procedures. It can be completed successfully only after careful preparation. Standards must be created for initial screenings using job-related criteria, which should include education, experience, and physical/personal attributes. They have changed relatively little over the past 20 years (see Paul Burton's *Corporate Public Relations*, and Nathaniel H. Sperber and Otto Lerbinger's *Manager's Public Relations Handbook*).

Criteria may be relatively brief or quite detailed. The Dow Chemical Company's Communications and Marketing Communications Departments, for example, use multiple interviews and a brief set of criteria for screening purposes (see Figure 14.1). Criteria in such cases must be general, however, in that they are designed for application in filling multiple positions.

Art Lobsenz, president of Lobsenz-Stevens, Inc., specified in a PRSA Counselor Academy newsletter 11 attributes he considers necessary to a successful career: (1) writing ability, (2) development and execution of plans, (3) innovativeness, imagination, and open-mindedness, (4) knowledge of client businesses necessary to counseling, (5) results orientation, (6) technical skills, (7) ability to create publicity through meaningful ideas, (8) ability to establish and maintain media relationships, (9) ability to learn and grow, (10) strong management skills, and (11) ability to communicate effectively with executives.

Sperber and Lerbinger offered lists of criteria for different categories of personnel in developing a handbook for managers (see Figure 14.2). Others could be added, most of them job-specific rather than generic. They should be contained in a second list. More demanding standards may be appropriate where applicants are interviewed for specialist positions.

FIGURE 14.1.

Communications and Marketing Communications Applicant Evaluation form Used by The Dow Chemical Company.

PLEASE COMPLETE EVALUATION IMMEDIATELY AFTER INTERVIEW

APPLICANT NAME: _____ _____

                  Last Name   First   Initial   Interview Date

ADDRESS: _____

           Street   City   State   Zip

Phone: _____

EVALUATION: How would this applicant *compete and compare* with other new hires?

	Poor	Difficult	Avg.	Above Avg.	Excel-lent	COM-MENTS
(1) Adaptability-Flexibility	[_____	[_____	[_____	[_____	[_____	]
(2) Education-Experience	[_____	[_____	[_____	[_____	[_____	]
(3) Human relations	[_____	[_____	[_____	[_____	[_____	]
(4) Communication Skills-Verbal	[_____	[_____	[_____	[_____	[_____	]
(5) Writing Competence	[_____	[_____	[_____	[_____	[_____	]
(6) Leadership-Managerial Skills Potential	[_____	[_____	[_____	[_____	[_____	]
(7) Energy Level & Self-Motivation	[_____	[_____	[_____	[_____	[_____	]
(8) Business Understanding	[_____	[_____	[_____	[_____	[_____	]
(9) Other	[_____	[_____	[_____	[_____	[_____	]

Writing Samples:

If you were able to review the applicant's writing samples, please give your evaluation to support (5) above.

OFFER-HIRE RECOMMENDATION:

[_____[_____[_____[_____]
NO   NO   UNCER-   YES   YES
Strong   Semi-   TAIN   Semi-   Strong
        Strong   Strong

Important characteristic(s) of this applicant that influenced your recommendation:

RECOMMEND FOR:

_____Communicator Development Program (CDP)   _____Summer Intern

_____Direct hire into _____

_____Other (explain) _____

FIGURE 14.1 (continued)

POTENTIAL:

(1) If your offer-hire recommendation was "yes," is applicant's potential as _____ Specialist _____ Manager.

(2) Name the highest level within Dow this applicant might achieve?

(3) Name the work and functions in which this applicant will make his/her greatest contribution.

Interviewer	Department

Reprinted by permission.

FIGURE 14.2.

Hiring PR Staff. Criteria for support, secretarial, and clerical staff as well as other components of the employment process in organizations are shown here.

Hiring PR Staff	Assigned to	Date/Time Assigned	Date/Time Completed
I. Once it is determined that there will be an in-house public relations department, consider the following for impact and effectiveness: 　1. Budget 　2. Centralized or division PR account executives 　3. Reporting lines 　4. A table of organization for the PR department (DPR straight line reporting to) CEO and dotted line responsibilities.	_____	_____	_____
II. Categorize personnel 　1. Account executives 　2. Support staff 　3. Secretarial clerical	_____	_____	_____
III. Account executives qualifications: 　1. Writing ability 　2. Articulation 　3. Creative ability 　4. Sales ability 　5. Integrity 　6. Reliability 　7. Aggressiveness 　8. Analytical capability 　9. Financial knowledge 　10. Decision-making quality 　11. Ability to see overall company posture 　12. Ability to handle day-to-day details 　13. General knowledge and frames of reference 　14. Personability (getting along with others) 　15. Implementability (carry through) 　16. Potential for senior leadership post 　17. Clear thinking in tense situations	_____	_____	_____

continued

FIGURE 14.2. (continued)

Hiring PR Staff	Assigned to	Date/Time Assigned	Date/Time Completed
IV. Staff support:	___	___	___
1. Skilled in pertinent specialty.			
2. Writing.			
3. Articulation.			
4. Planning ability.			
5. Attention to detail.			
6. Willingness to do homework.			
7. Ability to carry out and interpret research.			
8. Willingness to be a "go-fer."			
9. Potential for advancement.			
10. Willingness to accept leadership and responsibility.			
11. Compatability with team workers.			
12. Delivers more than asked for.			
13. Accepts pressure gracefully.			
V. Secretarial:	___	___	___
1. Secretarial skill.			
2. Feeling for language.			
3. Anticipate needs of superiors.			
4. Speed in executing secretarial duties.			
5. Gracious personal relationship.			
6. Responsible.			
7. Ability to keep confidence.			
VI. Clerical:	___	___	___
1. Attention to detail.			
2. Confidentiality.			
3. Gracefully accepts orders.			
4. Necessary skills.			

Source: From Nathaniel H. Sperber and Otto Lerbinger, *Manager's Public Relations Handbook*, © 1982, Addison-Wesley Publishing Company, Reading, Massachusetts. Reprinted with permission.

Knowledge Criteria

Another firm's industry-specific requirements provide insight into levels of nonprofessional knowledge necessary to success:

1. Economics
2. Distribution patterns
3. Technology
4. Business and consumer media serving the industry
5. Industry trade associations and their personnel
6. Legislative and administrative bodies, industry law, and legislative problems
7. Financial writers, analysts, and institutional investors specializing in the industry
8. Major companies in the industry
9. Any international trade factors pertaining to the industry, including competitors, tariff and trade barriers, and so on
10. Leading banks, lawyers, accountants, management consultants, and educators specializing in the industry
11. Labor unions active in the industry

These requirements are not easily met. They may be more demanding than necessary. They nevertheless indicate the importance managers assign to selection processes.

Before the Search

Recruiting begins when "ideal" candidates' profiles are complete. The process varies with type of organization. In corporate situations and larger counseling firms, personnel departments are involved. In smaller units recruiting is handled by principals or executive officers.

Several preliminaries are advisable in either case. First is a review of legal and regulatory requirements, which originate in federal and state statutes as well as executive orders and bar discriminatory employment practices. They change from day to day. Caution is advisable.

A Look Inside

Qualification inventories then should be used to identify employees who might be promoted to open positions. Those qualified should be given opportunities to fill positions on trial bases other than in unusual circumstances. They may arise from time pressures but managers should yield only under extreme duress. Giving existing employees "a try" enhances morale whether or not they succeed. Failure to provide opportunities may be seen by others as suggesting they look elsewhere for growth opportunities.

"Trial marriages" are not free of problems, especially where employees risk becoming known as having failed. Those of uncertain capability can be asked to "fill in until an appropriate candidate can be found." Few resent such offers. The search for the "appropriate candidate" then can be "delayed" until the "fill in" has had an opportunity to demonstrate ability to handle the job.

Preparing for the Search

In the absence of qualified employees, formal search procedures can begin as soon as compensation levels have been established. Starting wage rates and short-term increments based on successful completion of a probationary period should be determined in advance. This is information candidates require and to which they are entitled.

Sources of Personnel

All hiring should be governed by employment plans. Finding the right people, however, will be a constant challenge. Accelerating social change is producing mounting demand for public relations practitioners.

Except in organizations with in-house training programs, personnel searches tend to focus on colleges, universities, and organizations with public relations units—corporate, consultant, or otherwise. The media are a secondary source and produce few qualified applicants. Two factors are responsible. First, they are becoming more competitive in wages and fringe benefits. Second, their personnel are less and less qualified for public relations positions. Their experiential and/or their academic backgrounds are relatively narrow. They tend to be experienced in one medium but novices in others.

Beginning the Search

Formal searches can be accomplished through several channels. They include search or recruiting firms, personnel agencies, advertising, networking, resume files, and personal referrals. Each has advantages and drawbacks.

Professional search or recruiting firms specializing in public relations or communications disciplines can be of help. They can identify needs, clarify job specifications, and establish appropriate salary ranges. They generally operate on fee bases rather than commissions. They tend to be more selective than personnel agencies in referring candidates.

Personnel agencies require judicious use but need not be excluded. Managers should provide precise candidate profiles and caution agencies to refer only those who meet criteria.

Advertising

Advertising also requires discretion. It may produce a deluge of inquiries but few qualified applicants. The impact of the deluge can be limited through use of "blind" advertisements. They also may discourage qualified applicants.

Networking is most helpful where time permits. The "old boy-old girl" system is quite efficient. Those who recently have filled staff positions are ideal contact points. They may be able to refer qualified candidates who were not hired.

Maintaining a resume file can be beneficial. Managers often retain resumes of apparently qualified applicants received in the prior 90 days. They also may find qualified applicants through referral services of the Public Relations Society of America and the International Association of Business Communicators.

SELECTION PROCEDURES

Recruiting and selection are different processes. The former is designed to produce as many candidates as possible. The latter sorts out the most qualified among them. Both may involve policy matters that should be considered in advance. Can bright but young and inexperienced candidates be selected because they will be greater long-term assets than more experienced individuals? How should managers respond if promising applicants appear when no vacancies exist? Policy guidance is necessary in larger organizations.

Alternative Approaches

Selection processes usually involve one of two approaches. They can be viewed as a series of tests, each requiring passing scores. Applicants in the alternative can be taken holistically. Weaknesses in one area may be offset by strengths in others. Where the first approach governs, candidates are eliminated when the first failure occurs. In the second, they complete the process and are judged on overall results.

The Procedure

Selection processes should conform to organizational needs. They tend to be rigorous where failures are costly. Managers in some organizations are encouraged to overhire and weed out poor performers later, but this approach seldom is appropriate in public relations. The procedure most frequently involves a series of steps: preliminary interview, completion of application, selection testing, principal interview, background investigation, final selection interview, and induction.

The Process

Application blanks are information-gathering tools. They enable reviewers to identify prospective employees and perhaps draw inferences as to their suitability. Some contend content can be analyzed to produce information beyond data presented. Interviewers should consider any conclusions that might be drawn from applications to be tentative. Interviews, tests, and background investigations provide more reliable information.

Testing

Employment testing is a complex process with considerable error potential. Tests are inappropriate in public relations, especially where creative personnel are involved. They must be legally validated where used. They must measure what they are supposed to measure: individual candidate potential. Validity is almost impossible to establish without large numbers of employees in all categories involved.

Other Problems

Other factors also militate against tests in smaller units. They have been shown most useful in making selections from among candidates deemed likely to succeed. They have proven better predictors of failure than success. Where several applicants pass tests, those with the highest scores are not necessarily the best candidates. Relationships between abilities and scores are not always linear. In addition, a number of potential legal pitfalls exist.

Legal Risks

Legal dangers can not be understated. Suits brought by Blacks and Hispanics over cultural bias usually have been class actions. Courts in these cases may award back pay to existing and former employees. Employers also can be ordered to reinstate all involved.

Psychological testing services and in-house psychology services create no significant safeguards. When tests are found to produce discriminatory results, employers can be found guilty regardless of intent.

Safe Alternative

Perhaps the safest testing technique available involves paying applicants to handle free-lance assignments. Hiring decisions then can be based on quality of work performed. This approach creates no immunity to litigation but is likely to pass judicial scrutiny.

Legal constraints also exist as to physical examinations. They may be required only to the extent physical condition is important in the job.

About Portfolios

Testing at first glance may appear superfluous where candidates offer portfolios for inspection, but this is not the case. Portfolio content may demonstrate applicant capabilities. It may be equally representative of the skills of others. To differentiate, interviewers must determine where and under what circumstances samples were created. To what extent, in other words, do they represent the work of the applicant? To what extent are they the work of others?

The nature of the candidate's position may provide clues. Samples are more apt to be the result of applicant efforts in small organizations. The larger the organization, the less likely this will be the case. The circumstances are not unlike those where cub reporters work on metropolitan dailies. Articles appearing under their by-lines may be more representative of editorial than reporting skills.

Portfolio content thus may or may not be a fair reflection of candidate work. It should be supplemented with information from other sources.

Selection Interviews

Unlike testing, selection interviews are universal process components. Multiple interviews are common, especially for higher level positions. Interviewers alone can assess individual attributes and evaluate them with other information.

Objectives

Interviews are conducted for three purposes. Their primary objective is sufficient information to support a hiring decision. They also must provide information to applicants to enable them to evaluate the job. Finally, they should deal with candidates in a way that creates goodwill toward the organization.

Alternative Techniques

Interviews can be categorized as planned, patterned, and stress. For planned or in-depth interviews, interviewers prepare outlines of areas to be explored. Applicants are encouraged to speak freely on a range of subjects, such as home life, education, work experience, attitudes and social/recreational interests.

Patterned interviews are based on comprehensive questionnaires and are highly structured. This probably is the most popular approach. Research data indicate that it produces salutary results.

Stress interviews are difficult and dangerous. Interviewers assume hostile roles. Candidates tend to respond in kind. Results can be damaging if interviewers lose control. Stress interviews should be used only by highly trained interviewers and where stress is a factor in the job to be filled.

Interview results should be recorded regardless of technique. Records should relate to previously established criteria. They should include evaluative data amenable to use in comparing candidates.

Managing the Interview

Employment interviews are burdensome for applicants and managers. They should involve two-way communication. Information flows should be of near equal volume and should deal with substance rather than appearance. The latter requirement is difficult to achieve with both parties presumably "on good behavior." A relaxed atmosphere free of interruptions and beginning at the appointed hour is helpful. So is interviewer control of any tendency to dominate the conversation.

Interviews should begin with reviews of job specifications. These should be conveyed with information about the firm and job requirements. The occasion permits interviewers to sell the organization, but negatives should be covered as well. Pressures, time and effort requirements, and other potential sources of discouragement should be described. Both parties are better served if applicants then decide against the position.

Seeking Information

Untrained individuals seldom conduct interviews well. Interviews should elicit information. They do so only where candidates "open up." When this occurs, interviewers seek to identify professional, personality and thought patterns. They attempt to determine applicant values, professional views, and attitudes.

Questioning techniques vary but are best kept simple and direct. When patterned interviews are used, questions are prepared in advance and in detail. The process has become common because legal problems may arise where no detailed records are maintained. Where the planned interview is used, only a topic list is necessary.

A favored technique among interviewers using the planned approach is the so-called funnel device. Questions proceed from general to specific over a series of subject areas. The "exemplary approach" also tends to produce sought-after information. It involves requesting descriptions of memorable projects with which candidates have been involved.

Another technique incorporates apparently different but repetitive questions. Interviewers seek inconsistencies in responses. Consistency, intelligence, integrity, good judgment, and common sense are valued. They become evident where interviews are of sufficient length and detail.

Serial Interviews

Interviews often are undertaken in series; multiple interviewers occasionally are involved. First interviews seek to ascertain applicants' assessments of their strengths and weaknesses. Subsequent interviews may involve others in the organization for two reasons. First they may detect prospective personality conflicts between candidates and existing staff. More important, they can be training experiences for staff members.

Legal Constraints

Questions on many subjects are "off limits" under federal and state laws and regulations. One is most important: No information that might serve as a basis for discriminatory behavior can be elicited.

Background Investigations

When primary interviews are complete, backgrounds of candidates still under consideration are investigated. Legal constraints are substantial and counsel is advisable. Credit records, legal documents, and other material more or less readily obtained may not be considered in various jurisdictions.

References are a starting point in examining candidate credentials. Those provided by applicants seldom are of value. Former employers often provide no information other than hiring and termination dates and job titles. These circumstances arise out of potential for litigation. The "old boy-old girl" network is the best source of information concerning candidates under serious consideration. Many will not be wholly forthcoming but some may provide implied advice.

Other potential sources of information include counselors retained by candidates' former employers and practitioners who have left those employers.

End and Beginning

When a candidate has been selected, a final interview may be scheduled. This often is the case where management positions are involved and final decisions are handled by several individuals or by committee.

Mutual understanding at this point usually has been reached as to position requirements, compensation, and perquisites. Restatement of this verbal contract is advisable.

In the wake of a final interview, the induction process begins. It is both an end and a beginning. It concludes the employment process and begins the career development process.

IN SUMMARY

Human resources are organizations' most volatile component, and this will continue to be the case. Difficulties will compound through the early years of the twenty-first century as a result of impending manpower shortages. Human resources managers will be challenged by these circumstances to create nurturing environments for employees.

The employment process begins with examination of organizational strategic plans. They lead to development of strategic and employment plans for the human resources function.

The process requires care and diligence. It begins with development of recruiting profiles based on comparisons of organizational needs and employee skill/qualification inventories. Comparisons lead to selection criteria expressed in terms of knowledge and skills. Searches begin only after internal capabilities have been reviewed and existing employees are given opportunities for growth.

While tailored to individual organizational needs, selection procedures usually involve seven steps: preliminary interview, completion of application, selection testing, principal interview, background investigation, final selection interview, and induction. The latter process also marks the beginning of the new employee's career development in the organization.

ADDITIONAL READING

Burton, Paul. *Corporate Public Relations*. New York: Rheinhold, 1966.

Cantor, Bill, *Inside Public Relations: Experts in Action*, edited by Chester Burger. New York: Longman, 1984.

Cascio, Wayne F. *Managing Human Resources: Productivity, Quality of Work Life, Profits*. New York: McGraw-Hill, 1986.

Ettema, James S., and D. Charles Whitney, eds. *Individuals in Mass Media Organizations: Creativity and Constraint*. Beverly Hills, Calif.: Sage, 1982.

Glueck, William F. *Personnel: A Diagnostic Approach*, 3rd ed. Plano, Texas: Business Publications, 1982.

Katz, Daniel, and Robert L. Kahn. *The Social Psychology of Organizations*, 2nd ed. New York: John Wiley, 1978.

McCormick, Ernest J. *Job Analysis: Methods and Applications*. New York: AMACOM, 1979.

McGregor, Douglas. *The Human Side of the Enterprise*. New York: McGraw-Hill, 1960.

Naisbitt, John, and Patricia Aburdene. *Re-Inventing the Corporation*. New York: Warner, 1985.

Sperber, Nathaniel H., and Otto Lerbinger. *Manager's Public Relations Handbook*. Reading, Mass.: Addison-Wesley, 1982.

Stanton, Erwin S. *Reality-Centered People Management: Key to Improved Productivity*. New York: AMACOM, 1982.

15

Nurturing Employees

Employment is the first step in creating a human asset for the organization. Well-designed and executed, the process insures individuals are well-chosen. Whether they meet expectations is another matter. Their maturation is a product of several factors, which include organizational culture, personnel policies and procedures, career development programs, the performance evaluation system, the compensation system, and employee benefit programs. These are environmental components that create employee satisfaction or dissatisfaction.

ORGANIZATIONAL CULTURE

Developing nurturing environments begins with creation of an organizational culture: a vision of the future projected by a skilled manager and of sufficient attractiveness to induce exceptional employee performance. Visions need not be cast in glowing economic terms. The economics of employment rank low on lists of human motivators.

This especially appears to be so with younger generations of workers. They seek enjoyment in their work, a sense of accomplishment, of having contributed to the attainment of worthwhile goals. They want to exercise an entrepreneurial bent; to grow with their organizations. Under skilled managers, organizations and individuals grow together.

Public relations professionals may be best equipped to create such environments. Their backgrounds and work make them "people-oriented." They seek accommodation between clients and stakeholders. They need only apply in their own organizations the skills they offer to clients.

Beginning Points

Corporate or organizational cultures can be developed in any organization. They require two components: skilled leadership and worthwhile endeavors. Ethically pursued, public relations objectives meet the latter criterion. These circumstances suggest managers need only the necessary commitment to fashion shoes for the shoemaker's children. Those who identify with organizational purposes join in ownership of a shared vision. They become engaged in their life work rather than merely functioning in an organization.

Variation in organizational structure can limit ability to engender nurturing environments. Traditional corporate reward systems, for example, can be obstacles. So can traditional benefit programs and policy and procedure structures. Nurturing environments nevertheless can be created. Managers need only apply the tools at their disposal. Wage increases, bonuses, and promotions may or may not be among them. Ability to grant recognition, stature, and perquisites is universal.

Constructing the Environment

Near the top of most lists of effective motivational factors are several within managers' ability to control. They include a sense of belonging; of being in management's confidence or "in the know." They include recognition for a job well done.

Recognition

Rewards may be as simple recognition as "employee of the month" or as complex as unofficial status as departmental "second in command." Stature in organizations is as easily granted. Memoranda well-prepared by employees can be forwarded to senior managers with cover notes rather than under managers' signatures. Talented employees can be granted control of specific projects, or given responsibility for a client's work. Devices producing stature for employees are limited only by managers' imagination.

Responsibility

Frederick Herzberg suggests a set of seven elements that also can be used as motivators: removing controls, increasing accountability, granting control over a complete unit of work, granting additional authority, providing copies of report data direct to the worker rather than through a supervisor, introducing new and more difficult tasks not previously assigned, and assigning specialized tasks that enable the worker to become an expert.

Perquisites

Managers also control numerous perquisites. Almost all of them have the power to decide who receives preferred vacation dates. They control professional assignments and decide who goes south during the winter or north during the summer. Continuing education opportunities can be similarly apportioned. Those in resort areas can be granted to superior performers. Attendance at professional meetings and conventions can be handled in like manner. Organizational cultures thus are as readily created in public relations units as in corporations. The process requires only commitment by managers to get the job done.

Beginning the Process

Instilling the values of organizational cultures in new employees can begin in preemployment interviews. Where prospective immediate supervisors are involved, this should be the case. The process more often begins with orientation.

The typical orientation process is not well designed to achieve cultural results. It usually is conducted by personnel department representatives and deals primarily with mundane matters. Employee benefit programs are apt to be reviewed in detail; so are personnel policy and procedure manuals. New employees need considerably more. Their needs can be satisfied within departments or other operating units.

Orientation Programs

The orientation process was designed to introduce new employees to the organization, their jobs, their superiors, and their colleagues. The process may be simple or complex. It is intended to save time, reduce employee anxiety, and induce realistic expectations, positive attitudes, and job satisfaction.

Formal programs normally cover several areas, including organizational history and general policies, descriptions of products or services, structure, personnel policies, compensation and benefits, and daily routines.

Departmental

Orientation to public relations units varies with applicant backgrounds. Where they are newcomers to the community, the process may extend over a period of months. It may include introductions to vendors, media representatives, and others. Within the unit, new members should be introduced to colleagues and others with whom they will come in regular contact. Orientation of consultant firm employees to client organizations is equally important.

Potential Problems

The process can be complex from the employer's standpoint. It also may be inadequate in failing to address needs created by environmental change. Two are paramount: employer need to imbue employees with the corporate culture; and employee need to understand how the organization will meet his or her expectations. Employers who fail to meet these needs create future problems. Lower employee loyalty levels are produced, encouraging undue turnover.

Opportunity

Departmental orientation processes create opportunities for managers to introduce newcomers to the corporate culture. The term embraces all of the mores and folkways of the organization; its values and standards; its traditions and concepts of service. Introducing these concepts early assists employees to adapt to the environment. Long-term impact is enhanced where managers address employee concerns as well. These relate to economics and the nurturing process.

GUIDING EMPLOYEES

Organizational guidance to employees traditionally has been provided in two documents: the job description, and the personnel policy and procedure manual, which also may deal with benefit programs. They may or may not be adequate.

Job Descriptions

Personnel policy and procedure manuals produce fewer problems for managers than ambiguity in job definitions and management expectations. Many attempt to minimize potential difficulty through job descriptions. Unfortunately, these usually are generic in nature. They list every task every employee in a given category ever may be called upon to perform. They often conclude with a sentence incorporating the phrase "and other duties as may be assigned." As communication vehicles, job descriptions are all but worthless. They permit terms and conditions of employment to be set and modified by immediate superiors whose actions may not reflect management intentions.

If employees are to succeed, they must have precise definitions of position requirements, which should be expressed as priorities. Each task should be described in detail. Quantitative and qualitative criteria should be provided. It's inadequate, in other words, to tell a janitorial employee his or her primary task is to clean the floor. Minimum acceptable performance must be defined. Employees can be told how many square feet of floor must be cleaned. The word "clean" must be defined. Such words mean different things to different people. Mutual understanding can be accomplished only when standards have been demonstrated—when supervisors can step back and declare, "That's what I mean by clean."

Mutual understandings of job requirements also are a major asset in another way. Among criteria by which employees measure job satisfaction is the ability "to know where I stand." Those denied such knowledge are prone to become dissatisfied and less productive. Clarity in job requirements gives employees performance standards for their own use as well as management's.

Policy and Procedure Manuals

Policy and procedure or personnel manuals usually are introduced during orientation processes. They historically have been dedicated more to controlling policy abusers than to inspiring conscientious employees. Many therefore have become unnecessarily negative in tone. A relative few are striking exceptions. Among them are the policies and procedures of Burson-Marsteller, the world's largest counseling firm. Separated into policy and procedure sections, the Burson-Marsteller policy manual covers the following topics:

PERSONNEL POLICIES
    Equal opportunity
    Appearance
    Personnel Records
    Recruiting/Talent Search Award
    Confirmation Letter/Employee Agreement
    Relocation
    Performance Appraisals
    Resignations
    Exit Interviews
    Reference Checks/Credit Checks
    Severance Pay
    Pay and Overtime
    Education Reimbursement
    Claims Against Employees' Salaries
    Holidays
    Vacation
    Sick Time
    Attendance Bonus Plan
    Jury Duty
    Unpaid Leaves of Absence
    Sign-In Sheets

OPERATING PROCEDURES
   Legal Procedures
   Confidentiality
   Financial Public Relations
   Signing of Contracts
   Time Recording Procedures
   Expense Reports
   Travel
   Non-Reimbursed Expenses
   Gifts
   Press Relations
   Articles Written for Publication
   External Speaking Opportunities
   Outside Business Positions/Free-lancing by Employees
   Endorsements to Media and Suppliers
   Releases and Agreements
   Free-Lancers
   Use of Employees as Talent
   Purchasing Production Materials
   Prohibited Practices
   Subscriptions to Publications
   Private Club Use
   Operating Aircraft
   Public Service Activities*

The potential range of personnel policy/procedure manual content is almost limitless. It is governed by the needs of individual organizations. Periodic policy and procedure reviews are advisable. They are especially necessary where organizations are growing rapidly and while statutory requirements are in a state of flux.

Legal Risks

More and more judges are viewing these documents as employment contracts. Employers are being held liable for promises made, implied or implicit. Similar problems have arisen through court rulings giving employees proprietary interests in their jobs. The employee may in part "own" the job.

Corporate public relations organizations' legal departments presumably have reviewed personnel manuals to guard against such difficulties. Counselors should be aware that pitfalls exist and act accordingly. Periodic legal review of documents pertaining to employee-employer relationships is advisable.

Note: Reprinted by permission.

Employment Contracts

Legal interpretation of employee handbooks need not be a source of employer problems. Contracts of sorts always have existed between employer and employee. Employees agree to provide specific services to employers in return for specified wages and benefits. Difficulty has arisen from two sources.

The first has been employer attempts to perpetuate vestiges of paternalism in wage/benefit systems. Holidays, sick leave, and other "benefits" harken back to an era in which employers were socially obligated to care for employees for life.

The second source of difficulty is benefit system distortion arising out of efforts to control abuse. These have been especially prevalent in sick leave, absenteeism, tardiness, and the like. Employees, it seems, long ago set aside any obligations to which they once were socially committed.

Interpretation of employee-employer relationships as contractual is not necessarily contrary to employer interests. It creates an opportunity to rectify inequities tradition has made part of those relationships. Employment contracts can become part of the process.

Employment contracts have been used in public relations to protect against loss of business should employees be tempted to depart with clients. While perhaps less than ethical, such events have not been uncommon.

Legal Precedents

Considerable legal precedent upholds the validity of employment contracts within reasonable limitations. The latter arise from court rulings that employees may not contract away their rights to earn a livelihood. Employment contracts have been held legal where noncompete clauses are considered "reasonable." The reasonableness yardstick has been applied to duration, geographic limitations, and the scope of other provisions. Other sensitive areas include limitations on rights to solicit former employers' clients, prospective clients, and former clients. Employment contracts have been upheld where limited to less than five years, a geographic radius of no more than 100 miles, and clients and those under active solicitation.

The foregoing applies primarily but not necessarily to counseling organizations. Where employee "pirating" is common, employers have become concerned over former employees' ability to convey "trade secrets" to competitors. Contracts have been written to limit information transfer, but with limited effectiveness. Breach of a nonsolicitation clause can be proven in some circumstances. Breach of confidence is another matter. In the absence of tangible evidence, such as stolen documents, employers must prove information involved could have been received from no other source.

Burson-Marsteller, on the reverse side of the firm's employment application, provides the following agreement that successful applicants are asked to sign upon accepting employment:

Acceptance of Employment

I, _____accept employment by Burson-Marsteller and I understand that my starting compensation will be at the rate of $__ (monthly) (yearly).

I further attest to the accuracy of all information I have recorded on the "Burson-Marsteller Employment Application" form.

I hereby agree that in consideration of my employment by Burson-Marsteller I will hold in trust and confidence all information disclosed to me which relates to any and all entities (commonly referred to as "clients") for whom Burson-Marsteller may at any time provide services. Such confidential information shall include, but shall not be limited to, all information disclosed to me by clients or Burson-Marsteller which relates to clients' past, present and future research, development and business activities and the result of my work as it pertains to clients, excepting such information as is now known to me or is publicly disclosed either prior or subsequent to the disclosure to me and except such information as the client may release in writing from this prohibition. Upon termination of my employment, I shall return to Burson-Marsteller all written or descriptive material relating to clients including but not limited to marketing plans, media schedules, conference reports, copy, drawings, blueprints, artwork, descriptions or other papers or documents which contain any such information.

I will not, at any time during my employment and during a period of six (6) months immediately following termination of my employment, directly or indirectly, for myself or for or on behalf of any other person, firm, corporation or other entity, solicit any client of Burson-Marsteller to become an advertising or public relations client of anyone other than Burson-Marsteller, nor will I during the aforesaid period of time render any such advertising or public relations services, directly or indirectly, to or for any person, firm, corporation or other entity which has been a client of Burson-Marsteller at any time during a period of six (6) months immediately preceding my termination.

I further agree to prohibit the use of my title and Burson-Marsteller affiliation along with my name as any visual, verbal or printed matter of non-commercial organizations or ad hoc groups especially as they might relate to political or other organizations not operated for profit without the specific consent of Burson-Marsteller's Board of Directors.

In further consideration of my employment herein acknowledged, I hereby authorize Burson-Marsteller, its agents, successor and assigns, to use, reproduce and publish photographs or films or video tapes taken of me for Burson-Marsteller or promotional activities of clients including advertising or public relations services in all its forms.*

Signature _____
Date _____

As in other matters dealing with employee-employer relationships, legal

Note: Reprinted by permission.

advice is essential. Corporate managers should seek assistance in their legal departments. Counselors should call on their attorneys.

CAREER DEVELOPMENT

A new era in career development is taking shape. It is being created by a new generation of employees and their demands for personal growth. It arises out of organizational needs to maintain employee knowledge and skill levels. Impetus may be added, however, by increasing interest in licensure and certification in public relations.

At lease three separate organizations were studying licensure and certification in the late 1980s. The Public Relations Society of America, which took no action subsequent to a study in the 1960s, was considering a second look at the subject. The society's Counselor Academy also was preparing a study of prospective licensure of public relations firms. An independent committee chaired by public relations pioneer Edward Bernays was developing model legislation for introduction in the legislatures of the several states. The Bernays Committee was committed to licensure, certification, and significantly higher educational standards for entry level and senior practitioners.

The Process

Career development is a process undertaken by organizations and employees for mutual benefit. Employers' interests are enhanced employee and organizational effectiveness, minimal obsolescence, and reduced turnover and personnel costs. Employees' interests are in career growth and rewards that growth implies. In the "age of information," with the "half-life" of knowledge ever-declining in duration, career development is growing in importance.

As with human organisms and organizations, careers proceed through identifiable phases. They have been characterized as exploration, establishment, maintenance, and decline. Each creates specific needs as to career patterns, which vary in individuals. The variables include technical competence, managerial competence, security, creativity, and independence. In combination with organizational needs, they are applied in a matching process to guide career development programs. Organizational needs include staffing, growth and development, planning for the individual's maintenance phase, and planning for restaffing with his or her decline.

Four Developmental Approaches

Career development programs involve one or more of four processes. In order of frequency of use, they are individual activities, supervisory coaching, group activities, and formal career counseling.

Individual Activities

Personal readings and professional meetings and seminars constitute the bulk of individual activities. Few employers fund formal educational programs for employees although the number has been growing.

Where employers fund formal education, several restrictions often apply. Most common is a requirement that courses involved be "job-related." Others base reimbursement on academic grades and obligate employees to repay sums involved should they resign within predetermined times.

Funding personal readings and professional meetings varies in similar fashion. Larger organizations often maintain professional libraries. Many fund employee participation in professional organizations and their continuing education activities. Smaller units require employees to shoulder these burdens, a less-than-desirable approach where the half-life of knowledge rapidly is declining.

Supervisory Coaching

Supervisory coaching occurs to some extent in most organizations. Quality and quantity usually vary with supervisory accountability for unit performance and the skills of those involved. More progressive organizations often turn to colleges and universities for assistance.

Group Activities

Group activities or internal classes tend to be limited to larger public relations organizations. They long have existed in national and international counseling firms such as Burson-Marsteller, which numbers its personnel complement in the thousands. These activities are so intensive the firm recruits professional personnel from such disciplines as English and the social sciences. Education and training in public relations are provided internally.

Career Counseling

Career counseling also is becoming prevalent among larger organizations and in public relations units of major corporations. Small firms largely are without both group activities and career counseling.

Rewards

Appropriate rewards must accompany professional progress. Even junior practitioners can be given responsibility, as counselor Ann Klein told the 1986 Spring PRSA Counselor Academy meeting in Phoenix, and rewards for performance quickly should be forthcoming. Even a good month can be recognized with a bonus.

PERFORMANCE EVALUATION

Evaluating employee performance is a multifaceted process of marginal value in many organizations. Problems arise from evaluation systems and application of data they produce. Many organizations accurately call the exercise merit review. "Merit" defies measurement and "review" implies no further action. Systemic failure is compounded by the absence of supervisory accountability. This results in tendencies to grant all-but-identical "above average" ratings regardless of employee performance. The latter tendency is compounded by human preference to avoid conflict. Confrontation can develop out of more candid evaluation or resultant impacts on wage increases.

Creating Successful Systems

Successful performance evaluation systems exist where both employee and supervisor/evaluator compensation are involved. Mutual interest dampens tendencies toward emotionalism. Given such a system, evaluation variables are readily controlled.

Variables

In addition to evaluators, variables include criteria for evaluation, timing of the process, and techniques applied. Effective criteria must be performance-related, significant in context with organizational objectives, amenable to measurement, and understood by evaluator and employee at the start of the period in which performance is to be evaluated.

Evaluation Devices

A number of mechanical evaluation devices are available, including graphic rating scales as well as forced choice, essay, management by objective, and checklist systems. Each may be applied by one or more evaluators. Mechanics are less significant than criteria in governing the process. Evaluations should be based on job requirements and performance standards. The latter must be behaviorally based and understood by employees. Measurement scales should be brief and logical. The system should be validated, and an appeal mechanism provided. Abstract traits such as "attitude," "friendliness," and so on, should be avoided.

Given these criteria, performance evaluation—as opposed to merit review—can be simply handled. As few as six to eight primary criteria amenable to quantitative and qualitative measurement may be specified on priority bases for each employee. Where rewards are based on performance and supervisor-evaluator's rewards are based on unit performance, systems function.

Other Systems

More sophisticated systems involving performance tests, field review techniques, and the like may be logical or desirable in larger organizations. They are inappropriate in most public relations organizations.

COMPENSATION SYSTEMS

Compensation systems must meet several criteria to succeed. They must be fair, effective, and perceived as such by organization members. These objectives are realizable where rewards are equitably allocated.

Defining Terms

Effectiveness in compensation systems is a product of several factors, including adequacy, equity, balance, cost effectiveness, incentive, and security. Some of these terms require elaboration. "Balance" refers to the total reward package, including wages and benefits. "Cost effectiveness" implies compensation levels are satisfactory to employees and within employers' means. "Security" suggests compensation levels are adequate to meet employee needs that wages satisfy.

Comparable Wages

Equity is produced by establishing comparability of wage rates with those paid for similar jobs in other enterprises, different jobs in the same enterprise, and the same job within the same enterprise. The standards are not uniformly applicable. In smaller organizations, there may be only one individual in a specific capacity. In larger organizations, seniority may play a part. Compensation levels also may be influenced by organizational adoption of one of three wage strategies: high pay level, low pay level, and comparable pay level.

Wage Strategies

High-pay-level strategies involve paying somewhat higher wages than prevail in the market. They assume the organization will attract and retain better personnel. Low-level strategies are found where resources are limited or management seeks high short-term profits. The comparable pay strategy is a "match the competition" approach.

Bases for Compensation

Whichever approach is used, there must be a beginning point for determining compensation levels. Most plans are based on variation in job requirements. They include education, skill, effort, responsibility, and job conditions.

One of four basic evaluation systems usually is applied in calculating relative worth of jobs. Two are nonquantitative: the ranking or job comparison system and the grade description system. The others are quantitative, using point or factor comparison structures.

Ranking. Ranking systems are most suitable in smaller organizations. They are simple to use but have serious disadvantages: They do not show how far apart jobs are in content or difficulty; and perhaps more serious, they provide no means for recording evidence to support ratings.

Grades. Grade description systems are exemplified in the U.S. Civil Service System. Fixed written scales are used to compare jobs but grade descriptions are imprecise. In addition, the method provides no mechanism with which to weight factors involved in each job.

Points. The point system is most popular in the United States. It is more complex yet more precise. Eight to twelve factors usually are selected for inclusion in evaluation processes. Points are assigned to each based on degree. For example, were experience to be a factor, one point might be awarded for one year's service, two for two years' service, and so forth until a predetermined maximum is reached. The sum of the points then determines job worth in comparison to other jobs. The system has multiple advantages, among which are relative precision and documentation. It is difficult to install and maintain, however, and thus relatively expensive.

Factors. The factor comparison system is a combination of ranking and point systems. It is applied primarily to managers and professionals but can be used to grade others as well. Factor comparison yields points that can be converted directly into dollars. To this extent, the system is more analytical than the point approach. Results usually are applied in terms of existing wage rates. Since jobs change, errors may develop over time.

Shared weaknesses. All of the systems share several weaknesses. First, they establish direct or indirect limits on compensation levels. Employees who reach these limits have no incentive for further effort. Second, most impose fixed wage ranges, ignoring a broad range of capacities within individuals. Third, they assume performance will be rewarded with wage increases. These are permanent by definition. No provision is made for a variation in performance over extended periods; for the deterioration that, for example, may come with age. A compensation strategy with more flexibility is needed. In recent years, it has been developing in a few organizations.

A New Approach

The new strategy developed from increased pressure for productivity. Called "performance-based compensation," it is designed to encourage and reward productive employees. The system proceeds from the premise that compensation will be increased only to the extent employees exceed "minimum acceptable performance." It assumes "across-the-board" wage increments will be used only to maintain employee purchasing power in the face of inflation. All other rewards become a function of performance or productivity. They usually are granted as bonuses rather than wage increments. The latter are permanent and lead to the "what have you done for me lately" syndrome. The former are nonrecurring unless performance levels are maintained or improved upon.

Defining Performance

Proceeding from this point is difficult for manager and employee alike. Managers are required to specify their expectations of employees. Employees are required to meet expectations to move up the economic scale. Despite potential for difficulty, leaders in employee relations are incorporating the new concept into their performance appraisal systems.

Federal Express Corporation, for example, combines established performance parameters with managerially designed factors (see Figure 15.1). Established parameters for professionals relate to professional capabilities, leadership skills, personal qualities, and work output characteristics. As many as six managerially designed criteria may be added to two established criteria in the latter category.

Federal Express also directs performance appraisers to work with subordinates in improving their productivity. A "Performance Planner" is part of the discussion guide for this purpose (see Figure 15.2).

Managers' primary difficulty in implementing a productivity-based system occurs in specifying performance criteria, which only appear difficult to develop. The "product" of individuals in a public relations organization is difficult to measure. There are adequate relative if not absolute performance indicators available.

An Example

Consider, for example, the work of a typical account executive. Duties under the consultant model essentially are identical regardless of organizations involved. Client satisfaction is the primary performance criterion. It can be measured through periodic performance evaluations, which should be used in any event as a quality control device. Specific criteria might include timely completion of projects, level of creativity as perceived by clients, and indicators of results used in reporting to clients.

Timely delivery can be measured in the abstract. Client perceptions defy measurement. Evaluation must be based on relative rather than abstract data. Satisfaction levels for Period A are averaged across clients the employee serves and compared with like data for Period B.

Performance of support personnel, given adequate definition of duties

FIGURE 15.1.

	Outstanding	Well Above Satisfactory	Above Satisfactory	Satisfactory	Below Satisfactory	Well Below Satisfactory	Weak	Not Observed
	7	6	5	4	3	2	1	0

Importance Rating:

7. **Written Communications:** How effectively this person produces written material which is clear, concise, brief, and shows logical thought progression.

II. LEADERSHIP SKILLS

7	6	5	4	3	2	1	0

8. **Project Leadership and Coordination:** How effectively this person operates independently in delegating work to peers and coordinating the work of others when given project or assignment leadership responsibility.

7	6	5	4	3	2	1	0

9. **Promoting Group Teamwork and Motivation:** How effectively this person maintains and promotes positive work performance within/between departments regardless of the position or status of others and in both favorable and unfavorable or conflict situations.

7	6	5	4	3	2	1	0

10. **Public/Customer/Client/User Relationships:** How effectively this person handles complaints about services, promotes services, promotes the company and department, determines and understands the needs of others, and makes forceful efforts to cooperate.

III. PERSONAL QUALITIES

7	6	5	4	3	2	1	0

11. **Behavior Flexibility:** How effectively this person adapts behavior and approaches and controls emotion under the demands of time, multiple assignments, opposition, and changing priorities and directions.

7	6	5	4	3	2	1	0

12. **Dependability and Initiative:** How effectively this person performs routine job functions such as compiling and maintaining reports/records/documentation, follows through on assignments, requires the appropriate level of supervision, recognizes the needs for action and assumes responsibility without prompting.

Federal Express Corporation Individual Progress Discussion Guide.
Reprinted by permission.

270

FIGURE 15.2.

PERFORMANCE PLANNER

NAME _____

In this section of the Individual Progress Discussion Review, you are to work with your staff member in order to provide a developmental plan which is designed to improve areas of performance concern noted in your description of the staff member's performance (Step II). Areas of greatest concern would be those you rated as "regular parts of the job" in which the employee rated three or below. In addition, you will want to alert your staff member to areas you feel would be important in preparing this employee for future career opportunities.

Performance areas where improvement is needed (you may wish to consider only those categories where importance exceeds 3 and performance is rated less than Satisfactory).	Knowledge, skills or abilities that must be developed to result in the improvement.	Developmental Activities/ Assignments. These are activities you and the staff member plan to address the area of needed experience.	Projected Implementation date (month/ year).	Projected Completion date (month/ year).

Federal Express Corporation Performance Planner.
Reprinted by permission.

271

and responsibilities when they are employed, is more easily accomplished. How accurately is their work completed? On how timely a basis? With how many revisions necessary? Within budgetary parameters? Potential for criteria development is limitless. Only one universal requirement exists: Each must be mutually understood and agreed upon by managers and subordinates.

Mutual Benefits

Agreement is reached with relative ease where systems apply to all employees. Managers' incentives then are based on the sum of unit productivity. Their rewards become dependent on subordinates' performance. The system virtually guarantees managerial/supervisory fairness and equity in dealing with personnel. Tendencies toward favoritism or discriminatory conduct disappear as self-interest is engaged.

Managerial Control

This especially is true where managers delegate reward authority to supervisors within predetermined parameters. For example, $5,000 may be allocated to a unit for bonuses in a specified period. Supervisors may be given an upper limit in terms of bonus size but no others should apply. They then are faced with having to allocate the $5,000 on the basis of performance. Management can be certain the job will be done with exquisite care. Failure to distribute rewards in keeping with productivity would tend to reduce productivity in subsequent periods. Since unit productivity is the basis for supervisory rewards, skillful handling of the mechanism is assured. Management may be asked for—and should provide—any training that supervisors may need in handling the system. Nothing more should be required.

The philosophy underlying the approach is simple: Reward those who produce; deny rewards in the absence of productivity. Diligently applied the system produces an organization in which fewer employees earn higher wages. In other words, two highly productive employees can and should be paid far better than three drones. If the wages of the three were totaled and divided between the two productive employees, organizational profits necessarily would increase. The cost of most organizations' fringe benefit packages is about 30 percent of salaries and these funds go "straight to the bottom line."

Systemic Maintenance

Perhaps most important, the system "feeds on itself." It tends to attract the most productive applicants when positions become available. Where managers expand staffs, ample numbers of first-quality candidates apply,. The manager has the luxury of "picking and choosing" and can afford higher-than-average wage rates from the outset.

State of the Art System

Perhaps the most advanced performance appraisal system extant was introduced by Burson-Marsteller in 1986. Called "Job Portfolio Performance Appraisal," the system is designed to measure and reward performance and guide employee development. Its purposes, as specified in the 15-page appraisal document, are to:

1. Insure mutual understanding between staff professionals and Burson-Marsteller management of:
   —Activities that comprise individual employee job responsibilities
   —Personal and professional skills to be developed in preparation for promotion to next level of responsibility
2. Provide periodic documentation of each employee's progress.
3. Facilitate discussion of that progress between employee and the reviewer.
4. Provide planning for strengthening employee's performance.
5. Provide input to management for planning employee's future at B-M.

The Job Portfolio contains some 150 performance criteria in seven categories: professional capabilities, people management, account program management, money management, client management, internal business management, and self-management. Managers select relatively few of these in keeping with the responsibilities of individual employees, according to Burson-Marsteller Executive Vice-President Michael Morris. Each is identified as a "key priority" in the employee's current position or as a capability to be developed in the position. Employees are ranked as outstanding, above average, fully satisfactory, provisional, or not satisfactory only on "key priority" items (see Figure 15.3). A final page is provided on which evaluators summarize results in each category.

The final two pages of the Job Portfolio Performance Appraisal document are devoted to a "Plan for Personal Development." The plan identifies development or improvement areas most important in the ensuing rating period. It specifies how and when this will be accomplished and how results will be measured.

The personal or career development portion also identifies the next position in the Burson-Marsteller organization toward which the employee can work. It specifies training activities that will help him or her reach the specified level, as well as anticipated time of promotion and location involved.

The Burson-Marsteller program thus meets both employee and organizational needs. Systemic productivity necessarily is a function of managerial application rather than document content. Burson-Marsteller assures user commitment by arming evaluators with control over subordinate rewards and applying the same system to evaluators.

FIGURE 15.3.
Burson-Marsteller Job Portfolio Performance Appraisal.

	Job Priority K/D	Perf. Rating O/AA/FS/P/NS
Responsible for day-to-day client administration		
Communicates status of program and client sensibilities		
Keeps client abreast of all plans and consults with client on all aspects of the program		
Responsible for keeping client abreast of all plans and consulting with client on all aspects of the program		
Arbitrates and helps solve client relations problems		
Knows clients' business including buying influences, chain of distribution, key markets, technologies, customer base, competition and relevant media		
Knows clients' corporate needs, including financial relations, positioning, public affairs, media, internal communications		
Keeps abreast of outside issues and events and brings these to B-M and client		
Analyzes client's marketing situation and pinpoints key marketing problems and opportunities		
Challenges client when required		
Shows innovation/fresh ideas/creative solutions beyond clients' ideas		
Knows critical decision maker at client contact		
Responsible for senior client contact and counseling		
Maintains regular business contact with senior client management		
Maintains social contact with client personnel		
Attentive to client "personal side" (birthdays, children, hobbies)		
Helps client contact attain career goals		

Overall Rating & Comments

_____

_____

_____

Dealing with Obstacles

Considerable variation exists among managers in their ability to implement performance-based compensation systems. Proprietors of counseling firms have near-total latitude; corporate managers must operate within organizational policy. They can establish informal reward structures, however, to create incentives. Preferred assignments can be reserved for those with superior performance records. So can choices of vacation dates and other perquisites. The latter include convention trips, preferred office locations, and the like.

An even stronger set of incentives can be created through managerial delegation of responsibility and authority. Delegation usually is relatively unrestricted by corporate policy. It can be an intangible reward of great magnitude and a major incentive to further effort. It is especially useful where employees aspire to promotion.

Management talent must be identified early in any event, as the Chester Burger Company's Albert Geduldig points out. When candidates have been identified, responsibility, plans for the future, and rewards must be shared with them. The reward system thus can further organizational development.

Corporate managers also can enrich subordinates' intangible rewards by permitting greater contact with top management, as in presentation of their ideas in person or by endorsed memoranda. The possibilities are near limitless and mutually rewarding to the parties involved.

Managers operate with a variety of compensation systems. Most are imposed in corporate situations and large counseling firms. They usually are based on complex wage scales designed to maintain differentials between jobs. They suffer in that wage increments usually are limited by the structures involved. "Ceilings" exist that discourage exceptional performers. Managers have no choice but to comply. They nevertheless can enhance unit performance using nonmonetary rewards.

Avoiding Inequities

Regardless of the basic system, one question remains concerning job applicants: How much shall they initially be paid? Salaries always are negotiable, excessive demands must be resisted, even at the risk of losing a prospective "star." It is not unusual for new employees to "sign on" at rates higher than those paid their peers. Periodic reviews should be undertaken to identify and eliminate discrepancies.

EMPLOYEE BENEFITS

Benefits are an important component of compensation systems. They are valuable to employees and costly to employers. Whether they retain all their early importance among elements that attract and retain personnel is another question.

Employee and Employer Perspectives

Contemporary thought suggests nurturing environments will be employees' major concern during the 1990s and beyond; benefits may rank second. Considerable change may occur, however, in the relative attractiveness of benefits. This may arise out of tax law changes. Any action to make benefits taxable to employees, for example, would have a major impact. Emerging preferences for nurturing environments suggests that educational benefits— subject to tax concerns—may move higher on employees' preference lists. Employer concerns also have a bearing, however, on benefit packages. Since the 1980s, employers have become sensitive to escalating employee costs. Increases were created by over-use of health-care benefits and abuses in other areas.

Against this backdrop, many began reviewing benefit policies. Health-care programs were first impacted. Many previously wholly funded by employers were made participatory. Second opinions often were made mandatory prior to elective surgery. In others, greater percentages of costs were shifted to employees in the absence of second opinions.

Employers also reexamined absenteeism and tardiness costs. Liberal policies were tightened. "Universal leave" plans were adopted to supplant vacation time, holidays, sick leave, and other "time paid but not worked." Formulae often were established whereby leave time accrued on the basis of hours worked, further limiting employer liability.

Traditional Benefit Plans

In addition to pay for time not worked, employees in the United States amassed many other benefits during the latter years of the twentieth century. Among the more significant are:

1. Employee services
   A. Cafeterias
   B. Child care facilities
   C. Parking facilities
   D. Recreation facilities
   E. Product/service discounts
2. Health care programs
   A. Hospitalization
   B. Medical/surgical payments
   C. Paid sick leave
   D. Accident insurance

E. Dental care
F. Vision care
3. Other benefits
A. Pensions
B. Contributions to savings plans
C. Supplemental unemployment benefits
D. Separation pay
E. Guaranteed wages
F. Auto insurance
G. Homeowners insurance
H. Profit-sharing programs
I. Holiday gifts/bonuses
J. Service awards
K. Educational benefits
L. Prepaid legal services
M. Counseling services
N. Tax-deferred annuities

The list could go on. Most estimate total benefit costs at 30 to 40 percent of gross wages for the average employee.

Extent of benefits varies with several factors. They include cost and ability to pay, competitive factors, and tax/purchasing power considerations. The latter have been significant in that "bulk purchasing" can create savings for employees. Group insurance rates, for example, are lower than individual rates.

Taxes enter the equation because benefits traditionally have been tax-free to both employer and employee. Employers' pay in pretax dollars and benefit value need not be shown on employee tax returns. These circumstances may or may not continue. Costs inevitably will continue to increase, however, and will add to the popularity of a new benefit approach.

Flexible Benefit Plans

Many organizations have installed flexible or "cafeteria" benefit programs together with universal leave plans, which were designed to meet changing social patterns. Employees earn credits applicable to a broad range of optional benefits. In two-breadwinner households, fixed benefit plans produced expensive duplication of benefits such as health insurance.

Types of Benefits

Employee benefits may be mandatory or optional. Legally mandated are unemployment compensation, government retirement programs, and workman's compensation. Optional plans can be subdivided into those wholly paid by employers, those handled on participatory bases, and those funded exclusively by employees. The latter often include tax-sheltered annuity and optional group insurance plans. Employer-paid and jointly funded programs include life and health insurance, private pension, and retirement plans.

Benefits also may include educational programs, financial services such as credit unions, social and recreational programs, child care centers, prepaid legal services, counseling services, and group auto insurance.

Corporate Benefits

Corporate practitioners often enjoy more benefits than their counselor colleagues. Scope of counselor benefit programs usually is a function of organizational size.

Corporate managers and practitioners have little influence over benefit program design. For counselor firm principals, the reverse is true. Changing federal tax laws and competitive factors require their continuing attention.

Advantages in employer sponsorship arise out of tax benefits or group rates. If costs become taxable to employees, counselors may find employees will prefer cash to benefits. Unless organizations can develop "cafeteria" approaches at reasonable cost, combinations of larger paychecks and smaller benefit packages might best serve all involved.

"Cafeteria" Plans

Cafeteria plans offer a broader range of benefits than traditionally is available. They permit individuals to select those they prefer. The result is greater employee satisfaction per benefit dollar expended. As first developed, cafeteria plans were designed to meet employee needs or desires without increasing employer costs.

The rationale is simple. Young employees are disinterested in retirement plans. Older employees and singles are not interested in maternity benefits. In multiple-wage-earner households, benefits may be duplicated, a problem that is compounded in health insurance plans. Policies almost invariably include "coordination of benefit" clauses. They require insurers to share claim costs where individuals are covered by two policies. Both employers pay premiums; employees receive no greater benefits. Only insurance carriers "win."

In cafeteria plans, benefits other than those required by law are optional on the part of the employee. Employers usually offer multiple health insurance plans as well as a "no health insurance" option. They add a broad range of additional coverages, which may include vision, dental, automotive, and even mortgage insurance. On-premises child care, educational benefits, and any other program of interest to employees may be added.

Cafeteria plans also may include "time paid but not worked." Employees automatically receive no paid time off other than for holidays when offices are closed. Dollars involved accrue to their benefit accounts. Into these accounts also flow dollars that otherwise paid for fixed benefits. Employees then use "benefit funds" to "buy" any combination of time off and other benefits they desire. In some cases, benefit dollars may be withdrawn in cash although some must then be used to pay taxes.

Controlling Costs

Employers moving from traditional to cafeteria plans also may install mechanisms to benefit their organizations. Primary among these have been innovative benefit accrual systems. Most provide for benefit dollar accrual on the basis of hours worked—full, 60-minute hours. Accrual rates are based on numbers of hours employees are expected to work on annual bases.

These systems penalize those who fail to work anticipated numbers of hours. Also penalized are those who arrive late or depart early since 60-minute hours are required for accrual. The system thus discourages absenteeism and tardiness.

TERMINATION

The right to terminate employees at will—with or without cause—long has prevailed for employers. As of the mid–1980s, this "right" was deteriorating under legal attack; federal and state courts increasingly were tending to protect "at will" employees. Erosion of management rights began as courts agreed to hear appeals from discharged employees. Some early cases involved "whistle blowing" by personnel who had found their employers were in violation of law or governmental regulation. Others, as the courtroom doors opened wider, were only marginally in the "public policy" arena.

Implied Contracts

From personnel policies, the courts moved into interpretation of statements made during preemployment interviews. They often were viewed as promises; as parts of an implied contract. There also arose a legal theory accepted by the courts that held there is an inherent covenant between the parties requiring all dealings be conducted in good faith.

Termination Procedures

Broadening legal interpretations and legislation requiring "due process" have led managers to become more involved in the termination process. Their involvement focuses on a number of factors, principal among which are authority to terminate, the termination procedure, and documentation of the process.

Documentation

Termination is a process rather than an event; it begins with the employee's first failure to meet conditions of employment. This may have occurred during earlier months or within moments of the manager's decision. As a result, record-keeping is of critical importance. This is the case regardless of termination policy. Policies may require verbal or written notices prior to termination. The written must be filed; the oral must be documented—reduced to writing.

Conflicts

The "paper trails" that courts examine extend into other areas. Performance appraisal, compensation, and other records will be reviewed. Implied or implicit conflicts receive special attention. Employees who have been retained for years despite poor performance and then terminated without apparent cause may well be ordered reinstated.

A Matter of Equity

One further factor requires attention in context with all of the elements considered above: All programs and policies must be equitably applied. Successful organizations universally provide due process for employees. Due process is a legal term; applied organizationally, it means only that equity, fairness, and justice will apply in all employee-employer dealings. In most organizations it requires a formal process to be established, although these vary in complexity.

Better-designed policies share several features—two are especially important. First, the initial step in appeal procedures does not require employees to consult supervisors. They often are part of the problem. Moreover, employees perceive they will have to continue to "live with the supervisor" win or lose. Suppression of legitimate complaints often is the result.

Second, the process should provide for a terminal step that assures employees that management will tolerate no misconduct among middle managers. Some organizations establish external arbitration as an ultimate step. In others—even companies as large as Federal Express Corporation—the employee can appeal all the way to the chief executive officer. The mechanism is less important than employee perceptions of its effectiveness and of management's commitment to justice.

IN SUMMARY

Developing nurturing environments for personnel will be one of managers' primary challenges through the early years of the twenty-first century. They will find it essential to create strong organizational cultures in the face of competitive problems.

Personnel policies and procedures, career development programs, and other factors will have to contribute to the nurturing environment. So will evaluation and compensation systems and benefit programs.

Each can be a strength or a weakness. Contemporary policy and procedure documents often cause problems. The absence of career development opportunities also produces difficulties. Greatest existing weaknesses arise in terms of equity in performance appraisal and compensation systems.

Performance appraisal is all but lacking in many organizations. Compensation systems fail to reward performing employees. With corrective action in these areas and an employee-oriented benefit program, the public relations unit will be positioned to meet any competitive challenge.

ADDITIONAL READING

Cascio, Wayne F. *Managing Human Resources: Productivity, Quality of Work Life, Profits.* New York: McGraw-Hill, 1986.

Ellig, Bruce R. *Compensation & Benefits: Design and Analysis.* Scottsdale, Ariz.: American Compensation Association, 1985.

Fear, Richard A. *The Evaluation Interview*, 3rd ed. New York: McGraw-Hill, 1984.

Johnson, Robert G. *The Appraisal Interview Guide.* New York: AMACOM, 1979.

Kellogg, Marion S. *What to Do About Performance Appraisal.* New York: AMACOM, 1975.

Lefton, Robert E. et al., *Effective Motivation Through Performance Appraisal.* New York: John Wiley, 1977.

McCaffery, Robert M. *Managing the Employee Benefits Program.* New York: AMACOM, 1972.

Milkovich, George T., and Jerry M. Newman. *Compensation.* Plano, Tex.: Business Publications, 1984.

16

Public Relations and the Law

The practices of law and public relations come together in multiple situations. More often than not, they involve mutual clients. In an increasingly litigation-prone society, however, public relations practitioners find themselves calling on attorneys for counsel concerning their own practices. Managers most often seek legal counsel in four areas. The first occurs chronologically during the founding of public relations practices. The second involves relationships between organizations and three constituencies: employees, clients, and vendors. The third deals with an assortment of legal constraints, including copyright, ownership, and use of illustrative materials, and related items. The fourth involves multiple taxes and licenses with which practitioners must deal.

ESTABLISHING THE PRACTICE

Public relations practice, like most endeavors, creates benefits and risks, both of which are economic. They vary with the legal form of the enterprise. Most counselor firms are sole proprietorships, partnerships, or corporations, although benefits produced by the forms at times are combined.

Sole Proprietorships

The sole proprietorship legally is the simplest organizational configuration. It is individually owned and practitioners personally undertake attendant risks, which can be considerable. There are benefits, but most consider them too few to offset the risks.

Risks

Most risks in sole proprietorships are economic. Owners or their estates are liable for debts. Personal assets are at risk in connection with judgments against the business. The latter risks may be the greater, because potential for litigation involving practitioners is considerable. Juries have been liberal in damage awards. Insurance has increased in cost and become more difficult to obtain.

Benefits

Simplicity is the primary benefit of the sole proprietorship. Initial legal expenses are lower than in other situations. Accounting costs are reduced. Profits or losses are the proprietors'; they file only individual income tax returns.

Many professionals launch practices as sole proprietorships. Few elect to continue indefinitely in this form because of risks involved and/or benefits derived from other legal forms.

Partnerships

Other than in corporate form, partnerships may be least desirable among organizational formats. Potential for noneconomic difficulty is greater than in other circumstances.

Risks

Partnerships are as vulnerable to risk as sole proprietorships. Further problems tend to develop from disagreements between partners, which can be destructive to personal relationships. They also can be fatal to businesses in the absence of complex legal safeguards. Expressed in partnership agreements, these usually are more complex and costly than traditional corporate documents.

Benefits

Perhaps the only benefit of the informal partnership is ease of creation. Two or more individuals can agree to operate as partners and proceed to do so—nothing more is necessary. Difficulties, both personal and legal, arise later.

Many public relations firms are established as partnerships. More frequently than not, they become corporations. The corporation provides personal economic protection but creates no barrier to personal problems. As constant change among counselor organizations demonstrates, partners disagree as frequently in public relations as in other professions.

Corporations

Legal and economic protection provided by corporations make them the most popular organizational format among counselors. The corporate form can be used by sole proprietorships and partnerships as well as in circumstances involving many shareholders.

Risks

The only significant risk created in the corporate form involves minority owners. No individual, it has been said, is quite so powerless as a minority shareholder in a closely held corporation. The term "closely held" refers to corporations in which stock is not publicly traded. Minority owners who wish to sell seldom find it possible to dispose of their holdings. They also are powerless to influence corporate direction.

Benefits

The primary attribute of the corporation is its legal standing as a "person." Legal judgments against corporations in most cases are not collectible from shareholders. Corporate debts are not personal debts.

Offsetting these benefits are greater costs and, perhaps, greater tax liabilities. Corporate tax returns must be prepared and filed even where owners elect "Subchapter S" status. The latter option enables corporations to "pass through" profits or losses to shareholders who pay applicable taxes.

Hybrids

A majority of public relations organizations are hybrids. Most are sole proprietorships or partnerships that have adopted the corporate form for any of several reasons. Primary among them, other than legal protection, are potential tax savings.

Tax Advantages

Over the years, multiple advantages have accrued to those who use the corporate form. Some involve using pretax dollars to provide benefits that individuals have to buy with after-tax dollars. Examples include educational benefits for owners and their dependents and liberal company-paid health insurance benefits. Others include a variety of tax shelters.

"Self-Employment"

Those who can be categorized as "self-employed" also have been able to take advantage of Keogh Plans. These are retirement programs similar to Individual Retirement Accounts (IRAs) but are available only to the self-employed. They are free to use IRAs as well.

Since tax laws constantly are changing, practitioners should consult attorneys and/or accountants as to these and other dollar-saving devices currently available.

Protective Devices

Where partnerships are constituted as corporations, several legal safeguards should be considered. Most significant are "buy-sell agreements" and other devices designed to limit stock ownership to founders and/or those they designate.

Buy-Sell Agreements

Buy-sell agreements are created to guard against two eventualities. First and most common is a falling out among partners. The second is the death of a partner. Buy-sell agreements limit the manner in which ownership interests can change hands.

In the event of disagreement, most require those seeking to sell first to offer their shares to the corporation or other shareholders. These agreements also may directly or indirectly govern selling prices, which usually are limited in one of two ways. The first involves specific formulae established by owners, often based on the book value of corporate stock. Where this system is used, corporate by-laws require shareholders to restate values periodically.

The second is based on "market value." This method permits owners to offer their shares for sale. The corporation or other stockholders hold an option to preempt any transaction by acquiring the stock at the best price offered.

Inheritance Provisions

A price formula approach also may be used where owners decide to keep corporate stock out of their estates. This device prevents surviving owners from being forced into partnership with heirs. It usually is specified in a buy-sell agreement and requires the deceased's stock be sold to the corporation or remaining stockholders. The provision may be another "first option" arrangement or it may be mandatory.

Where purchase by the corporation or surviving shareholders is mandatory, additional terms and conditions, usually designed to prevent economic hardships, may be attached. They may permit purchase over an extended period of time or authorize payment over a like period at below-market interest rates.

Buy-sell agreements also may include mechanisms to resolve stockholder conflicts. They are most applicable in partnerships cast in corporate form. Where disputes require dissolution of partnerships, one partner sets a "buy or sell" price. The other has the option to buy his partner's shares or sell his own.

An almost limitless number of variations is possible. Competent legal and accounting counsel is essential.

EMPLOYEES, CLIENTS, AND VENDORS

Laws and regulations governing public relations practice change from day to day. Change continues even when neither federal nor state legislative bodies are in session. Civil laws are implemented through regulations and procedures established by federal and/or state agencies. Court decisions also modify statutes and requirements of regulatory and administrative bodies. Competent legal counsel is vital to those who would avoid pitfalls involved. This especially is true as to relationships between public relations organizations and their clients, vendors, and employees. They are governed primarily by federal law and state statute, although "common law" and trade practices in some circumstances may be equally binding.

Client Relationships

Relationships between counselors and clients should be reduced to contractual form. Counselors' obligations are not limited, however, by such contracts. A number of more-or-less generic duties and obligations are produced by the basic agency relationship. Attorneys consider them to include the following.

Conflict of interest. Conflict of interest situations are prohibited by law under definitions of agency. They also are barred by the code of ethics of the Public Relations Society of America. The code refers primarily to serving clients whose interests may be in conflict. Legal constraints also bar counselors from ownership interests in vendor organizations. These restrictions legally can be eliminated only by prior knowledge and consent of all involved.

Financial responsibility. Public relations organizations almost inevitably purchase materials and services for clients. These items remain client property subject to any contractual conditions. Counselor organizations thus serve as clients' trustees. They are responsible for protecting and preserving clients' property and for its delivery to clients on termination of relationships. Special conditions apply where photography, printing, and other materials are involved. Photographers' negatives, printers' negatives and plates, and similar items may remain the property of those parties unless other arrangements are made before work begins. Conscientious practitioners frequently make such arrangements as a matter of course. Their clients or employers then own the materials involved.

Confidentiality. Considerable confidential information concerning client activities comes into the possession of public relations practitioners, and they are obligated to safeguard such information. The obligation extends beyond the term of any contract since information, unlike property, can not be returned. The same principle applies to relationships between public relations organizations and their employees.

Accountability. Public relations organizations are accountable for funds conveyed to them by clients. This principle applies specifically to monies transferred as a result of counselor billings to clients. They may produce no hidden benefits or secret profits to counselors. Commissions, rebates, or markups must be remitted to clients in the absence of contrary agreements. Public relations organizations' books and records pertaining to clients must be made available to client accountants on request.

Responsibility. Practitioners must confine their actions within limits imposed by clients. Most contracts specify client approval prior to any undertaking. The legal obligation exists in any event. Where counselors proceed beyond authorized limits, they become liable to litigation. Clients also are free to cancel contracts in these circumstances.

Disclosure. The nature of counselor-client relationships requires practitioners immediately to convey to clients any information that comes to their attention and may influence the client's business. The requirement is not limited to potential conflicts of interest; it applies to all information. For counselor organizations in major media and governmental centers, it can be burdensome.

Contract Provisions

In a booklet entitled "The Management of the Public Relations Firm," published by the Counselor Academy of the PRSA in 1983, Chester Burger recommended that inclusion of a number of provisions be included in contracts between counselors and clients. These included:

1. Minimum charges on hourly or other bases.
2. A "Hold Harmless" clause designed to protect counselors against inadvertent disclosure of inaccurate or incomplete information while providing financial relations services.
3. An arbitration clause to facilitate resolution of any disputes that may arise.
4. A general description of services to be provided by the counselor.
5. An agreement not to hire the counselor's employees.
6. A provision making counselor records available to clients.

Attorney Morton J. Simon listed the following primary components of counselor-client agreements: description of services, payment of fees, payment of staff time and expenses, special project provisions, duration of retainer, client approval and control, assignment of personnel, maintenance of records, and termination provisions. While presenting samples of all of them, he cautioned against use of any of the samples in counselor contracts:

"These suggestions, as with any so-called 'drugstore' or 'form book' forms may be misapplied. They must be used intelligently and consonantly with the needs of the relationship which they are to serve."

Simon's caution should ring true to experienced public relations managers. Attachment of unique meanings to everyday words is a common occurrence in most professions and law is no exception.

Vendor Relationships

Legal requirements arising out of relationships between counselors and vendors they hire in behalf of clients are relatively clear. They fall into two categories: relationships with the mass media and relationships with other vendors.

Where paid advertising is placed by counselors for clients, counselors may be responsible for payment. The words "may be" are appropriate since the agency relationship under common law would leave clients responsible. Counselors may undertake this responsibility by contract with media involved.

In the case of other vendors—printers, graphic designers, and the like—the responsibility ultimately is the client's. The client, in legal terms, is a "disclosed principal." The counselor legally is merely the client's agent in the transaction.

Employee Relationships

Public relations organizations' relationships with employees are growing more complex. These circumstances result in part from the nature of public relations practice but more so from expanding government intervention. Employee turnover constitutes an area of potential damage to counselors since accounts may depart with employees. Legal safeguards can be made a part of employment contracts but these often are of questionable value. Potential difficulties arising in other areas can be equally troublesome.

Litigation based on alleged civil rights violations has been common in recent years. Race and age discrimination cases predominated for a time. More recently, sexual harassment has become a major issue.

Employee rights of privacy and of free speech in the work place also have been a source of litigation. The privacy issue promises to become increasingly troublesome. It has been raised in connection with drug testing and screenings for acquired immune deficiency syndrome (AIDS).

Regulatory Problems

Civil rights litigation is based in federal and state legislation barring discrimination in employment. Most statues involved cover employment and termination practices as well as on-the-job discrimination. In addition, all public relations managers are susceptible to difficulties arising out of regulatory action. Agencies with which managers are most apt to come in contact include:

1. The Securities and Exchange Commission (SEC), which would be most interested in trading on insider information involving a public relations organization's employees.
2. The Occupational Safety and Health Administration, which could become involved in work place violations.
3. The National Labor Relations Board, which guards employees' collective bargaining rights.
4. The Federal Trade Commission (FTC) and the Food & Drug Administration (FDA), which frequently are involved in cases involving misleading public information.

Knowledge Essential

Public relations organizations seldom are involved with regulatory bodies other than in behalf of clients. Practitioners whose work involves regular contact with them should become familiar with their regulations. They also should be familiar with laws governing lobbying or other activities designed to influence legislation. Most states and the federal government require lobbyists to be registered. The process is not burdensome but compliance is essential.

Practitioners' greatest areas of risk relate to the SEC, FTC, and FDA. Several SEC complaints have alleged insider trading on the part of consultants. Most often, SEC challenged securities trading on the basis of information concerning client firms. FTC and FDA problems usually have arisen over allegations concerning release of misleading information concerning client products.

Errors and Omissions

Bernard E. Ury, president of a PRSA Counselor Academy Firm Management Committee, compiled a list of potential legal problems covered by errors and omissions insurance. Clients, third parties, members of the public, and government agencies all may take legal action against the counselor, he said in a presentation of PRSAs 1985 annual meeting in Detroit. Clients may claim:

1. Information was not released on time.
2. Information omitted important data.
3. Information contained data not authorized for release.
4. The entire release was unauthorized by the client.
5. The information was not used by the media or was used to the client's dissatisfaction. (PR firms have no control over use of their material by the media, but an unsophisticated client may not accept this.)

6. Collateral material handled by the firm was not produced or delivered on time.
7. Collateral material contained errors.
8. Collateral material contained data unauthorized for use.
9. The client received counsel that proved to be wrong.
10. The firm exceeded the budget or incurred unauthorized expenses.

Third parties, including a client's employee, supplier, or customer, may sue over:

1. Unauthorized use of the third party's name, likeness, or statement, especially if the statement is a testimonial.
2. Wrong data or statement attributed to the third party.
3. Damage suffered by the third party as a result of being included in a client release, even though the third party approved that use.

A member of the public may sue on the basis of acting on information contained in material prepared by the public relations firm [Ury continued]. Such actions can include buying a security or a product that turned out to be unsatisfactory. Or a price contained in a press release may be out of date by the time the release is published by the media, and the customer sues because he/she can't buy at the new price.

Finally, there are the actions government (local, state, federal) may take against a PR firm on the basis of material distributed for a client. The Securities & Exchange Commission may sue for wrongful or untimely disclosure; the Federal Trade Commission may sue for unsupported product claims; the Food and Drug Administration may sue for wrongful health claims.

Some firms require clients to review and approve all materials, Ury said, and others use "hold harmless" clauses in their contracts as well, "But what if the client can't or won't pay?" Litigation over these clauses in some jurisdictions also suggests they provide less protection than some had assumed.

OTHER LEGAL PITFALLS

Legal problems in public relations practice can arise from many sources. Those indigenous to the profession include copyright, trademarks, right of privacy, use of illustrative materials, and potential libel or slander. They can be considered only briefly here. Practitioners who become managers presumably are aware of potential problems and will be governed accordingly.

Copyright

A copyright protects tangible expressions of ideas, which may be expressed in writing or any other art form. In general, the copyright exists under common law until a legal copyright is obtained or the material involved goes into the public domain.

There exists in copyright law a concept known as "fair use." This permits limited use of copyrighted work without permission. It does not apply to commercial or promotional applications.

Where even as much as a few sentences of a copyrighted work are contemplated for use in promotional material, permission must be obtained. Failure to obtain permission may expose practitioners and their organizations to litigation.

Trademarks

Trademarks are words, symbols, or other devices that serve to identify product origin. Trademarks may be registered with the federal government subsequent to initial use in interstate commerce. Registration essentially grants ownership in and exclusive rights to use the trademark.

Public relations practitioners often are involved in creating trademarks and may assist in "policing" them as well. This is one of few areas in which interests of attorneys and practitioners coincide.

Policing—or writing cautionary letters to infringers or misusers—is vital in trademark protection. When permitted to become "generic," words involved may be lost as trademarks. Failure to capitalize Coca-Cola or Coke thus inevitably brings a letter from the trademark owner.

Developmental Considerations

Trademark development involves multiple considerations, including uniqueness, brevity, memorability, and ease of application in all media. When appropriate marks have been developed and narrowed to a relative few, a search must be conducted at the U.S. Patent Office and elsewhere to insure they are not already in use.

Trademarks need not be registered to be in conflict with proposed marks. Searches thus must extend beyond the Patent Office, but the best of searches does not eliminate potential problems. They occasionally have arisen, creating considerable expense for the parties involved.

Protective Measures

Trademark protection includes letters of the sort described above and several other steps. Most important is use of the familiar circled R (®) beside the trademark. Others include written protests to publishers and educational advertising. Coca-Cola is a major user of advertising, especially in trade publications read by potential infringers.

Trademark manuals are used more and more frequently by large organizations with multiple trademarks. They often are designed for internal and external use to prevent errors that might erode owner's legal positions in protecting trademarks.

Right of Privacy

The right of privacy protects names, portraits, or pictures of individuals from unauthorized use. The principle applies even to public figures where the user's purpose is commercial or promotional. It also applies to employees and the deceased.

Employees do not waive their rights as a condition of employment. Use of their photos in employee newsletters probably would not be a violation, but public circulation of the newsletter might be construed as such.

In general, any use of individuals' names or photos in advertising without prior permission is a violation. The only satisfactory device for avoiding attendant liability in these or questionable circumstances is a duly-executed legal release.

Illustrative Materials

When photography, artwork, and graphics of various kinds are used in public relations practice, legal questions may arise. Ownership, copyright, and right of privacy all may be involved. So may questions concerning libel and responsibility for loss. So complex are the circumstances that Simon recommends maintaining control files including the following information:

1. Source, including name, address, and telephone number.
2. Whether full or limited reproduction rights or license have been acquired and, if the latter, the account/program/story involved.
3. Name and address of copyright holder if different from the source.
4. Privacy releases if necessary.
5. Evidence of purchase, at minimum the purchase order used.
6. Approval from legal counsel.

Simon also emphasizes a number of major distinctions of which public relations practitioners should be aware in handling graphic materials. Major legal differences exist, he says, between:

1. Ownership of physical graphic property and copyright ownership.
2. Full title and ownership with unlimited rights to use and reproduce versus limited and transient rights.
3. A finished photograph versus the negative, plate, proof, or other materials required to reproduce the photo.
4. Ownership or right to use graphic material versus any right of privacy that may be involved.

The complexities need not be explored in detail here. This is an area in which legal guidance is essential to those who wish to avoid potential difficulties.

Libel and Slander

Libel essentially is published defamation while slander is verbal defamation. Defamation can be construed broadly as any action that tends to hold an individual up to ridicule or contributes to disrepute.

In general, plaintiffs in litigation arising out of either alleged offense must prove damages have occurred. Where the mass media are accused, malice also must be shown.

Public relations managers presumably are familiar with both general definitions and specific cases bearing on the profession. The body of pertinent case law is steadily expanding.

"If in doubt, don't" probably is the best guideline for practitioners. Legally actionable events in public relations practice almost always result from error. All materials should be reviewed prior to publication or broadcast. Where doubt exists, legal counsel should be consulted.

Public Releases

During the 1985 Annual Conference of the Public Relations Society of America in Detroit, attorney Alan J. Berkeley outlined liability risks in issuance of public releases. He specified nine areas of vulnerability.

Obligation and exposure of counsel. Public relations firms are obligated to conduct reasonable investigations to determine the truth of information supplied by clients (*SEC* v. *Pig 'N Whistle Corp.*, 1972). "To the extent that the standard for accuracy and completeness embodied in the anti-fraud provision is not met," SEC reminded in 1984, "the company and any person responsible for the statements may be liable under the federal securities laws...."

Accurate disclosures. Public statements, including any public releases, negotiations, or filings not part of SEC reports, must not be "false or misleading." Those making public statements must make diligent efforts to verify information (*Texas Gulf Sulphur*, 1968).

Complete disclosures. Public disclosures must be sufficiently complete so as not to be misleading. There is no obligation to disclose every material fact but information disclosed must not mislead (*Staffin* v. *Greenberg*, 1982).

Updating previous disclosures. Where the public is relying on a previous disclosure there is a duty to correct or update any prior statement that has become misleading due to subsequent events. (*Ross* v. *A.H. Robins*

Co., 1984). Depending on the significance of events, the correction may be held until a quarterly or annual report.

Disclosure to prevent improper trading. When companies suspect persons with inside information are improperly trading securities, the company may have to disclose the information to prevent further abuse. Where selective disclosure of significant information occurs, intentional or inadvertent, disclosure becomes especially important (*Sharon Steel Corp.*, 1981).

Correcting rumors. Companies need not correct rumors other than where they result from company action (*Electronic Specialty Co.* v. *International Controls Corp.*). Any response to a rumor, however, must be accurate and complete.

Correcting third parties' misstatements. There generally is no duty to correct but any correction must be accurate and complete. A duty may arise where there is a special relationship between the company and the third party or where the company is entangled in information disclosure and dissemination processes.

Timing. Timing of disclosures often is critical. News of new products, discoveries, mergers, and so on, usually is required in quarterly or annual reports. Disclosure of corporate transactions should follow an agreement as to "price and structure" (*Reiss* v. *Pan American World Airways,* 1983). Disclosure of negative news may not be necessary other than in special circumstances although both the SEC and the stock exchanges strongly encourage prompt disclosure.

Public response. Because "price and structure" had not been agreed upon, the court in *Greenfield* v. *Heublein* approved a statement by the company that it knew of no reason for unusual market activity. Previously, in *Carnation*, SEC held "no knowledge" and "no negotiations" statements unacceptable even where the corporate treasurer acted in good faith.

Each of the specified cautions arises out of a legal or administrative decision. Each can be changed or reversed by subsequent decisions. Counselors must stay abreast of such changes and conduct themselves accordingly.

TAXES AND LICENSES

Taxes and licenses seldom will be of concern to organizational public relations managers. They do, however, require the attention of counselors. Both may be required or imposed at any level of government. Taxes may be imposed by federal, state, county, and municipal authorities and by special taxing districts. Licenses may be required as well.

Taxes

Most business taxes are imposed on income, real property, inventories, and sales. The primary federal tax involving counselors is the income tax. Some states, counties, and cities also impose income taxes. Real estate taxes are common at county and municipal levels. Inventory taxes often are found at state levels. Sales taxes may originate with cities, states, or counties.

Sales Taxes

Sales taxes typically are added to client statements. They apply in some cases only to merchandise or otherwise exclude professional services. Where the latter conditions obtain, counselors should handle billings so as to minimize tax burdens on their clients. This can be accomplished by separately itemizing taxable and nontaxable components.

Counselor organizations usually absorb other taxes or recover amounts involved through adjustments in fee structures. Before entering into practice, prospective counselors should become knowledgeable concerning tax structures and their prospective impacts. They vary from one jurisdiction to another. Office locations often can be selected to minimize their impact.

Advice Needed

Most counselors consult qualified accountants for advice on tax matters. Advice is especially necessary where real estate ownership is involved. Many have found it advantageous to own real estate individually and lease it to their companies.

Accounting advice also can be helpful in dealing with personal property taxes. Where rates are high, leasing may be more attractive than purchasing equipment. The same may be true of automotive equipment. State statutes and county/municipal ordinances vary considerably.

Licenses

Licenses seldom are required of individual public relations practitioners. They rarely are required, in fact, of counselor firms. This apparently results from the fact that public relations firms are relative newcomers to the business community. Their advent apparently was not anticipated by those who drew up licensing codes and ordinances.

IN SUMMARY

Public relations counselors find themselves involved with legal matters from the inception to the liquidation or sale of their practices. Many practices are established as sole proprietorships or partnerships; most ultimately assume corporate form for the protection of the individuals involved.

Further long-term protection is necessary to protect the parties and their heirs. This includes buy-sell and first option provisions. To function as planned, they must include formulae through which practices can be equitably valued.

Employee, client, and vendor relationships also should be of concern to counselors in an increasingly litigous society. Of special interest in client relationships are conflict of interest, financial responsibility, confidentiality, accountability, responsibility, and disclosure. Counselor-client relationships should be reduced to formal contracts for the protection of both parties.

Vendor relationships are governed by the agency principle. Obligations undertaken by the counselor in behalf of the client are the client's rather than the agency's unless legally changed.

Employee relationships are especially complex, as are regulatory problems. Both are governed by rapidly changing bodies of law and administrative regulation.

Errors and omissions insurance may protect against many of the pitfalls involved. They arise as to clients, third parties, and members of the public as well as regulatory bodies.

Potential legal difficulties for the public relations practitioner also can be created by copyright and trademark legislation and by violations of individuals' right to privacy. Libel and slander laws also are of special significance to counselors.

A massive body of law and regulatory interpretation governs the activities of practitioners who deal with financial public relations. Change is ongoing in this area as well. The same is true as to tax and licensing laws.

ADDITIONAL READING

Moore, Russell F. *Law for Executives.* New York: American Management Association, 1968.

Nelson, Harold L., and Dwight L. Teeter, Jr. *Law of Mass Communications.* Mineola, N.Y.: Foundation Press, 1982.

Simon, Morton J. *Public Relations Law.* New York: Appleton-Century-Crofts, 1969.

Writer's Digest. *Law and the Writer.* Cincinnati: Writer's Digest Books, 1978.

Zuckman, Harry, and Martin J. Gaynes. *Mass Communication Law In a Nutshell.* St. Paul, Minn.: West, 1977.

17
Planning for the Future

Life cycles occur in individuals, in careers, and in organizations. They parallel one another but differ as well. While individuals and their careers proceed from birth through adolescence and maturity to senility and death, organizations may be reborn through development of a new leadership. Rebirth processes occur in organizations and their components, including public relations departments. Together with professional careers, they require management if success is to be achieved.

CAREER PLANNING

Linkages between professional careers and organizations seldom are obvious but nevertheless exist. Most obvious is a link between managers' individual performance and professional futures. Those who perform well achieve greater recognition. This usually leads to greater opportunities, internally or externally.

Internal Factors

Practitioner growth potential is a major organizational variable. Professional opportunities are few where organizational public relations units are small, with one exception. The exception arises where managers' growth preferences are not confined to public relations practice; where they are willing to consider pure managerial roles. The same option arises in large counseling firms.

Where either of these alternatives is viewed favorably, managers should plan accordingly. In most cases, planning has a bearing on organizational as well as practitioner success. Those who succeed in management roles accomplish organizational objectives and more.

The "more" is often overlooked. It involves creating internal structures that make managers dispensable parts of public relations units. Dispensable in this case refers to managerial availability for other assignments. Those most available in the eyes of senior managers have developed their own units to a point at which they continue to function in managers' absence. Where practitioners have successfully applied professional development programs for their subordinates, this will be the case.

Managers most eligible for promotion, in other words, have achieved several objectives. They have succeeded in their current roles and trained their successors. They then become senior managers' most logical choices for greater responsibility as organizations grow. The process also prepares managers to capitalize on external opportunities should they arise.

External Factors

The development process also is beneficial to managers looking toward personal opportunities outside the organization. For them. professional visibility becomes most important. It is most readily achieved through involvement in community and professional affairs at local, regional, and national levels.

Community and professional involvement requires time away from occupational settings. This in turn requires subordinates able to perform in the professional's absence. Managers' success entails developing and executing long-range plans for individuals and professional practices.

The two in large part are parallel but not identical. Career and organizational development path lines proceed together during individuals' early practice years. This especially is so where those involved are founders or early members of the organization. The lines tend to separate as individuals enter their middle years. Speed of separation is governed by the organizational life cycle and the individual career cycle. Where managers have provided for organizational renewal or regeneration, growth continues. More often than not, organizational growth creates opportunities for individual growth. Few change jobs for the sake of change. They instead tend to remain with organizations that can satisfy their career objectives.

In smaller public relations units, growth potential is limited by organizational size. Practitioners then must chart career paths that ultimately lead away from their organizations. Whether or not this is the case, planning is necessary in two contexts: One involves the individual, the other concerns the organization.

Success in careers, as in business ventures, is a function of planning. Individuals must complete such plans early in their careers. The plans should include assessment of organizational ability to meet individual goals. Approximate dates for job changes should be forecast, within the organization or otherwise. Internal potential will vary with personal preference as well as the size of the public relations unit. Those interested in senior management positions often will find greater internal potential than otherwise would be the case.

In either event, planning for the public relations unit should coincide with managerial plans. Managers' responsibilities include preparation for problem-free transitions. They are better remembered as having had trained successors in place than for leaving disorganization in their wakes.

Orderly transitions are at least equally necessary in counselor practice where practitioners also are proprietors. Circumstances in the latter situation, however, are considerably more complex.

ORGANIZATIONAL PLANNING

Planning for the future of organizations and their leaders should be undertaken concurrently. As one leadership generation plans for retirement, the rebirth or dissolution of the organization should be planned as well. Either objective can be accomplished without undue trauma. Major organizational alternatives include sale or merger, transfer to employees, co-owners, or heirs, and liquidation.

Each requires careful planning. Counsel from attorneys, accountants, insurance experts, and others also is required. Individuals involved often are not those with whom owners worked at the founding of their organizations. Specialists in tax and estate matters must be called upon. Skilled counsel is essential.

Developing the Plan

The planning process often involves reexamining the organizational structure of businesses. Practitioner objectives may require change in organizational form. This in turn may necessitate "liquidating" one entity to establish another.

The tax implications of these changes require careful examination. The interests of multiple owners also must be considered where they exist. Adequate protection of those interests may require new agreements. They should specify the rights of each relative to others under the proposed new structure and in the event of withdrawal or death.

Liquidity Problems

Liquidity always is a source of concern in business transfers. Unless anticipated in advance, illiquidity may afflict any who assume ownership. Existing owners' concerns involve family members who will inherit businesses or receive sale proceeds. Potential difficulties are created by federal and state inheritance taxes or long-term financing that existed prior to the death of the owner(s). They can be avoided through careful planning.

Family Considerations

Where family members are to inherit, transitions can be eased by several methods. These include reliance on marital deductions in estate tax laws, purchase of life insurance policies, and sections of the Internal Revenue Code that offer special relief provisions.

Stock can be transferred by married couples to their children in amounts up to $20,000 annually. Under a "unified credit" option available beginning in 1987, up to $600,000 can be transferred without gift or estate taxes. Gifts can be in the form of corporate shares, partnership interests, or otherwise. A careful review of options with qualified counsel is essential.

Transfer to Others

Transfer of professional practices to relatives is less practical than in other businesses. They are more frequently transferred to other owners or employees. Occasionally they are liquidated.

Transfer arrangements should be made early other than where liquidation is the owner's choice. They usually include one of two vehicles where multiple owners are involved. The first is a "buy-sell" or "cross purchase" agreement under which surviving owners acquire the interests of the deceased. The second is a redemption agreement, which requires the corporation or partnership to purchase their interests. Decisions in either case must be made as to how the purchase is to be financed and what terms will apply.

Terms and financing are important. Corporate acquisition of the deceased's shares is preferable from a tax standpoint to individual purchase. Funds flowing through corporations other than the Subchapter S variety are taxed at corporate and individual levels. This distinction may not apply where partnerships are involved. Insurance-funded purchases in some circumstances may eliminate the distinction as to corporations.

Buy-Sell versus Redemption

Neither the buy-sell agreement nor the redemption approach is perfect. Redemption may result in a dividend to the estate of the deceased; it also can reduce corporate liquidity. This approach generally favors surviving owners in terms of tax liability.

Buyout agreements usually include insurance funding and extended purchase terms. Where insurance exists, down payments or purchase prices often equal insurance proceeds. Organizations often provide insurance in anticipation of these circumstances. Buyout terms usually range from three to five years. Interest often is charged but rates vary.

Employee Acquisitions

Many counselors elect to sell their businesses to employees. Two advantages are created: First, employee acquisition often is most effective in assuring continuity. Where owners retain minority interests or become creditors, security is enhanced as well. Second, established plans through which employees can obtain ownership encourage them to remain with the practice.

Employee stock ownership plans (ESOPs) have become popular vehicles for ownership transfer. They are appropriate only where owners intend transferring stock to many or most employees rather than a selected few. Other available devices include:

1. Below-value stock sales. This approach fails to create employee incentives and, in addition, creates added tax liabilities for employees involved.
2. "Golden handcuff" plans under which employees may acquire stock that can be retained only while they remain on the payroll. These plans usually provide for repurchase at cost should the employee resign.
3. A number of stock plans ranging from incentive options to stock bonuses and including ESOPs.

Most important from an owner's standpoint is that there be a plan. Decisions must be made as early as possible. Ample time should be allowed to explore all options and select that which best suits the circumstances.

BUYING, SELLING, AND MERGING

Ownership transfer involves several complexities—some are human, others are financial. Other than where a firm's stock is publicly traded, most relate to value or—more technically—valuation.

Many meanings have been attached to the word "value." Where sale of property is involved, buyer and seller are most concerned with "fair market value." The most popular of definitions, which originated in a 1928 legal case, defines this term as meaning "what an intelligent and reasonable seller and an intelligent and reasonable buyer would in their fairly mercenary interests have been most likely to agree upon as a fair price for the property in question."

Establishing Value

These words underlie what has become known as the "willing buyer-willing seller" concept. It unfortunately is often inadequate in establishing the value of a practice. This results from several intervening factors. They include the nature of individuals involved and the business at hand.

Individual characteristics are most troublesome. The attachment entrepreneurs come to have for their enterprises can make "value" as much a product of emotion as reason. Avarice may be present; so can suspicion. No one likes to feel taken advantage of in a business transaction.

Technical Concerns

Beyond these human factors are multiple technical concerns, which arise where shares in the business are not publicly owned and traded. In the latter situation, the "willing buyer-willing seller" concept is readily applied. The value then is the number of outstanding shares multiplied by the share price at the close of the prior day's trading.

Where shares are not publicly traded, the impact of technical factors compounds. They relate primarily to cost efficiency or return on investment. Also involved are several of the varying definitions of value.

Components of "Return"

When examining return on business investments, investors are concerned with year-to-year yield and potential for enhanced value. They calculate return on investments and prices at which they might be liquidated. Calculated values are compared with those of alternative investments to determine attractiveness.

Another factor influencing prospective buyers is the asset or liquidated value of the business. What might the components bring at a forced sale?

These standards are not readily applied to public relations practices. Client and employee loyalty are their most valued assets. Clients seldom are legally bound beyond 12 months. In practical terms, they may sever their relationships at will. Employees are equally uncontrollable. Other than as constrained by employment contracts, they may become competitors overnight.

Personal Loyalties

These factors and one other—personal loyalties—pose major problems for prospective buyers. Public relations is a personal endeavor. Client loyalties more often are to individuals rather than firms. The sale of a practice or the retirement of the founder may be perceived by clients as relieving them of any obligations.

All these elements must be dealt with in arriving at the value of a practice. Agreement on value is essential to sale or merger. A number of other elements common to valuation of a business also require attention, however. They include economic influences and general valuation factors other than those mentioned above.

Economic Influences

A number of general economic factors must be weighed in evaluating a business. General economic trends, the economics of particular industries, and government policies are among them.

Economic Trends

Long-term and current economic influences must be weighed in establishing business values. Long-term factors include government fiscal policies, defense expenditures, social programs, and the like. Short-term factors include government tax policies, Federal Reserve Board credit policies, and wage/price trends.

Relative conditions at the time of the proposed sale or merger provide bases for forecasting potential change. Economic change creates varying impacts. Increasing social programs funded by new taxes, for example, tends to enhance incomes in one component of the population at the expense of others.

Client Analyses

Analyses of trends and clients' endeavors create insights into the economic future of organizations. Where tax rates are increasing, for example, disposable income tends to decline and leisure-oriented industries may suffer.

Practice balance thus is significant to prospective practice buyers. Client diversity becomes a relative strength. Well-balanced practices are not apt to suffer unduly with changing economic times.

Specific Factors

Among specific factors considered in establishing values for most businesses are earnings, assets, and market values of securities. The first is most significant and most elusive.

Earnings

High earnings or profit figures may be desirable when organizations are offered for sale. The reverse is true at other times, except where organizations are publicly owned. The reasons originate in the nation's tax laws. Corporate profits are taxed before being paid to owners and then taxed again as personal income.

Many if not most public relations counseling firms use the corporate form. With the tax structure designed to capture as much as 75 percent of profits, every effort is made to reduce them. Higher salaries or bonuses and liberal benefits are favored devices. Other than as deemed excessive by the Internal Revenue Service, wages and bonuses are taxed as ordinary income to the individual. They also are business expenses to the corporation, however, and thus are subject to only one income tax. Many benefits are tax-free to both employer and employee.

Report versus Reality

Reported profits of public relations firms for these reasons usually are lower than "real" profits. The latter are important in establishing business values. Considerable time and effort thus are required of buyers, sellers, and accountants in establishing valid "bottom line" data for evaluation purposes.

Physical assets, consisting of furnishings and equipment, usually are of negligible value. In some cases, substantial investments in computers may create greater than average asset values. Occasionally, a firm may occupy its own building. Building titles usually are held individually by owners, again for tax purposes.

Other Attributes

The desirability of a public relations practice to a buyer is not necessarily confined to traditional elements considered in valuing businesses generally. Several others can make the practice quite attractive.

Specialized skills among practice personnel may attract prospective buyers. The nature of clienteles may be an unusually good "fit" for a particular merger-seeker. Acquisitions often are preferred vehicles in expanding counselor practices and in acquiring staff with specialized backgrounds.

SETTING A PRICE

A price ultimately must be set. Each party to the proposed transaction will have a strong opinion on this point. They almost necessarily will be in disagreement if not in conflict. Given a willing buyer and a willing seller, however, agreement can be reached.

A Strategic Approach

Many begin by establishing two preliminary figures: minimum and maximum. This process creates a range within which further negotiations can proceed.

Minimum Value

Most owners and prospective buyers would agree the value of a business is no less than its net worth. Assets and liabilities at worst might be revalued to reflect their economic worth—the tangible net worth of the business. This much usually can be agreed upon.

Liquidation value of assets may be substituted for market values. This seldom is appropriate except where the business is doing nothing more than generating a reasonable income for the owner. In these circumstances, there are no profits. Profit accrues only after expenses have been paid. A reasonable owner's salary is part of business expenses.

Maximum Value

Maximum value is more difficult to determine. Most appraisers consider a business worth no more than five times pretax profits. Resulting figures almost invariably will be too low where firms have been growing.

The above "rule of thumb" usually is applied to retail and other businesses where future volume and profit rationally can be projected based on past performance. In public relations, this is less likely to be the case. Addition of a relatively few profitable accounts can compound profit levels for a future year. Profits also are subject to rapid erosion through loss of business. Longevity of client relationships can serve as indicators of potential change.

Negotiating the Price

Appraisers generally expect businesses to sell at a price between tangible net worth and a multiple of profits, usually about five times profits. Between these extremes, noneconomic values come into play. These may include how well established the business is and, more importantly, how transferable its goodwill may be. In a public relations practice, the latter factor might better be termed client loyalty.

Writing in the *Business Valuation Handbook*, Glenn M. Desmond and Richard E. Kelley suggest that the value of goodwill for an advertising agency should be lower than for insurance agencies or legal/accounting practices because of greater risk of client turnover. They suggest two price formulae: market value of tangible assets less liabilities plus 30 to 50 percent of annual billings or 8 to 12 times monthly profits after owner salaries. The same logic might be applied to public relations practices.

Gerald C. Wollan of Padilla & Speer, Inc., described several other options during the 1984 Spring Conference of the Counselor Academy of the Public Relations Society of America. They included the prior year's net fee income, three to five times after-tax earnings plus book value, two times pretax earnings plus book value, and formulae based upon performance over a three-to five-year period.

Some plans have been based on earnings potential before taxes, bonuses, and, perhaps, unusual owner perquisites, Wollan said. Most of them are based on historical performance over periods from two to five years.

Padilla & Speer, in establishing a plan through which the firm was to be sold to employees, finally established a formula involving three primary factors: weighted average annual earnings, desired return on investment, and net worth:

$$\text{Value} = \frac{\text{weighted average annual earnings}}{\text{desired \% return on investment}} + \text{net worth}$$

The weighted average over five years is calculated by multiplying the most recent year's earnings by five, next most recent year's by four, and so on. Total weighted earnings then are divided by the sum of the weights applied (15) to produce the weighted average. The weighted average is divided by the percentage return required. Net worth then is added. The Padilla & Speer formula is noteworthy in that it can be used to project values based on varying rates of return on investment.

Any of these approaches might be worthy of consideration in the typical public relations practice. Recent transactions in several cities suggest disagreements over practice pricing also can be overcome through alternative strategies.

Overcoming Conflicts

A number of barriers exist between an "agreement in principle" and conclusion of a sale. Most involve conflicts concerning price and how an agreed-upon price will be paid. The latter element is important from a tax standpoint.

Tax Considerations

Business sales generally involve assets or equities, the latter in the form of stocks or partnership interests. Equity sales usually are simpler and, from sellers' standpoints, relatively attractive. Profits are taxed as long-term capital gains. Equity sales limit tax planning potential, however, and many thus prefer to sell assets.

Asset sales tend to create greater conflicts, especially as to allocation of purchase prices. Sellers seek maximum capital gains. Buyers want depreciable assets. The two viewpoints are in conflict. Dollars paid for goodwill, for example, qualify for capital gains treatment but goodwill may not be amortized.

Buyer and seller together must determine how purchase dollars will be allocated to tangible property, real estate, inventories, customer lists, and both consulting and non-competition agreements. Since negotiations are adversarial in nature, the Internal Revenue Service usually accepts such allocations for tax purposes.

Other Conflicts

Most other conflicts concerning practice values arise over their futures rather than their pasts. Owners tend to emphasize future potential rather than past performance. Among prospective buyers, the reverse is true.

Over the years, a number of strategies have been developed to protect both parties' interests. Most involve extended payment plans or continuing ownership interests for sellers.

Extended Payments

Sellers prefer to receive 100 percent of purchase prices when sales are closed. Buyers prefer to make no "front end" payments. They would rather defer compensation until anticipated profits are being collected. Extended payment plans are a compromise between these positions.

The plans often provide for adjusted compensation levels based on developments subsequent to closing dates. Where sales volume or profits increase, prices are adjusted upward. Where they decline, the reverse is true.

Extended or deferred payments usually cover two to five years. Compensation formulae vary. They differ primarily as to base periods from which changes are calculated. A typical plan provides for compensation to the seller in five equal payments, each adjusted upward or downward from the year prior to the closing date.

Increases or declines in compensation can be based on the performance of the business as a whole or on accounts existing or in negotiation before the sale.

Ownership Plans

Ownership plans differ from deferred compensation plans. They give sellers an interest in buyers' businesses. Ultimate compensation thus is dependent as much on the buyer's success as the seller's prior efforts.

Stock received by sellers in some cases is sold back to buyers over predetermined periods. A mutually agreeable formula for determining per share values is essential where this procedure is followed.

The basis for calculating results also is important to sellers. Buyers manage businesses and may manipulate profit levels. Most ownership plan outcomes therefore are predicated on sales volume rather than profit.

Closing Arrangements

After price and terms have been agreed upon, there remains one question that may produce conflict: amount to be paid at closing. Buyers prefer large payments. They want the cash and seek to minimize potential collection problems. Sellers prefer to conserve cash and are concerned over hidden practice weaknesses that may become known only after closing.

Multiple Dollar Sources

Dollars involved at closing originate from several sources. First are physical assets, whose values traditionally have been relatively low. They can be significant, however, where practitioners have invested heavily in production equipment and facilities. Second are accounts receivable, consisting of services performed for which the organization has not been paid. Third is the premium over assets that the buyer has agreed to pay for the business.

Payment at Closing

Buyers in most cases compensate sellers for physical assets and accounts receivable at closing. Receivables that prove uncollectable may be charged back to sellers. Sellers' tax circumstances may make other arrangements preferable. Professional counsel is necessary on both sides.

Advice Essential

Buyer and seller will want counsel from attorneys and accountants in completing transactions. Potential tax consequences make any other course of action foolhardy.

Exchanges of stock, for example, can be beneficial from a tax standpoint. On the other hand, the value of stock received is a function of variables beyond buyer ability to control. Sellers can manipulate these values in close-held corporations.

IN SUMMARY

Long-term planning is necessary to the success of public relations practitioners and the organizations with which they are involved. Individuals require career plans. Organizational development in counselor practice should include planning preparation for long-term continuation or disposition of the business. Organizational practitioners must meet similar needs in preparing for the next steps on their career paths.

In varying degrees, practitioner and organizational paths parallel one another. They diverge only as professionals find it necessary to seek opportunities outside the organization or as entrepreneurs prepare to dispose of practices.

Advance planning is necessary for either the rebirth or dissolution of the practice. The latter objective is readily accomplished. The former is considerably more complex in any of several forms.

Owners may elect to prepare for conveyance to their heirs or others. The organizational form under which the practice has been operating requires review in either event. Change may prove necessary or advisable for tax reasons.

Liquidity problems also can arise in the absence of planning. They can be burdensome to heirs or others who might acquire the practice but a number of remedies are available.

Valuation of practices for sale or merger is a difficult task. The problem is especially complex where corporate stock is not publicly traded. Human and technical problems are equally troublesome. The first include owners' emotional attachments to their businesses. The latter occur where tax avoidance practices render "profit" figures inaccurate. Economic trends, client histories, and other factors must be considered in establishing practice values.

Most resolve the valuation problem by establishing a formula. Formulae often are based on the economic performance of the practice for a two-to five-year period subsequent to the sale. They often are calculated to meet the parties' individual situations with regard to taxes and liquidity.

ADDITIONAL READING

Desmond, Glenn M., and Richard E. Kelley. *Business Valuation Handbook*. Llano, Calif.: Business Valuation Press, 1977.

Gallesich, June. *The Profession and Practice of Consultation*. San Francisco: Jossey-Bass, 1982.

Greiner, Larry E., and Robert O. Metzger. *Consulting to Management: Insights to Building and Managing a Successful Practice*. Englewood Cliffs, N.J.: Prentice-Hall, 1983.

Lasser, J. K., Tax Institute. *How to Run a Small Business*, 5th ed. New York: McGraw-Hill, 1983.

Meyers, Herbert S. *Minding Your Own Business: A Contemporary Guide to Small Business Success*. Homewood, Ill.: Dow Jones-Irwin, 1984.

Epilogue

Public relations promises to be one of the growth occupations of the future. Environmental assessment suggests multiple stimuli will be responsible.

Numbers of business and industrial crises appear to be increasing. Social problems are compounding. The advance of science is raising moral as well as environmental issues. Available evidence suggests these issues will compound rather than diminish in number and complexity.

Professionally, public relations appears well-equipped to handle them. Knowledge of the applied social sciences has increased and colleges and universities are graduating more students adequately equipped in these areas and in communication.

Practitioners thus appear relatively well-equipped to meet process challenges. Whether they are equally well-prepared to manage their practices is another matter.

Institutions of higher education have attempted to remedy this weakness. More and more business courses—especially in management and marketing—are required of public relations students. Colleges and universities, unfortunately, are not equipped to meet the challenge alone and professional organizations have yet to react adequately.

The problem consists of two components: Limitations on higher education curricula constitute one of them; the absence of adequate postgraduate educational opportunities is another.

Public relations for the most part is taught at the undergraduate level. Curricula consist of 120 to 132 semester hours or their equivalent. The total arguably is adequate to cover a lower-division core curriculum and upper-division coursework in public relations and selected business areas.

Public relations pioneer Edward Bernays long has espoused undergraduate degrees in the social sciences followed by a master's in public relations. A national committee chaired by Mr. Bernays and committed to licensure and certification of practitioners is considering a similar approach. The committee's first draft of a model statute prescribed 30 hours of appropriate postgraduate study as a prerequisite to licensure.

Given appropriate course work, a requirement of this sort might initially equip entry-level practitioners with adequate educational backgrounds. Maintenance of skill and knowledge levels in a fast-changing society is another matter.

Opportunities for continuing education in public relations are almost nonexistent beyond the limits of New York, Chicago, and a few other large cities. The Public Relations Society of America is experimenting with new approaches. Professional development seminars in other cities were launched on an experimental basis in 1985. The same year saw the advent of PRLink, an on-line informational utility accessible via CompuServe. Unfortunately, no more than a few hundred were participating in these activities as of this writing.

Success in meeting the needs of tomorrow's public relations professionals—especially those who aspire to management—will require comprehensive action by educators and practitioners. Ideally, it would consist of three components:

1. An undergraduate curriculum with a strengthened social science component but including basic skills courses.
2. A master's degree program consisting of further public relations courses as well as extensive work in subjects including management, marketing, finance, and human resources.
3. A generally available set of continuing education programs designed to achieve two objectives:
   a. Maintenance of state-of-art knowledge in areas covered by the baccalaureate and master's programs.
   b. Provision of further knowledge and skills necessary to deal with practice problems as they arise.

Availability of appropriate continuing education programming will be a function of demand. Few postsecondary educational institutions would turn away from an opportunity to meet practitioners' needs were numbers of participants adequate to support developmental efforts.

The demand need not be geographically concentrated. Adequate technology exists today to permit a broadly distributed audience to participate in electronically mediated programs, which can be delivered through existing computer-based systems such as CompuServe or The Source. Satellite-based teleconferencing systems also might be used.

With academic developmental resources and technology in place, only the demand factor remains to be created. It may well develop through contemporary efforts toward licensing of public relations practitioners.

The author is an advocate of licensing and certification as espoused by Bernays and others. Burgeoning demand and declining numbers of college and university graduates in the years ahead will multiply problems in public relations. Counselors and organizational practitioners will experience difficulty in hiring adequately skilled employees. These conditions also will invite a new generation of charlatans to misuse the words "public relations."

Practitioners concurrently are exerting an ever-increasing influence on the nation. Significant portions of the information purveyed daily by the media pass through the hands of public relations professionals. We are a democratic society governed by a constitution that assumes the existence of an informed electorate. If the integrity of communication channels is to be assured, public relations practitioners ultimately must be licensed.

With associated continuing education requirements, licensing would go far toward assuring users of public relations services of practitioner credentials. More importantly, such requirements would create sufficient "demand" to encourage program development on the part of educational institutions and/or professional organizations.

Neither expanded educational curricula nor universal access to continuing education would assure the success of any individual in public relations or public relations management. Such developments could, however, be expected to radically improve what today appear to be poor odds on entrepreneurial success.

New counseling practices announced in the professional media but never heard of again are legion. In some few cases, names of founders are later mentioned as having been appointed to an organizational or other position. Organizational practices appear somewhat more durable but relatively few achieve their potential.

Basic, advanced, and continuing education in public relations and in management are needed; they ultimately will become available. It is hoped that this book will be of some assistance in the interim to students, managers, and entrepreneurial practitioners.

Selected Bibliography

The following bibliography augments the Additional Reading lists provided at the close of each chapter of the text. It is designed to assist those who want to pursue specific subject matter in still greater depth.

Aiken, Michael, and Paul E. Mott, eds. *The Structure of Community Power*. New York: Random House, 1970.

Allen, T. Harrell. "PERT: A Technique for Public Relations Management." *Public Relations Review*, Summer 1980.

American Institute of Certified Public Accountants. *The Management of Corporate Social Performance*. New York: 1977.

Atchison, Thomas J., and Winson W. Hill. *Management Today: Managing Work in Organizations*. New York: Harcourt, Brace, Jovanovich, 1978.

Babbie, Earl R. *The Practice of Social Research*. Belmont, Calif.: Wadsworth, 1979.

Belkner, Loren B. *The First Time Manager: A Practical Guide to the Management of People*. New York: AMACOM, 1978.

Bernard, Jessie. *The Sociology of Community*. Glenview, Ill.: Scott, Foresman, 1973.

Black, Sam, ed. *Public Relations in the 1980's: Proceedings of the Eighth Annual Public Relations World Congress*. Oxford: Pergamon, 1979.

Bradshaw, Thornton, and David Vogel. *Corporations and Their Critics: Problems of Corporate Social Responsibilities*. New York: McGraw-Hill, 1982.

Bramson, Robert M. *Coping With Difficult People*. Garden City, N.Y.: Anchor Press/ Doubleday, 1981.

Bretz, Rudy. *Media for Interactive Communication*. Beverly Hills, Calif.: Sage, 1983.

Brown, James K. *The Business of Issues: Coping with the Company's Environment*. New York: The Conference Board, 1979.

———. *Guidelines for Managing Corporate Issues Programs*. New York: The Conference Board, 1981.

Buchholz, Rogene A. *Business Environment and Public Policy*. Englewood Cliffs, N.J.: Prentice-Hall, 1982.

Burger, Chester. *The Chief Executive: Realities of Corporate Leadership*. Boston: CBI Publishing, 1978.

Camillus, John C. *Budgeting for Profit: How to Exploit the Potential of Your Business*. Radnor, Pa.: Chilton, 1984.

Carroll, Archie B. *Business and Society*. Boston: Little, Brown, 1981.

Castells, Manuel, ed. *High Technology, Space and Society*. Beverly Hills, Calif.: Sage, 1985.

Chase, Howard. *Issues Management: Origins of the Future*. Stamford, Conn.: Issues Action Publications, 1984.

Clifford, Donald K., Jr., and Richard E. Cavanagh. *The Winning Performance: How America's High-Growth Midsize Companies Succeed*. New York: Bantam, 1985.

Comer, James M., and Alan J. Dubinski. *Managing the Successful Sales Force*. Lexington, Mass.: Lexington Books, 1985.

Crable, Richard E., and Steven L. Vibbert. *Public Relations as Communication Management*. Edina, Minn.: Bellwether, 1986.

Cunningham, William H. *Marketing: A Managerial Approach*. Cincinnati: Southwestern, 1981.

Curtiss, Ellen T., and Philip A. Untersee. *Corporate Responsibilities/Opportunities to 1990*. Lexington, Mass.: Heath, 1979.

D'Aprix, Roger. *Communicating for Productivity*. New York: Harper & Row, 1982.

Davis, Dennis K., and Stanley J. Baran. *Mass Communication and Everyday Life: A Perspective on Theory and Effects*. Belmont, Calif.: Wadsworth, 1981.

Deal, Terrence, and Allan A. Kennedy. *Corporate Cultures*. Reading, Mass.: Addison-Wesley, 1982.

DeFleur, Melvin L., and Sandra Ball-Rokeach. *Theories of Mass Communication*, 4th ed. New York: Longman, 1982.

Dillman, Don A. *Mail and Telephone Surveys: The Total Design Method*. New York: John Wiley, 1978.

Domhoff, G. William. *Who Really Rules* New Brunswick, N.J.: Transaction Books, 1978.

Donnelly, Robert M. *Guidebook to Planning: Strategic Planning and Budgeting Bases for the Growing Firm*. New York: Van Nostrand Reinhold, 1984.

Duncan, W. Jack. *Essentials of Management*, Hinsdale, Ill.: Dryden Press, 1978.

Dunn, S. Watson. *Public Relations: A Contemporary Approach*. Homewood, Ill: Richard D. Irwin, 1986.

Etzioni, Amitai. *An Immodest Agenda*. New York: McGraw-Hill, 1981.

Fendrock, John F. *Managing in Times of Radical Change*. New York: American Management Association, 1971.

Gellerman, Saul W. *Management by Motivation*. New york: American Management Association, 1968.

George, Claude S. *Supervision in Action: the Art of Managing Others*. Reston, Va.: Reston, 1979.

Goldhaber, Gerald. *Organizational Communication*. Dubuque, Iowa: Brown, 1979.

Gollner, Andrew. *Social Change and Corporate Strategy: The Expanding Role of Public Affairs*. Stamford, Conn.: Issues Action Publications, 1984.

Groesbeck, Kenneth. *The Advertising Agency Business*. Chicago: Advertising Publications, 1964.

Guttentag, Marcia, and Elmer Struening. *Handbook of Evaluation Research*. Beverly Hills, Calif.: Sage, 1975.

Hage, Jerald. *Communication and Organizational Control: Cybernetics in Health and Welfare Settings*. New York: John Wiley, 1974.

————. *Theories of Organizations: Form, Process and Transformation*. New York: Wiley Interscience, 1980.

Harman, Willis. *An Incomplete Guide to the Future*. San Francisco: San Francisco Book Company, 1976.

Harris, Marvin. *America Now*. New York: Simon & Schuster, 1981.

Haynes, W. Warren, Joseph L. Massie, and Marc J. Wallace, Jr. *Management: Analysis, Concepts, and Cases*, 3rd ed. Englewood Cliffs, N.J.: Prentice-Hall, 1975.

Health, Robert L., and Richard A. Nelson. *Issues Management: Corporate Public Policymaking in an Information Society*. Beverly Hills, Calif.: Sage, 1986.

Hersey, Paul, and Kenneth W. Blanchard. *Management of Organizational Behavior: Utilizing Human Resources*, 3rd ed. Englewood Cliffs, N.J.: Prentice-Hall, 1977.

Herzberg, Frederick. *Work and the Nature of Man*. Cleveland: World, 1966.

Herzberg, Frederick, Bernard Mausner, and Barbara Snyderman. *The Motivation to Work*. New York: John Wiley, 1959.

Hill and Knowlton Executives. *Critical Issues in Public Relations*. Englewood Cliffs, N.J.: Prentice-Hall, 1975.

Hills, P. J., ed. *Trends in Information Transfer*. Westport, Conn.: Greenwood Press, 1982.

Hodgetts, Richard H. *Introduction to Business*. Reading, Mass: Addison-Wesley, 1977.

Koehler, Jerry W., Karl W. E. Anatol, and Ronald L. Applebaum. *Organizational Communication: Behavioral Perspectives*, 2nd ed. New York: Holt, Rinehart and Winston, 1981.

Lewis, Phillip V. *Organization Communication: The Essence of Effective Management*, 2nd ed. Columbus, Ohio: Grid, 1980.

Lovell, Ronald P. *Inside Public Relations*. Boston: Allyn & Bacon, 1982.

Maccoby, Michael. *The Leader*. New York: Simon & Schuster, 1981.

Marting, Elizabeth, Robert E. Finley, and Ann Ward, eds. *Effective Communication on the Job: A Guide for Supervisor and Executives*. New York: American Management Association, 1963.

Mason, Richard O., and Ian I. Mitroff. *Challenging Strategic Planning Assumptions: Theory, Cases and Techniques*. New York: John Wiley, 1981.

Masuda, Yoneji. *The Information Society as Post-Industrial Society*. Tokyo: Institute for the Information Society, 1980.

McConkey, Dale T. *No-Nonsense Delegation*. New York: AMACOM, 1974.

McDonald, James O. *Managing Without Tears: A Guide to Coping with Everyday Organizational Problems*. Chicago: Crain, 1981.

McLean, Adrian et al. *Organization Development in Transition*. New York: John Wiley, 1982.

McWilliams, Peter A. *The Personal Computer Book*. Los Angeles: Prelude Press, 1983.

―――. *The Word Processing Book: A Short Course In Computer Literacy*. Los Angeles: Prelude Press, 1982.

Miller, Lawrence M. *Behavior Management: The New Science of Managing People at Work*. New York: John Wiley, 1978.

Mitchell, Terrence R. *People in Organizations: Understanding their Behavior*. New York: McGraw-Hill, 1978.

Moore, H. Frazier, and Frank B. Kalupa. *Public Relations: Principles, Cases and Problems*, 9th ed. Homewood, Ill.: Richard D. Irwin, 1985.

Nagelschmidt, Joseph. *Public Affairs Handbook*. New York: American Management Association, 1982.

Naisbitt, John, and Patricia Aburdene. *Re-Inventing the Corporation*. New York: Warner, 1985.

Newman, William H., and James P. Logan. *Strategy, Policy and Central Management.* Cincinnati: Southwestern, 1981.

Nolte, Lawrence W., and Dennis L. Wilcox. *Effective Publicity: How to Reach the Public.* New York: John Wiley, 1984.

Ouchi, William. *Theory Z.* Reading, Mass.: Addison-Wesley, 1981.

Paluszek, John. *Will the Corporation Survive?* Englewood Cliffs, N.J.: Prentice-Hall, 1977.

Pascarella, Perry. *Industry Week's Guide to Tomorrow's Executive: Humanagement in the Future Corporation.* New York: Van Nostrand Reinhold, 1981.

Patton, Michael Q. *Qualitative Evaluation Methods.* Beverly Hills, Calif.: Sage, 1978.

Peake, Jacquelyn. *Public Relations in Business.* New York: Harper & Row, 1980.

Perrow, Charles. *Complex Organizations: A Critical Essay,* 2nd. ed. Glenview, Ill: Scott, Foresman, 1979.

Perry, Joseph B., and M. D. Pugh. *Collective Behavior: Response to Social Stress.* Minneapolis: West, 1978.

Peters, Tom, and Nancy Austin. *A Passion for Excellence: The Leadership Difference.* New York: Random House, 1985.

Ray, Michael L. *Advertising and Communication Management.* Englewood Cliffs, N.J.: Prentice-Hall, 1982.

Rejda, George E. *Principles of Insurance.* Glenview, Ill: Scott, Foresman, 1982.

Reuss, Carol, and Donn Silvis, eds. *Inside Organizational Communication.* New York: Longman, 1981.

Rice, Ronald E. et al. *The New Media: Communication, Research and Technology.* Beverly Hills, Calif.: Sage, 1984.

Rifkin, Jeremy. *The Emerging Order.* New York: G.P. Putnam's Sons, 1979.

Roalman, A. R. *Profitable Public Relations.* Homewood, Ill: Dow Jones-Irwin, 1961.

Robinson, Edward J. *Public Relations Survey Research.* New York: Irvington, 1969.

Rogers, Everett M., and Rekha Agarwala-Rogers. *Communication in Organizations.* New York: The Free Press, 1976.

Rosenblum, Jerry, and Victor G. Hallman. *Employee Benefit Planning.* Englewood Cliffs, N.J.: Prentice-Hall, 1981.

Roxe, Linda A. *Personnel Management for the Smaller Company: A Hands-On Manual.* New York: AMACOM, 1979.

Rubel, Stanley M. *Guide to Selling A Business,* Chicago: Capital, 1977.

Rubin, Brent D., ed. *Information and Behavior.* New Brunswick, NJ.: Transaction Books, 1985.

Rubin, David M. and David P. Sachs. *Mass Media and the Environment.* New York: Praeger, 1973.

Scott, William G., and David K. Hart. *Organizational America.* Boston: Houghton Mifflin, 1979.

Sethi, S. Prakash, and Carl L. Swanson. *Private Enterprise and Public Purpose.* New York: John Wiley, 1981.

Simon, Morton J. *Public Relations Law.* New York: Appleton-Century-Crofts, 1969.

Simon, Raymond. *Public Relations Management: A Casebook.* Columbus, Ohio: Publishing Horizons, 1986.

Snider, H. Wayne. *Employee Benefits Management.* New York: Risk and Insurance Management Society, 1980.

Stanton, William J. *Management of the Sales Force*. Homewood, Ill.: Richard D. Irwin, 1983, 6th ed.

Stempel, Guido H. III, and Bruce H. Westley, eds. *Research Methods in Mass Communication*. Englewood Cliffs, N.J.: Prentice-Hall, 1981.

Stonich, Paul J. *Implementing Strategy: Making Strategy Happen*. Cambridge, Mass.: Ballinger, 1982.

Stonich, Paul J., and John C. Kirby. *Zero-base Planning and Budgeting: Improved Cost Control and Resource Allocation*. Homewood, Ill.: Dow Jones - Irwin, 1977.

Toffler, Alvin. *Preview and Premises*. New York: William Morrow, 1983.

————. *The Third Wave*. New York: William Morrow, 1980.

Trentin, H. George, and Reginald Jones. *Budgeting General and Administrative Expenses: A Planning and Control System*. New York: American Management Association, 1966.

Tuleja, Thaddeus. *Beyond the Bottom Line*. New York: Facts on File, 1985.

Walsh, Frank. *Public Relations Writer in a Computer Age*. Englewood Cliffs, N.J.: Prentice-Hall, 1986.

Weinbauch, J. Donald, and William E. Piland. *Applied Marketing Principles*. Englewood Cliffs, N.J.: Prentice-Hall, 1979.

Weiss, Carol H. *Evaluation Research: Methods for Assessing Program Effectiveness*. Englewood Cliffs, N.J.: Prentice-Hall, 1972.

Yankelovich, Daniel. *New Rules*. New York: Random House, 1981.

Zander, Alvin. *Making Groups Effective*. San Francisco: Jossey-Bass, 1985.

Index

About the Author

E. W. BRODY teaches public relations in the Department of Journalism at Memphis State University in Tennessee and maintains a public relations counseling practice in Memphis.

Dr. Brody's articles on public relations have appeared in *Public Relations Journal*, *Public Relations Quarterly*, *Public Relations Review*, *Journalism Quarterly*, *Legal Economics*, *Health Care Management Review*, the *Journal of the Medical Group Management Association*, *Modern Healthcare*, and *Hospital Public Relations*.

He holds degrees from Eastern Illinois University, California State University, and Memphis State University and is accredited by the Public Relations Society of America and the International Association of Business Communicators.